9.00/mm

SURVEYS OF CONSUMERS 1971·72

CONTRIBUTIONS TO BEHAVIORAL ECONOMICS

BY

LEWIS MANDELL
GEORGE KATONA
JAMES N. MORGAN
JAY SCHMIEDESKAMP

SURVEYS OF CONSUMERS 1971·72

CONTRIBUTIONS TO BEHAVIORAL ECONOMICS

ISR Code No. 3454

Library of Congress Catalog Card No. 72-619718
ISBN 0-87944-139-9 paperbound
ISBN 0-87944-140-2 clothbound

Published by the Institute for Social Research
The University of Michigan, Ann Arbor, Mich. 48106

Cover Design by Mary Kay Krell

PREFACE

The *Surveys of Consumers 1971-72* is the first volume of a new series of annual monographs published by the Economic Behavior Program of the Survey Research Center. Its predecessor, the annual *Survey of Consumer Finances,* was published continuously from 1960 through 1970.

The Survey Research Center began to collect data on the distribution of incomes, major assets, and debt, as well as on expenditures on durable goods and related major transactions, in 1946. This practice continued annually through 1971. Periodic surveys, conducted for the purpose of ascertaining changes in consumer attitudes and expectations, were begun over twenty years ago and have been carried out quarterly over the past decade. While interest in studies of the psychological factors which influence economic demand has grown and support for these studies continues, comparable data collected by the Census Bureau and others have greatly reduced the demand and support for the Survey Research Center's annual collection of financial data. Consequently, 1971 marks the last year in which these financial data were collected on an annual basis. Hopefully, these surveys can be repeated on a less frequent basis in the future in order to monitor further many of the trends which scholars and others have thought to be significant during the past several years.

This new series of monographs and its subtitle "Contributions to Behavioral Economics" reflect the growing diversity of the research which is conducted under the Economic Behavior Program. Beyond the collection of financial data and the quarterly collection of consumer outlook data, the Economic Behavior Program is now completing a major five-year study of poverty and changes in income, directed by James N. Morgan. It is also pursuing a program to develop measures of economic incentives, values and subjective well-being under the direction of Burkhard Strumpel. It conducts studies of housing and the environment, directed by Robert W. Marans, and studies of consumer knowledge and information, under the direction of Lewis Mandell.

The format of this volume has both similarities to, and divergences from, the earlier *Survey of Consumer Finances* volumes. There are four parts to this monograph. The first part reports on the financial survey which was conducted in February of 1971. This survey interviewed a total of 1,327 families across the United States and asked questions relating to family income, debt, assets, and other components of family finance. It must be noted that the relatively small number of interviews which were conducted in 1971 make the population estimates somewhat less reliable than they were during earlier years.

Part Two contains a summary of the findings of the quarterly surveys of consumer sentiment for five quarters. These reports have also been included in previous volumes. Part Three is an innovation in the annual monographs of the Program; it contains substantive theoretical and methodological articles, based on the diverse research projects of the Economic Behavior Program. Part Four outlines the survey methodology and procedures which are used by the Survey Research Center.

The Economic Behavior Program of the Center is directed by James N. Morgan in conjunction with Burkhard Strumpel. Lewis Mandell has directed the analysis of the financial data for the past three years and served as senior editor of this volume. Burkhard Strumpel and Jay Schmiedeskamp are responsible for the quarterly surveys of consumer sentiment. George Katona, although officially retired from his University responsibilities, remains in residence and continues to make valuable contributions to all of the facets of the Economic Behavior Program, which he founded.

Toby Clark assisted in the compilation and analysis of the financial data in this volume. Assisting Jay Schmiedeskamp in the collection and analysis of the consumer sentiment data were Charles Cowan and Alicia Szuman. In addition, thanks are due to many of the authors' colleagues in the Economic Behavior Program. These include Janet Keller, Susan Schwartz, Richard Curtin, Jonathan Dickinson, Katherine Dickinson, Nancy Baerwaldt, Jacob Benus and Anthony Jiga. Special thanks are due to Evelyn Hansmire, the Administrative Assistant for the Program who coordinates much of the activity, and also to Margaret Hinz, who was of great help in preparing the manuscripts.

The samples used in the Economic Behavior Program surveys were drawn under the direction of Irene Hess. The interviewing was conducted under the direction of John Scott, and the coding was directed by Joan Scheffler. The authors are especially indebted to several hundred interviewers, as well as to Marlene Lipschutz who served as the editor of this volume, and William V. Haney who is the Managing Editor at the Institute for Social Research, and Douglas Truax and Linda Stafford who helped prepare the manuscript for publication. Proofreading was done by Grace Truax and Toby Clark.

The data management and computation upon which this book is based employed the OSIRIS computer software system, which was jointly developed by the component Centers of the Institute for Social Research, the University of Michigan using funds from the National Science Foundation, the Inter-University Consortium for Political Research and other sources.

A national advisory committee of experts in economic behavior consistently provides substantial help on the annual surveys. In 1971, the following scholars aided the Economic Behavior Program. Petter de Janosi, Robert Ferber, Lawrence Klein, Scott Maynes, Guy Orcutt, James Tobin and Arnold Zellner.

TABLE OF CONTENTS

PART
1
FINANCIAL
DATA

INTRODUCTION

Since 1946, the Survey Research Center has collected annual data on the distribution of major financial variables among families in the United States. Sample sizes in nearly all of these years were between 2,500 and 3,000.

In 1971, financial data were obtained from only 1,327 families. This reduction in sample size had the effect of increasing the sampling variability of the data, particularly if the data are presented not only for all families but also for subgroups of the population. Consequently, many of the tables and trends which have appeared in previous volumes of the *Survey of Consumer Finances* have either been eliminated or condensed in this volume.

The traditional chapter on the distribution of income has been entirely omitted. While data on family income are still collected, they now serve the purpose of indicating income differences in other data collected in the survey among major income groups. Data on the distribution of family income per se are collected by the Bureau of the Census on the basis of sample sizes that are many times larger than those of the Survey Research Center.

The major aim of Part I of the *Surveys of Consumers 1971-72* is to present national survey data on installment debt, housing, automobiles, household durables and financial assets which are not available from any other source. Furthermore, it will present some major trends which traditionally have been presented in the *Surveys of Consumer Finances*. The sample sizes of the subgroups used in the analysis of the financial data can be found in Chapter 17.

1

INSTALLMENT DEBT

Installment borrowing decreased during the last two years when measured in terms of the proportion of families with outstanding debt or in terms of the median outstanding debt for families with debt. The table below shows that only 48 percent of American families had outstanding installment debt in 1971 while 51 percent had outstanding debt early in 1969.

Early in:	1966	1967	1968	1969	1970	1971
Amount of installment debt outstanding						
None	51%	52%	52%	49%	51%	52%
$1-199	8	9	8	7	8	9
$200-499	9	8	7	8	8	8
$500-999	10	9	10	10	9	8
$1,000-1,999	12	12	12	13	11	10
$2,000 or more	10	10	11	13	13	13
Total	100%	100%	100%	100%	100%	100%
Median debt for families with debt	$850	$880	$960	$1020	$940	$900

The median outstanding debt for borrowing families continued to decrease in 1971 to an average of $900 per family. In 1970 the median debt was $940, and in 1969 it was $1,020. Possibly part of the decrease in 1971 may have resulted from an increase in the use of revolving credit and credit cards as instruments of finance. Of the vast array of goods that families purchase on credit, only the biggest one, the automobile, is now purchased exclusively on

5

a straight installment plan; the rest of the items may be purchased either on an installment plan or with the use of revolving credit.

Early in 1971, as in previous years, the use of credit was most heavy among upper middle class families. Those families with incomes between $10,000 and $15,000 a year were the greatest users of credit: 60 percent of families in this income range used credit as compared to only 46 percent among families with incomes of more than $15,000 per year (Table 1-2). Younger families typically are more prone to borrow than are older families. For example, 66 percent of families with heads under the age of 25 and 67 percent with heads between 25 and 34 had outstanding installment debt early in 1971. This proportion decreased with each age group after the age of 35.

A measure of a family's involvement with installment debt is determined by the ratio of annual installment debt payment to the previous year's annual income. Table 1-3 shows that while 52 percent of all families had no outstanding debt, 13 percent had less than 5 percent of their income committed to debt repayment, 13 percent had between 5 and 9 percent of this income committed; 13 percent had 10 to 19 percent of their incomes pledged in this fashion, and 7 percent of American families had at least a fifth of their income committed to the repayment of installment debt. Younger family heads were both more frequently involved in installment borrowing and also more frequently burdened with a heavy debt to income ratio. For example, for family heads under the age of 25, 39 percent paid at least 10 percent of their annual income to installment lenders. The comparable figure for family heads between 25 and 34 years of age paying 10 percent of their annual income to installment lenders was only 26 percent.

The use of credit cards by American families is increasing each year. The 1971 Survey of Consumer Finances did an extensive analysis of the use of the various types of credit cards by American consumers. In early 1971, 33 percent of families used a gasoline credit card, and half of all families used a non-gasoline credit card. Table 1-8 shows that of the families who used a non-gasoline credit card, 30 percent used one such card, 22 percent used two such cards, and 48 percent used three or more non-gasoline credit cards.

Both the use and the number of non-gasoline credit cards used is highly dependent upon incomes. Only 19 percent of families making $25,000 a year did not use at least one non-gasoline credit card, while 65 percent of those used bank credit cards, 45 percent used store credit cards, and 5 percent used travel and entertainment credit cards.

TABLE 1-1

DISTRIBUTION OF INCOME AMONG THOSE WITH INSTALLMENT DEBT
AND THOSE WITHOUT INSTALLMENT DEBT

(Percentage distribution of families)

Annual family income	All families					Families with installment debt					Families without installment debt				
	Early 1967	Early 1968	Early 1969	Early 1970	Early 1971	Early 1967	Early 1968	Early 1969	Early 1970	Early 1971	Early 1967	Early 1968	Early 1969	Early 1970	Early 1971
Less than $3,000	19	18	17	14	11	10	7	7	5	6	28	29	28	22	15
$3,000–4,999	15	14	14	12	15	13	12	10	7	12	17	16	17	16	17
$5,000–7,499	20	18	16	16	17	23	21	19	17	18	18	15	13	15	16
$7,500–9,999	18	17	17	16	14	23	22	21	20	15	13	12	12	12	13
$10,000–14,999	19	22	23	24	23	23	27	31	33	29	15	17	16	17	18
$15,000 or more	9	11	13	18	20	8	11	12	18	20	9	11	14	18	21
Total	100	100	100	100	100	100	100	100	100	100	100	100	100	100	100

TABLE 1-2 (Sheet 1 of 2)

AMOUNT OF INSTALLMENT DEBT OUTSTANDING

(Percentage distribution of families)

	Amount of installment debt							
	Early 1971						Early 1970	
	Any debt	$1-199	$200 -499	$500 -999	$1,000 -1,999	$2,000 or more	Any debt	$2,000 or more
All families	48	9	8	8	10	13	49	13
Annual family income								
Less than $3,000	29	16	7	3	1	2	19	1
$3,000-4,999	39	12	11	5	6	5	31	5
$5,000-7,499	51	12	8	10	13	8	52	9
$7,500-9,999	53	9	9	10	8	17	61	15
$10,000-14,999	60	6	11	8	16	19	65	19
$15,000 or more	46	6	5	9	7	19	49	20
Age of family head								
Under age 25	66	13	10	12	19	12	59	21
25-34	67	8	10	15	15	19	67	22
35-44	62	11	13	9	14	15	63	13
45-54	51	8	8	6	9	20	56	14
55-64	36	11	8	5	4	8	36	7
65-74	18	7	4	3	3	1	14	1
75 or older	8	6	*	*	*	2	6	*

TABLE 1-2 (Sheet 2 of 2)

AMOUNT OF INSTALLMENT DEBT OUTSTANDING
(Percentage distribution of families)

Life cycle stage of family head	Amount of installment debt							
	Early 1971						Early 1970	
	Any debt	$1-199	$200-499	$500-999	$1,000-1,999	$2,000 or more	Any debt	$2,000 or more
Under age 45								
Unmarried, no children	41	16	3	8	9	5	41	11
Married, no children	66	6	8	9	18	25	63	17
Married, youngest child under age 6	68	10	12	12	17	17	71	21
Married, youngest child age 6 or older	70	8	16	18	14	14	71	22
Age 45 or older								
Married, has children	60	11	12	6	8	23	57	16
Married, no children, head in labor force	34	8	4	5	7	10	43	10
Married, no children, head retired	16	8	6	1	1	*	15	3
Unmarried, no children, head in labor force	34	10	3	7	5	9	29	2
Unmarried, no children, head retired	12	6	2	2	*	2	14	*
Any age								
Unmarried, has children	63	13	18	9	10	13	56	9

Note: The term no children, appearing frequently in this chapter, means no children under age 18 living at home. Unemployed people and housewives age 55 or older are considered retired; unemployed people and housewives under age 55 are considered to be in the labor force.

TABLE 1-3 (Sheet 1 of 2)

RATIO OF ANNUAL INSTALLMENT DEBT PAYMENT TO PREVIOUS YEAR'S ANNUAL INCOME – WITHIN SPECIFIC GROUPS

(Percentage distribution of families)

	No payments; No debt	Less than 5 percent	5-9 percent	10-19 percent	20-39 percent	40 percent or more	D.K., N.A. amount of payment	Total
All families	52	13	13	13	5	2	2	100
Annual family income								
Less than $3,000[a]	70	1	4	12	5	8	*	100
$3,000-4,999	62	11	8	8	7	3	1	100
$5,000-7,499	49	11	12	15	12	*	1	100
$7,500-9,999	47	14	12	15	7	1	4	100
$10,000-14,999	40	17	17	21	2	*	3	100
$15,000 or more	54	17	19	7	*	*	3	100
Age of head								
Under 25	34	12	15	26	11	2	*	100
25-34	35	14	22	15	9	2	3	100
35-44	38	23	19	14	4	1	1	100
45-54	49	14	12	16	4	2	3	100
55-64	64	10	9	8	3	3	3	100
65-74	82	5	2	7	2	1	1	100
75 and over	92	2	2	3	*	*	1	100

* Less than 0.5 percent.

[a] Includes families with zero or negative incomes.

TABLE 1-3 (Sheet 2 of 2)

RATIO OF ANNUAL INSTALLMENT DEBT PAYMENT TO PREVIOUS YEAR'S ANNUAL INCOME – WITHIN SPECIFIC GROUPS

(Percentage distribution of families)

Life cycle stage of family head	No payments; No debt	Less than 5 percent	5-9 percent	10-19 percent	20-39 percent	40 percent or more	D.K., N.A. amount of payment	Total
Under age 45								
Unmarried, no children	58	8	11	11	11	1	*	100
Married, no children	34	8	29	21	8	*	*	100
Married, youngest child under age 6	33	17	16	22	8	1	3	100
Married, youngest child age 6 or older	29	30	20	12	6	1	2	100
Age 45 or older								
Married, has children	40	16	15	19	1	2	7	100
Married, no children, head in labor force	66	12	8	9	2	2	1	100
Married, no children, head retired	84	3	4	5	3	1	*	100
Unmarried, no children, head in labor force	67	7	5	9	8	3	1	100
Unmarried, no children, head retired	88	2	2	3	2	1	2	100
Any age								
Unmarried, has children	37	14	22	14	4	8	1	100

* Less than 0.5 percent.

TABLE 1-4 (Sheet 1 of 2)

MONTHLY INSTALLMENT DEBT PAYMENTS

(Percentage distribution of families)

	Amount of monthly debt payments							Early 1970
	Early 1971							
	None	$1-24	$25-49	$50-74	$75-99	$100 or more	D.K., N.A. amount of payment	$100 or more
All families	52	9	8	7	8	16	2	16
Annual family income								
Less than $3,000	71	12	11	1	2	3	*	1
$3,000-4,999	62	16	8	7	2	5	1	4
$5,000-7,499	49	10	11	10	7	13	1	10
$7,500-9,999	47	10	8	8	7	16	4	18
$10,000-14,999	40	6	8	8	14	21	3	24
$15,000 or more	54	3	5	6	10	20	3	26
Age of family head								
Under age 25	34	9	15	11	13	18	*	22
25-34	34	8	9	14	13	19	3	27
35-44	38	13	9	9	9	21	1	19
45-54	49	7	11	3	8	19	3	16
55-64	64	9	6	5	5	8	3	8
65-74	82	7	5	2	2	1	1	2
75 and over	92	7	*	*	*	*	1	*

* Less than 0.5 percent.

TABLE 1-4 (Sheet 2 of 2)

MONTHLY INSTALLMENT DEBT PAYMENTS

(Percentage distribution of families)

Life cycle stage of family head	Amount of monthly debt payments							Early 1970
	Early 1971							
	None	$1-24	$25-49	$50-74	$75-99	$100 or more	D.K., N.A. amount of payment	$100 or more
Under age 45								
Unmarried, no children	59	9	8	13	7	4	*	15
Married, no children	34	8	3	7	20	28	*	22
Married, youngest child under age 6	32	8	11	12	11	23	3	24
Married, youngest child age 6 or older	30	10	12	15	12	19	2	30
Age 45 or older								
Married, has children	40	7	14	7	6	19	7	20
Married, no children, head in labor force	66	7	4	3	7	12	1	13
Married, no children, head retired	84	8	4	1	2	1	*	3
Unmarried, no children, head in labor force	67	10	4	5	5	8	1	4
Unmarried, no children, head retired	87	6	3	1	1	*	2	1
Any age								
Unmarried, has children	37	23	17	6	3	13	1	13

* Less than 0.5 percent.

TABLE 1-5

AMOUNT OF INSTALLMENT DEBT OUTSTANDING

(Percentage distribution of families)

	Any debt	$1–199	$200 –499	$500 –999	$1,000 –1,999	$2,000 or more
Housing status and duration						
House owner, bought 1967–1970	58	6	9	8	15	20
House owner, bought before 1967	40	7	7	6	8	12
House renter, moved in 1967–1970	60	13	10	13	12	12
House renter, moved in before 1967	51	14	9	8	9	11
Race						
White	46	8	8	8	10	12
Black	68	17	18	11	7	15

TABLE 1-6

AMOUNT OF INSTALLMENT DEBT OUTSTANDING BY CHANGE IN FINANCIAL POSITION

(Percentage distribution of families)

Amount of installment debt outstanding, early 1971	All families	All families – financial situation compared to year ago is:			1970 family income under $10,000 – financial situation compared to year ago is:			1970 family income $10,000 or more – financial situation compared to year ago is:		
		Better	Same	Worse	Better	Same	Worse	Better	Same	Worse
No debt	52	44	62	48	44	67	52	44	53	40
$1–199	9	9	9	11	14	10	13	5	7	6
$200–499	8	8	9	9	10	8	10	7	10	7
$500–999	8	10	6	7	10	7	6	10	6	10
$1,000–1,999	10	14	6	10	13	3	9	15	10	12
$2,000 or more	13	15	8	15	9	5	10	19	14	25
Total	100	100	100	100	100	100	100	100	100	100
Percent of sample	100	31	36	31	13	22	20	18	14	11
Number of families	1,327	410	482	418	172	298	272	238	184	146

TABLE 1-7

USE OF GASOLINE CREDIT CARDS BY AGE AND INCOME

(Percentage distribution of families)

	Early 1971		Early 1967
	Use gasoline credit cards	Don't use gasoline credit cards	Use gasoline credit cards
All families	33	67	30
Age of head			
Under 25	17	83	21
25-34	39	61	32
35-44	33	67	40
45-54	43	57	35
55-64	35	65	32
65-74	28	72	22
75 and over	10	90	5
Annual family income			
Less than $3,000	5	95	5
$3,000-4,999	21	79	15
$5,000-7,499	20	80	27
$7,500-9,999	26	74	38
$10,000-14,999	43	57	47
$15,000-19,999	50	50	67
$20,000-24,999	64	36	67
$25,000 or more	77	23	67

TABLE 1-8

USE OF NON-GASOLINE CREDIT CARDS BY INCOME

(Percentage distribution of families)

	Number of Non-Gasoline Credit Cards Used			
	None	One	Two	Three or more
Annual family income				
Less than $3,000	83	9	5	3
$3,000-4,999	70	14	7	9
$5,000-7,499	61	16	10	13
$7,500-9,999	50	17	15	18
$10,000-14,999	34	22	11	33
$15,000-19,999	28	12	18	42
$20,000-24,999	24	11	15	50
$25,000 or more	19	3	13	65
All families	50	15	11	24

TABLE 1-9

USE OF BANK CREDIT CARDS BY AGE AND INCOME

(Percentage distribution of families)

	Use bank credit cards	Don't use bank credit cards
All families	19	81
Age of head		
Under 25	12	88
25–34	26	74
35–44	27	73
45–54	23	77
55–64	15	85
65–74	11	89
75 and over	4	96
Annual family income		
Less than $3,000	2	98
$3,000-4,999	9	91
$5,000-7,499	10	90
$7,500-9,999	16	84
$10,000-14,999	29	71
$15,000-19,999	38	62
$20,000-24,999	35	65
$25,000 or more	36	64

TABLE 1-10

USE OF STORE CREDIT CARDS BY AGE AND INCOME

(Percentage distribution of families)

	Use store credit cards	Don't use store credit cards
All families	45	55
Age of head		
Under 25	27	73
25–34	47	53
35–44	51	49
45–54	56	44
55–64	48	52
65–74	37	63
75 and over	24	76
Annual family income		
Less than $3,000	17	83
$3,000–4,999	28	72
$5,000–7,499	35	65
$7,500–9,999	43	57
$10,000–14,999	57	43
$15,000–19,999	65	35
$20,000–24,999	72	28
$25,000 or more	74	26

TABLE 1-11

USE OF TRAVEL AND ENTERTAINMENT CREDIT CARDS BY AGE AND INCOME

(Percentage distribution of families)

	Use travel & entertainment credit cards	Don't use travel & entertainment credit cards
All families	5	95
Age of head		
Under 25	*	**
25-34	6	94
35-44	5	95
45-54	8	92
55-64	5	95
65-74	2	98
75 and over	1	99
Annual family income		
Less than $3,000	1	99
$3,000-4,999	*	**
$5,000-7,499	*	**
*7,500-9,999	1	99
$10,000-14,999	6	94
$15,000-19,999	4	96
$20,000-24,999	14	86
$25,000 or more	37	63

---

*Less than 0.5 percent.

** More than 99.5 percent.

2

HOUSING

Purchases of houses fell off somewhat in 1970, reflecting the continuation of the tight money market and the high interest rates which had prevailed in recent years. Only 4 percent of non-farm families purchased a house in 1970 and an additional 1 percent purchased a trailer. The median purchase price of houses bought in 1970 was $16,500, a decrease from 1969. A much larger proportion of persons buying houses bought them entirely with cash during 1970 than during most of the recent years. Nearly one-third of those families buying a house paid cash. The average mortgage debt incurred by those families who borrowed to finance the purchase of their houses also fell sharply.

Partially to compensate for their inability to purchase new houses, a larger proportion of families made additions and repairs to their existing housing. Forty-three percent of all non-farm families made some additions and repairs to their housing in 1970 while only 39 percent made additions and repairs the year before.

Respondents appeared to have upgraded the value of their houses, somewhat in keeping with the increased level of prices. In 1971, the median reported value for a house was $18,000, a slight increase from the previous year. The median mortgage debt outstanding remained the same as it was in 1970.

Tables 2-3 and 2-4 show that housing costs rose somewhat for both homeowners and renters during 1970. The median mortgage payment for homeowners was $108, an increase of $1 per month from the previous year. Rent increased more rapidly to a median of $90 per month, while the median stood at $85 per month during the previous year.

The housing status of non-farm families remained fairly constant in 1971. Sixty-two percent of those families interviewed lived in their own home, a fig-

Total family income, 1970	Percent of nonfarm owner families making expenditures on houses		
	1967	1969	1970
Less than $5,000	39	41	48
$5,000-7,499	55	54	56
$7,500-9,999	57	56	52
$10,000-14,999	57	59	64
$15,000 or more	63	63	60
All families	53	55	57

aTrailer owners are excluded.

ure which has not deviated much since the beginning of the 1960s. Four percent of families lived in trailers, 31 percent were renters and 3 percent neither owned nor rented. Whether a family owns or rents is highly dependent upon the age of the family head. Table 2-7 shows that while 66 percent of all families owned their own home (or trailer), only 17 percent of those families with a family head under the age of 25 were homeowners. Alternatively, while only 31 percent of all American families rented, fully 77 percent of those families headed by young persons below the age of 25 rented housing. Even among family heads between the ages of 25 and 34, a smaller proportion than the national average owned their own homes. After the age of 35 the proportion of families owning their own homes was higher than the national average.

Another determinant of whether a family owns or rents is total family income. Lower income families are more prone to rent, and those families with higher incomes are more likely to own their own homes. For example, of those families making less than $3,000 a year, only half owned their own home and 40 percent rented. Those families whose income was a least $15,000 a year, however, fully 84 percent owned their own homes and only 16 percent rented.

Persons who live in trailers constitute a particularly interesting group within our society. In 1971, trailer owners were largely in the lower middle income group—they earned between $3,000 and $10,000 a year—and they were often very young. Table 2-9 shows that 16 percent of those families headed by persons under the age of 25 lived in trailers, while this proportion was not above 4 percent for families with heads 35 years of age or older. Also, families with no children or with only one child were far more likely to live in a trailer than were families with two or more children. Another interesting set of statistics was that while 5 percent of white families lived in trailers, less than 1 percent of black families lived in this type of housing.

TABLE 2-1

TRENDS IN HOUSING TRANSACTIONS - 1959-1970

	Transaction Year						
	1959	1961	1965	1967	1968	1969	1970
Housing purchases of nonfarm families							
Percent buying houses	5^a	5^a	6	5	6	5	4
Percent buying a trailer	--	--	1	*	*	2	1
Median purchase price, excluding trailers (in thousands)	$12.9^a	$13.0^a	$15.9	$15.0	$15.0	$18.0	$16.5
Mortgage debt incurred by house purchasers							
Percent of buyers incurring mortgages	91	89	75	79	76	87	68
Median mortgage debt incurred (in thousands)^b	$10.7	$9.9	$13.3	$13.1	$13.9	$14.0	$11.7
Additions and repairs transactions							
Percent of all nonfarm families making additions and repairs	40	34	42	38	35	39	43

---

*Less than 0.5 percent.

[a]Includes trailer purchases in 1959 and 1961.

[b]Includes only those families who incurred mortgage debt.

TABLE 2-2

VALUE OF HOUSES OWNED, MORTGAGE DEBT AND NET EQUITY - 1960-1971

(Percentage distribution of owner-occupied nonfarm houses[a])

House value[b]	1960	1962	1967	1969	1970	1971
Less than $5,000	12	9	9	6	5	4
$5,000-7,499	9	9	8	8	5	4
$7,500-9,999	13	13	9	8	6	7
$10,000-12,499	20	19	16	15	12	11
$12,500-14,999	11	11	10	8	10	7
$15,000-19,999	20	20	22	20	20	20
$20,000-24,999	15	19	26	35	13	18
$25,000 or more					29	29
Total	100	100	100	100	100	100
Median (in thousands)	$11.1	$12.4	$14.6	$15.0	$17.8	$18.0
Mortgage debt						
Zero	40	37	47	44	42	43
$1-2,499	11	10	6	7	7	6
$2,500-4,999	12	10	9	7	7	7
$5,000-7,499	14	11	8	8	7	7
$7,500-9,999	9	10	9	8	8	8
$10,000-12,499	8	12	9	9	9	11
$12,500-14,999	3	4	4	6	7	5
$15,000 or more	3	6	8	11	13	13
Total	100	100	100	100	100	100
Median[c] (in thousands)	$6.4	$7.5	$8.4	$9.0	$10.0	$10.0
Net equity in house						
Under $1,000	d	d	3	4	3	1
$1,000-4,999	d	d	21	19	17	13
$5,000-9,999	d	d	28	26	22	25
$10,000-14,999	d	d	40	40	21	20
$15,000-24,999					23	26
$25,000 or more	d	d	8	11	14	15
Total	d	d	100	100	100	100
Median (in thousands)	d	d	$9.6	$10.0	$11.5	$12.0

[a] Trailers are excluded.

[b] As valued by respondents early in the year indicated, except that houses purchased during the preceding year were valued at purchase price.

[c] For mortgaged houses only.

[d] Not available.

TABLE 2-3

MONTHLY MORTGAGE PAYMENTS FOR SELECTED YEARS

(Percentage distribution of nonfarm homeowning families)[a]

Monthly mortgage payment	1960	1962	1967	1969	1970	1971
Have no mortgage	40	37	47	44	42	43
Have mortgage	60	63	53	56	58	57
$1-24	2	2	1	1	1	*
$25-49	9	7	4	3	3	3
$50-74	21	15	12	11	9	8
$75-99	16	20	14	13	12	13
$100-124	7	12	10	11	12	12
$125-149	3	4	6	7	7	5
$150 or more	2	3	6	10	14	16
Total	100	100	100	100	100	100
Median monthly payment	$73	$90	$90	$100	$107	$108

---

*Less than 0.5 percent.

[a]Trailers are excluded.

TABLE 2-4

MONTHLY RENT PAYMENTS FOR SELECTED YEARS

(Percentage distribution of rent-paying nonfarm families)

Monthly rent payment[a]	1960	1962	1967	1969	1970	1971
$1-24	9	7	5	4	4	3
$25-49	28	26	20	12	10	11
$50-74	34	35	28	28	21	20
$75-99	18	17	24	25	26	22
$100-124	6	6	11	13	15	16
$125-149	2	4	7	10	12	11
$150 or more	3	5	5	8	12	17
Total	100	100	100	100	100	100
Median monthly rent	$59	$65	$72	$75	$85	$90

---

[a]Rents are tabulated for all nonfarm renters,. excluding those who rent
part of another family's dwelling (roomers and roommates for example).

TABLE 2-5

MONTHLY MORTGAGE AND RENT PAYMENTS - EARLY 1971

(Percentage distribution within income groups of
nonfarm homeowning families and rent-paying families)

		Family income, 1970					
		Nonfarm homeowning families[a]					
	All	Less than $3,000	$3,000 -4,999	$5,000 -7,499	$7,500 -9,999	$10,000 -14,999	$15,000 or more
Monthly mortgage payment							
Do not have mortgage debt	43	80	73	59	36	24	32
Have mortgage	57	20	27	41	64	76	68
$1-24	*	*	1	1	*	*	*
$25-49	3	9	5	5	3	1	1
$50-74	9	6	13	9	15	12	1
$75-99	12	3	3	11	25	17	10
$100-124	12	1	*	7	11	24	12
$125-149	5	*	2	2	3	6	9
$150 or more	16	1	3	6	7	16	35
Total	100	100	100	100	100	100	100

Monthly rent payment[b]		Nonfarm rent-paying families					
$1-24	3	15	4	*	*	*	*
$25-49	11	24	12	14	4	10	*
$50-74	20	28	26	29	12	10	10
$75-99	22	17	21	21	40	19	12
$100-124	17	9	21	18	21	11	15
$125-149	11	2	9	10	14	16	15
$150 or more	16	5	7	8	9	34	48
Total	100	100	100	100	100	100	100

---

* Less than 0.5 percent.

[a] Trailer owners are excluded.

[b] Rents are tabulated for all nonfarm renters, excluding those who rent part of another family unit's dwelling (roomers, etc.) who get no rental value at all.

Note: For early 1970 data, see Table 3-11 in the 1970 Survey of Consumer Finances.

TABLE 2-6

HOUSING STATUS OF NONFARM FAMILIES

(Percentage distribution of nonfarm families)

Housing status	1960	1963	1966	1967	1969	1970	1971
Home owner[a]	58	61	62	60	61	62	62
Trailer	*	*	3	2	2	4	4
Primary renter	36	32	30	33	32	30	31
Secondary renter[b]	2	3	2	2	2	2	
Other[c]	4	4	3	3	3	2	3
Total	100	100	100	100	100	100	100

---

[a] Includes families who own their own apartments or are joint owners.

[b] Secondary renters are families who rent a part of another family's dwelling unit, such as roomers and roommates.

[c] Includes families who receive housing as compensation for employment or as a gift.

* Less than 0.5 percent.

TABLE 2-7

HOUSING STATUS - 1971

(Percentage distribution of nonfarm families)

		Housing Status			Percent of nonfarm families
	Total	Own[a]	Rent	Other	
All families	100	66	31	3	100
Age of family head					
Under age 25	100	17	77	6	9
25-34	100	51	47	2	19
35-44	100	71	27	2	19
45-54	100	78	21	1	19
55-64	100	74	22	4	15
Age 65 or older	100	76	19	5	19
Life cycle stage of family head					
Under age 45					
Unmarried, no children	100	15	78	7	6
Married, no children	100	42	54	4	8
Married, youngest child under age 6	100	62	35	3	18
Married, youngest child age 6 or older	100	76	22	2	10
Age 45 or older					
Married, has children	100	79	17	4	12
Married, no children, head in labor force	100	87	12	1	15
Married, no children, head retired	100	78	20	2	9
Unmarried, no children, head in labor force	100	61	39	*	6
Unmarried, no children, head retired	100	67	26	7	10
Any age					
Unmarried, has children	100	35	61	4	6
Total family income, 1969					
Less than $3,000	100	50	40	10	11
$3,000-4,999	100	54	42	4	15
$5,000-7,499	100	51	46	3	17
$7,500-9,999	100	65	34	1	14
$10,000-14,999	100	73	24	3	23
$15,000 or more	100	84	16	*	20

---

*Less than 0.5 percent.

[a]Includes trailer owners.

TABLE 2-8

HOUSING STATUS - 1949-1971

(Percentage distribution of nonfarm families)[a]

	Own						Rent					
	1949	1954	1960	1965	1970	1971	1949	1954	1960	1965	1970	1971
All nonfarm families	50	56	58	63	62	64	40	37	36	29	30	33
Family income quintile												
Lowest quintile	40	45	42	46	45	51	38	34	42	36	44	42
Second quintile	43	46	47	47	46	50	46	47	46	42	44	46
Third quintile	47	51	55	64	63	62	45	44	41	32	32	37
Fourth quintile	55	65	68	74	74	73	41	32	28	23	22	23
Highest quintile	69	71	77	86	83	84	28	28	21	13	16	16
Age of family head												
Under age 25	21	17	14	19	12	10	48	58	70	63	63	84
25-34	35	42	44	47	48	47	53	52	50	45	44	50
35-44	53	57	64	69	72	70	42	38	33	25	24	27
45-54	59	63	69	75	74	77	34	31	27	19	21	22
55-64	62	66	62	71	77	74	32	28	29	23	18	22
Age 65 or older	59	63	65	71	71	76	27	23	27	22	21	19
Race												
White	53	57	61	67	65	67	38	35	34	26	29	29
Nonwhite	31	40	38	37	43	42	51	52	53	50	51	58

[a]Percentages do not add to 100 because families who own trailers, rent part of another family's dwelling or receive housing as part of compensation are not shown.

TABLE 2-9

TYPE OF HOUSING STRUCTURE WITHIN INCOME, AGE, LIFE CYCLE, AND RACIAL GROUPS

(Percentage distribution of families)

	Type of Structure								
	Single family house		Duplex, row house, 2-4 family structure		Apartment of five or more units		Trailer		Total
	1970	1971	1970	1971	1970	1971	1970	1971	
Family income									
Under $3,000	64	72	18	14	13	12	5	2	100
$3,000-4,999	61	66	18	14	15	13⁻	6	7	100
$5,000-7,499	65	61	13	17	15	15	7	7	100
$7,500-9,999	69	67	16	19	11	7	4	7	100
$10,000 or more	79	77	10	12	9	8	2	3	100
Age of head									
Under age 25	34	36	26	28	27	20	13	16	100
25-34	66	62	14	20	14	11	6	7	100
35-44	80	75	12	14	6	9	2	2	100
45-54	78	81	12	12	7	5	3	2	100
55-64	77	75	10	10	10	12	3	3	100
65 or older	75	75	11	10	11	11	3	4	100
Life cycle stage of family head									
Under age 45									
Unmarried, no children	29	33	21	24	40	36	10	7	100
Married, no children	48	45	20	19	23	23	9	13	100
Married, youngest child under age 6	74	70	15	19	6	4	5	7	100
Married, youngest child age 6 or older	88	86	7	8	3	4	2	2	100
Age 45 or older									
Married, has children	87	87	7	9	4	3	2	1	100
Married, no children, head in labor force	79	80	10	10	8	7	3	3	100
Married, no children, head retired	81	82	10	8	6	5	3	5	100
Unmarried, no children, head in labor force	60	65	19	17	17	14	4	4	100
Unmarried, no children, head retired	67	65	13	10	16	21	4	4	100
Any age									
Unmarried, has children	55	56	25	31	16	12	4	1	100
Race									
White	73	73	12	13	10	9	5	5	100
Nonwhite	59	50	23	26	18	24	*	*	100
All families	71	71	14	14	11	11	4	4	100

*Less than 0.5 percent.

3

AUTOMOBILE PURCHASES
AND OWNERSHIP

Purchases of new automobiles fell sharply in 1970. According to the Survey of Consumer Finances, only 9 percent of American families purchased a new car during that year as contrasted with 13 percent who purchased one in the previous year. The decline in purchases of new automobiles was due primarily to two factors: the recession which encompassed the entire calendar year 1970, and the General Motors strike which sharply diminished American automobile production in the last half of the year. The average expenditure per car did not reflect the upward trend of recent years, in part because of the introduction of the lower priced American subcompacts.

Purchases of used cars increased slightly to 19 percent of all families. Table 3-2 indicates that during 1970, many families purchased late model used cars instead of new cars. Only 9 percent of all families purchased a car less than one year old as contrasted with 14 percent who purchased one during the previous year. 45 percent of those families purchasing a used car purchased one whose age was between 2 and 4 years, as contrasted with the 36 percent of used car buyers who purchased one that age in the previous year. Because some people purchased both a new and a used car, 26 percent of all families purchased either a new or a used car, while 28 percent were in this category in the preceding years. Sixty-nine percent of new car purchases and 37 percent of used car purchases involved the trade-in or sale of an automobile.

The proportion of new car purchasers who paid for their car in cash was 17 percent in 1970, as compared with less than half that proportion in 1969. On the other side of the coin, the proportion who used installment borrowing was 57 percent in 1970, as compared with 66 percent who used it during the

31

Year of Purchase	Cars purchased as a proportion of families (in percent)	
	New	Used
1970	9	19
1969	13	· 18
1968	12	21
1967	11	20
1966	13	19
1965	13	19
1964	12	19
1963	11	20
1962	10	23
1961	8	20
1960	10	20
1959	10	17
1958	8	18
1957	9	18
1956	10	18

aDomestic and foreign cars purchased by private households, in possession of buyers at the beginning of the following year.

Financing Method	New car purchases					Used car purchases				
	1966	1967	1968	1969	1970	1966	1967	1968	1969	1970
Cash only	12%	10%	10%	8%	17%	38%	35%	37%	40%	41%
Cash plus trade-in or sale	26	21	24	26	26	15	15	14	12	9
Installment or other borrowing only	4	3	3	2	2	9	7	9	7	12
Installment or other borrowing plus trade-in, sale, or cash	57	65	63	64	55	36	41	37	38	35
Gift	1	1	*	*	*	2	2	3	3	3
Total	100%	100%	100%	100%	100%	100%	100%	100%	100%	100%

*Less than 0.5 percent.

previous year. Purchasers of used cars used installment borrowing in a proportion similar to that of the previous year. Historically, recessions have always had a great impact on the percentage of purchases made on the installment plan.

Table 3-6 shows that the trend away from automobile-less families continued during 1970. Early in 1971, only 17 percent of American families did not own a car; this figure was lower than any figure previously recorded by the Survey of Consumer Finances. Twenty-eight percent of families owned 2 or more cars; this figure has remained fairly constant over the past several years. Automobile ownership is directly related to family income. While the proportion of families owning two cars was less than a half of one percent among families with incomes under $3,000 a year, it was somewhat over 50 percent among families earning at least $15,000 a year.

Table 3-8 shows that a sizable proportion of American families owned truck vehicles of some sort. When the ownership of trucks was added to the ownership of regular passenger automobiles, the proportion of families without a vehicle dropped to only 15 percent.

TABLE 3-1 (Sheet 1 of 2)

PRICE PAID AND NET OUTLAY FOR NEW AND USED CAR PURCHASES

(Percentage distribution of purchases)

Amount for new cars	Price					Net Outlay[a]				
	1966	1967	1968	1969	1970	1966	1967	1968	1969	1970
Less than $2,000[b]	6	8	3	3	*	27	25	22	22	20
$2,000–2,499	11	11	13	10	14	27	28	20	22	22
$2,500–2,999	25	18	12	11	16	24	18	25	16	17
$3,000–3,499	27	26	28	23	18	22	29	33	40	41
$3,500 or more	31	37	44	53	52					
Total	100	100	100	100	100	100	100	100	100	100

*Less than 0.5 percent.

[a]Price minus trade-in or sale.

[b]Includes cars received as gifts and payment in kind.

Note: This table is based on the figures for all cars owned by respondents at the time of the interview in January-February, 1967, 1968, 1969, 1970, or 1971, which had been purchased during the previous calendar year.

TABLE 3-1 (Sheet 2 of 2)

PRICE PAID AND NET OUTLAY FOR NEW AND USED CAR PURCHASES

(Percentage distribution of purchases)

Amount for used cars	Price					Net Outlay[a]				
	1966	1967	1968	1969	1970	1966	1967	1968	1969	1970
Less than $500[b]	44	39	40	32	31	50	43	44	35	36
$500-999	22	20	21	20	18	21	20	22	24	19
$1,000-1,499	12	15	13	17	18	14	17	14	16	20
$1,500-1,999	10	10	12	12	11	8	10	11	12	10
$2,000 or more	12	16	14	19	22	7	10	9	13	15
Total	100	100	100	100	100	100	100	100	100	100

*Less than 0.5 percent.

[a] Price minus trade-in or sale.

[b] Includes cars received as gifts and payment in kind.

Note: This table is based on the figures for all cars owned by respondents at the time of the interview in January-February 1967, 1968, 1969, 1970, and 1971, which had been purchased during the previous calendar year.

TABLE 3-2

AGE DISTRIBUTION OF USED CARS PURCHASED

(Percentage distribution)

Age[a] of car at time of purchase	Year of purchase					
	1965	1966	1967	1968	1969	1970
1 year or less	11	13	14	12	14	9
2-4 years	29	27	34	30	36	45
5-7 years	29	32	25	32	29	34
8-10 years	20	17	16	15	14	11
11 or more years	11	11	11	11	7	1
Total	100	100	100	100	100	100
Mean age (years)	6.8	6.8	6.4	6.7	6.0	5.9

[a]Based on year model; one year or less for 1970 stands for 1969, 1970, or 1971 model year cars.

TABLE 3-3

TRADE-IN ACTIVITY - 1966, 1967, 1968, 1969, 1970

(Percentage distribution of families)

	1966	1967	1968	1969	1970
Did not purchase a car	72	71	71	72	74
Purchased a new car[a]	12	11	11	12	9
Traded in a car bought new	6	5	6	7	4
Traded in a car bought used	3	2	2	2	2
No car traded in	3	4	3	3	3
Purchased a used car[a]	16	18	18	16	17
Traded in a car bought new	1	1	2	1	2
Traded in a car bought used	5	7	5	5	5
No car traded in	10	10	11	10	10
Total	100	100	100	100	100

[a]Families buying more than one car are classified only once according to the newest car purchased.

TABLE 3-4

PROPORTION OF TRADE-INS AND DISTRIBUTION OF TRADE-IN ALLOWANCES
FOR NEW AND USED CAR PURCHASES

(Percentage distribution of purchases)

	New car purchases				Used car purchases			
	1967	1968	1969	1970	1967	1968	1969	1970
Proportion of purchases involving trade-in or sale in private	69	70	72	69	40	35	34	37
Amount received for trade-in (in percent of all trade-ins)								
Less than $500	29	24	16	23	72	72	60	57
$500–999	24	20	31	26	16	18	25	24
$1,000–1,499	19	22	17	20	9	5	8	14
$1,500–1,999	15	14	15	16	1	4	5	4
$2,000 or more	13	20	21	15	2	1	2	1
Total	100	100	100	100	100	100	100	100

TABLE 3-5

PROPORTION OF FAMILIES PURCHASING CARS - WITHIN FAMILY INCOME GROUPS

| | Proportion of families buying cars in percent | | | |
| | New cars | | Used cars | |
	1969	1970	1969	1970
Annual family income				
Less than $3,000	1	*	12	7
$3,000-4,999	4	1	12	15
$5,000-7,499	6	5	18	21
$7,500-9,999	12	6	20	18
$10,000-14,999	19	10	16	20
$15,000 or more	23	20	17	16
All families	12	9	16	17

TABLE 3-6

NEW, USED, AND MULTIPLE CAR OWNERSHIP - 1957-1971

(Percentage distribution of families)

Car Ownership	1957	1959	1961	1963	1965	1967	1968	1969	1970	1971
Own one car, bought new	28	27	26	26	27	27	27	27	27	28
Own one car, bought used	34	32	32	32	28	26	26	25	27	27
Own two or more cars	13	15	18	22	24	25	26	27	28	28
Do not own car	25	26	24	20	21	22	21	21	18	17
Total	100	100	100	100	100	100	100	100	100	100

TABLE 3-7 (Sheet 1 of 2)

CAR OWNERSHIP IN EARLY 1971 - WITHIN VARIOUS GROUPS

(Ownership as a percentage of families in specified groups)

	Own at least one car		Own one or more cars bought new		Own two or more cars	
Annual family income	1970	1971	1970	1971	1970	1971
Less than $1,000	25	13	3	6	3	*
$1,000-1,999	41	34	17	9	1	*
$2,000-2,999	50	52	13	25	7	*
$3,000-3,999	60	61	25	34	6	9
$4,000-4,999	70	71	27	32	9	10
$5,000-5,999	75	83	28	29	9	12
$6,000-7,499	86	89	40	37	15	19
$7,500-9,999	92	89	44	45	26	26
$10,000-14,999	96	95	63	58	41	40
$15,000 or more	96	97	76	73	60	54
Life cycle stage of family head						
Under age 45						
Unmarried, no children	69	71	33	36	8	5
Married, no children	96	95	55	55	34	31
Married, youngest child under age 6	95	93	46	42	31	29
Married, youngest child age 6 or older	96	94	53	48	44	41
Age 45 or older						
Married, has children	91	93	53	48	51	49
Married, no children, head in labor force	92	97	62	69	42	43
Married, no children, head retired	78	82	54	54	16	15
Unmarried, no children, head in labor force	65	64	41	29	11	5
Unmarried, no children, head retired	39	42	25	30	2	3
Any age						
Unmarried, has children	55	54	24	25	9	12
All families	82	83	47	47	28	28

---

* Less than 0.5 percent.

TABLE 3-7 (Sheet 2 of 2)

CAR OWNERSHIP IN EARLY 1971 - WITHIN VARIOUS GROUPS

(Ownership as a percentage of families in specified groups)

	Own at least one car		Own one or more cars bought new		Own two or more cars	
	1970	1971	1970	1971	1970	1971
Age of head						
Under age 25	82	86	32	28	15	13
25-34	88	87	46	47	26	26
35-44	89	86	48	46	38	34
45-54	90	91	55	54	44	44
55-64	80	83	53	51	27	31
Age 65 or older	60	65	40	44	10	12
Education of head						
0-8 grades	66	67	29	32	14	14
9-11 grades	80	79	36	33	27	24
12 grades	87	91	53	54	30	30
Some college	90	89	53	56	35	37
College degree	92	93	71	65	41	43
Race						
White	86	86	50	50	31	30
Nonwhite	60	53	26	20	13	14
Region						
Northeast	82	79	50	50	31	28
North Central	84	86	50	46	28	29
South	78	82	42	45	24	26
West	87	85	50	46	37	31
Belt						
Central cities of 12 largest SMSA's	62	61	44	39	18	15
Central cities of other SMSA's	66	78	39	39	27	30
Suburban areas of 12 largest SMSA's	91	91	63	65	46	41
Suburban areas of other SMSA's	89	90	56	50	35	34
Adjacent areas of SMSA's	86	89	47	51	29	29
Outlying areas of SMSA's	83	82	37	38	20	18
All families	82	83	46	47	28	28

TABLE 3-8

TRUCK OWNERSHIP IN EARLY 1971 – WITHIN FAMILY INCOME GROUPS

(Percentage distribution of families)

Annual family income	Number of trucks owned[a]			Total
	None	One	Two or more	
Less than $5,000	90	10	*	100
$5,000–7,499	82	16	2	100
$7,500–9,999	76	24	*	100
$10,000–14,999	79	21	*	100
$15,000 or more	81	15	4	100
All families	82	17	1	100

[a]Includes trucks, pick-ups, vans, and jeep-type vehicles.

TABLE 3-9

VEHICLE[a] OWNERSHIP – WITHIN FAMILY INCOME GROUPS

(Percentage distribution of families)

Annual family income	Number of vehicles owned						Total
	None		One		Two or more		
	1970	1971	1970	1971	1970	1971	
Less than $5,000	42	42	46	46	12	12	100
$5,000–7,499	15	12	55	56	30	32	100
$7,500–9,999	6	7	50	47	44	46	100
$10,000–14,999	4	5	40	38	56	57	100
$15,000 or more	4	2	28	31	68	67	100
All families	16	15	43	43	41	42	100

[a]Includes cars, trucks, pick-ups, vans, and jeep-type vehicles.

4

HOUSEHOLD DURABLES

Purchases of household durables in 1970 increased somewhat from the year before, with 47 percent of all families reporting that they purchased at least one household durable. The average expenditure per buying family did not increase significantly from the previous year, even though the price level showed a significant increase. Based upon preliminary population estimates, the Survey of Consumer Finances found that American families spent some 16.8 billion dollars on household durables during 1970, a greater amount than they had spent in any previous year. The proportion of families buying on credit showed a sizeable increase to 43 percent in 1970 as compared with only 39 percent in 1969 (Table 4-1).

In the past, purchases of household durables have proven to be directly related to family income and inversely related to the age of the family head. In 1970 this pattern was not disturbed. However, proportionately larger increases in purchases of household durables were found among lower rather than among higher income groupings. Table 4-3 shows that 30 percent of those families making less than $3,000 per year purchased at least one household durable in 1970, as compared with only 21 percent in 1969. Similarly, 41 percent of those families making between $3,000-$5,000 per year purchased a durable in 1970, as compared with 35 percent the year before.

A good indication as to whether or not a family will buy a household durable is the family's present financial position, as compared to their financial situation in the recent past. For example, 56 percent of those families who said that their present financial situation was better than a year ago made a purchase of a household durable, while only 42 percent of those families who said that their financial situation was worse than a year ago made such a purchase (Table 4-5). When both a family's income and its relative financial position are considered, it is possible to predict accurately the likelihood with which they will purchase a household durable. For example, of the 18 percent of families who earn more than $10,000 per year, and who also said that their financial position was better than a year ago, fully 63 percent purchased a household durable. In contrast to this proportion, of the fifth of the sample whose incomes were under $10,000 a year, and who said that their present financial position was worse than it was a year ago, only 35 percent purchased durable goods during 1970.

Table 4-6 shows that although family heads were more likely to buy durables during 1970, the average amount spent on such durables was somewhat higher among family heads who were at least 25 years of age. In the 18 to 24 year old group, the median expenditure on household durables was only $290, as contrasted with $450 for the 25 to 34 year old age group. The life cycle of a family is another good predictor of the likelihood of household durables purchases. Table 4-7 shows that young married couples were more likely to purchase household durables than were other groups. Seventy-two percent of married families whose head was under 45 years of age and who did not have children, purchased a household durable during 1970, and 62 percent of married families in this age bracket with children under age 6 made such a purchase. These figures contrast sharply with those for unmarried family heads who are retired and have no children. In this latter category, only 20 percent of those families surveyed purchased a durable good.

With regard to the purchase of specific household durables, the largest proportion of families, 18 percent, bought furniture. Eleven percent purchased a black and white television set, 9 percent purchased a washing machine, and only 5 percent purchased a color television set. In 1971, a special analysis was made of those families who owned and who purchased both black and white and color television sets. It was found that 51 percent of all families had only black and white television sets, while 21 percent owned only color television sets, and 23 percent owned both black and white and color television sets. The ownership of a color television set was highly dependent upon both income and age, while it was only slightly dependent upon the education of the family head. Early in 1971, of those families making more than $15,000 a year, more than two-thirds owned at least one color television set, as compared with only 13 percent who owned one among those families with incomes of less than $3,000. Neither very young or very old families were as apt to own color televisions as were families in their middle years. Notably, nearly 50 percent of all families in each age group between 25 and 64 years of age had at least one color television set. Only 17 percent of those families with heads under 25, and 29 percent of those families with heads over age 75 owned a color television set.

Although the level of education of the family head is highly correlated with family income, color television set ownership is not as directly related to the level of education as it is to income. While 49 percent of those families headed by a college graduate and 44 percent of those families headed by a holder of an advanced degree had a color television set, fully 55 percent of those families headed by a person who began, but did not complete college, and 54 percent of those families headed by a high school graduate with non-college training, owned color television sets.

TABLE 4-1

PURCHASES OF HOUSEHOLD DURABLES[a] - 1964-1970

(Percentage distribution of families)

Families purchasing	Purchases of household durables					
	1965	1966	1967	1968	1969	1970
Percentage	46	48	43	48	45	47
Estimated number (in millions)	27.4	28.9	26.7	29.8	28.5	30.6
Percent using credit (buyers only)	44	43	40	42	39	43

[a]Includes purchases of new and used household appliances. Durables other than cars refer to all items of movable furniture and all electrical and gas appliances not permanently built-in or attached to the dwelling structure. Personal effects, recreation items, non-household items (like lawn mowers), and non-appliance household items are not included.

TABLE 4-2

AMOUNTS SPENT FOR HOUSEHOLD DURABLES - 1964-1970

(Percentage distribution of families)

Amount spent[a]	1964	1965	1966	1967	1968	1969	1970
Zero	56	54	52	57	52	55	53
$1-99	4	4	5	5	5	3	4
$100-199	9	8	11	8	8	7	7
$200-299	9	9	8	7	7	7	8
$300-499	9	10	9	9	11	10	10
$500-749	6	7	8	7	8	9	8
$750-999	2	3	3	3	4	3	4
$1,000 or more	4	5	4	4	5	6	6
Amount not ascertained	1	*	*	*	*	*	*
Total	100	100	100	100	100	100	100

*Less than 0.5 percent.

[a]Before deduction for trade-in; includes amount borrowed.

TABLE 4-3

PURCHASES OF HOUSEHOLD DURABLES
WITHIN INCOME, AGE, AND LIFE CYCLE GROUPS

(Percentage distribution of families)

	Proportion that purchased					
	1965	1966	1967	1968	1969	1970
Annual family income						
Less than $3,000	26	28	20	23	21	30
$3,000-4,999	35	42	40	39	35	41
$5,000-7,499	46	49	42	48	41	39
$7,500-9,999	58	54	49	55	49	53
$10,000 or more	60	61	56	59	56	56
Age of family head						
Under age 25	47	61	62	56	51	60
25-34	62	64	57	65	57	57
35-44	56	58	50	54	53	58
45-54	48	47	49	50	47	44
55-64	37	39	37	39	39	44
Age 65 or older	26	28	21	27	25	29
Life cycle stage of family head						
Under age 45						
Unmarried	36	37	42	43	31	39
Married, no children	60	65	65	64	57	72
Married, children	62	63	57	64	58	60
Age 45 or older						
Married, has children	53	57	53	47	48	55
Married, no children	41	39	36	43	40	39
Unmarried	a	a	a	24	22	26
All families	46	48	43	48	45	47

---

[a]Not available.

Notes: The term no children, which appears frequently in this chapter,
means no children under age 18 living at home. Unemployed people and
housewives age 55 or older are considered retired; unemployed people and
housewives under age 55 are considered to be in the labor force.

TABLE 4-4

PURCHASES OF HOUSEHOLD DURABLES – WITHIN INCOME GROUPS

(Percentage distribution of families)

		Annual family income				
	All	Less than $3,000	$3,000 -4,999	$5,000 -7,499	$7,500 -9,999	$10,000 -14,999	$15,000 or more
Did not purchase in 1970	53	71	60	61	47	44	44
Purchased in 1970	47	29	40	39	53	56	56
Spent[a]							
Less than $100	4	6	7	4	2	3	1
$100–199	7	7	11	7	9	6	5
$200–299	8	6	7	7	9	10	6
$300–499	11	6	8	7	15	14	11
$500–749	9	4	6	6	10	13	11
$750–999	4	1	1	4	4	5	8
$1,000 or more	6	*	1	4	4	6	14
Total	100	100	100	100	100	100	100
Percent using credit[b]	43	56	45	50	51	48	24
Percent of sample	100	11	15	17	14	23	20
Number of families	1327	149	192	225	184	309	268

---

*Less than 0.5 percent.

[a]Before deduction of trade-in; includes amount borrowed. Subtotals do not necessarily add up to totals because of rounding.

[b]Based only on families making a purchase; includes purchases of all durables.

TABLE 4-5

PURCHASES OF HOUSEHOLD DURABLES IN 1970 BY CHANGE IN FINANCIAL POSITION

(Percentage distribution of families)

Amount spent on durables in 1970	All families[b]	All families - financial situation compared to a year ago[a]:			1970 family income under $10,000 - financial situation compared to a year ago[a]:			1970 family income $10,000 or more - financial situation compared to a year ago[a]:		
		Better	Same	Worse	Better	Same	Worse	Better	Same	Worse
None	53	44	56	58	52	58	65	37	53	44
Some	47	56	44	42	48	42	35	63	47	56
$1–99	4	4	2	4	5	3	6	3	1	1
$100–199	7	7	9	5	9	10	5	6	7	3
$200–299	8	10	8	7	11	8	5	9	7	9
$300–499	11	14	9	9	12	10	7	16	8	12
$500–749	9	11	8	8	6	6	7	13	11	10
$750 or more	10	11	8	10	7	4	4	15	13	21
Total	100	100	100	100	100	100	100	100	100	100
Percent of sample	100	31	36	32	13	22	20	18	14	11
Number of families	1,327	410	482	418	172	298	272	238	184	146

[a] The question asked was: "We are interested in how people are getting along financially these days. Would you say that you and your family are better off or worse off financially than you were a year ago?"

[b] Includes 2 percent of families whose relative financial position was unknown or not ascertained.

TABLE 4-6

PURCHASES OF HOUSEHOLD DURABLES – WITHIN AGE OF FAMILY HEAD GROUPS

(Percentage distribution of families)

	All families	Age of family head						
		18–24	25–34	35–44	45–54	55–64	65–74	75 or older
Did not purchase in 1970	57	41	43	42	57	56	68	77
Purchased in 1970	43	59	57	58	43	44	32	23
Spent[a]								
Less than $100	4	10	4	3	2	3	3	2
$100–199	7	10	8	8	4	7	7	7
$200–299	8	11	7	8	10	6	7	6
$300–499	11	10	12	15	9	12	8	5
$500–749	9	11	15	9	6	9	5	1
$750–999	4	3	4	6	6	3	2	1
$1,000 or more	6	5	8	8	7	3	2	*
Total	100	100	100	100	100	100	100	100
Percent using credit[b]	43	46	57	48	42	31	17	32
Median amount spent[b]	$400	$290	$450	$400	$400	$390	$300	$250
Percent of sample	100	9	19	18	20	15	13	6
Number of families	1,327	116	254	243	261	203	167	83

*Less than 0.5 percent.
[a]Before deduction of trade-in; includes amount borrowed.
[b]Based only on families making one or more purchases.

TABLE 4-7

PURCHASES OF HOUSEHOLD DURABLES IN 1970 – WITHIN LIFE CYCLE GROUPS

(Percentage distribution of families)

	All families	Under age 45				Age 45 or older					Any age Unmarried
		Unmarried	Married			Married			Unmarried		
		No children	No children	Youngest child under age 6	Youngest child age 6 or older	Has children	No children		No children		Has children
							Head in labor force	Head retired	Head in labor force	Head retired	
Did not purchase in 1970	53	65	28	38	44	46	60	63	71	80	53
Purchased in 1970	47	35	72	62	56	54	40	37	29	20	47
Spent[a]											
Less than $100	4	7	7	3	2	3	*	4	4	3	9
$100–199	7	4	8	10	10	6	6	7	4	6	4
$200–299	8	5	12	7	9	12	7	8	9	3	8
$300–499	11	11	13	11	16	9	13	7	3	7	14
$500–749	9	4	13	17	10	12	6	4	4	1	5
$750–999	4	4	7	6	4	5	5	4	3	*	4
$1,000 or more	6	*	11	8	6	8	4	4	3	1	4
Total	100	100	100	100	100	100	100	100	100	100	100
Percent using credit[b]	43	39	45	52	53	47	23	14	41	30	70
Median amount spent[b]	$400	$300	$450	$500	$400	$425	$400	$320	$280	$240	$320
Percent of sample	100	6	8	18	10	12	16	9	6	9	6
Number of families	1,327	75	109	239	135	162	217	115	75	122	78

*Less than 0.5 percent.

aBefore deduction of trade-in; includes amount borrowed.

bBased only on families making one or more purchases.

TABLE 4-8

PURCHASES OF HOUSEHOLD DURABLES – WITHIN HOUSING STATUS AND DURATION OF HOUSE OCCUPANCY GROUPS

(Percentage distribution of families)

| | All families | Housing status and duration of house occupancy[a] | | | | |
| | | Own house | | Rent house | | Neither own nor rent |
		Bought house 1968-1971	Bought prior to 1968	Moved in 1968-1971	Moved in prior to 1968	
Did not purchase in 1970	53	40	56	49	55	59
Purchased in 1970	47	60	44	51	45	41
Spent[b]						
Less than $100	4	4	2	6	5	12
$100-199	7	9	7	6	7	9
$200-299	8	7	8	8	12	3
$300-499	11	9	12	9	10	12
$500-749	9	15	8	10	2	3
$750-999	4	5	3	4	8	3
$1,000 or more	6	11	4	8	2	*
Total	100	100	100	100	100	100
Percent purchasing two or more items[c]	39	28	15	23	17	9
Percent using credit[d]	43	44	33	57	62	37
Median amount spent[d]	$400	$500	$400	$440	$280	$220
Number of families	1,301	193	679	282	118	34

*Less than 0.5 percent.   [a]Includes primary families only.   [b]Before deduction of trade-in; includes amount borrowed.
[c]Refers to specific appliances (see footnote to Table 5-9).   [d]Based only on families making one or more purchases.

TABLE 4-9

NUMBER OF APPLIANCES[a] PURCHASED, 1968–1970

(Percentage distribution of families)

| | Did not purchase | Families purchasing | | Total |
		One item	Two or more items	
All families				
1970	53	29	18	100
1969	63	26	11	100
1968	62	24	14	100
Annual family income				
Less than $3,000				
1970	70	23	7	100
1969	82	14	4	100
1968	82	14	4	100
$3,000–4,999				
1970	59	27	14	100
1969	70	23	7	100
1968	71	22	7	100
$5,000–7,499				
1970	61	22	17	100
1969	66	24	10	100
1968	61	26	13	100
$7,500–9,999				
1970	47	36	17	100
1969	62	25	13	100
1968	56	27	17	100
$10,000–14,999				
1970	44	32	24	100
1969	55	31	14	100
1968	54	28	18	100
$15,000 or more				
1970	44	30	26	100
1969	54	30	16	100
1968	52	27	21	100

[a]Includes only the following items: TV (color or black and white), re-frigerator, washing machine, cooking range, clothes dryer, dishwasher, air conditioner, sewing machine, radio, record-playing equipment, tape recorder, freezer, humidifier and dehumidifier.

TABLE 4-10 (Sheet 1 of 2)

PURCHASES OF SPECIFIC HOUSEHOLD DURABLES, PRICES PAID, AND USE OF CREDIT – 1966-1969

(Percentage distribution of purchases)

	TV				Refrigerator				Washing machine			
	1967	1968	1969	1970	1967	1968	1969	1970	1967	1968	1969	1970
Proportion purchasing	13	16	14	15	7	8	8	7	8	8	7	9
Total price paid												
$1-99	11	9	8	11	13	15	11	11	12	10	10	14
$100-199	26	25	20	18	8	11	16	12	23	28	27	25
$200-249	7	7	6	5	17	11	11	12	41	29	32	25
$250-299	4	5	3	5	18	24	18	19	11	20	14	23
$300-399	8	10	12	11	28	22	26	25	7	10	14	10
$400-499	10	14	12	18	7	11	10	12	4	2	1	3
$500 or more	34	30	39	32	9	6	8	9	2	1	2	*
Total	100	100	100	100	100	100	100	100	100	100	100	100
Proportion of purchases involving:												
Credit	44	39	39	41	36	39	33	31	34	38	36	37
Cash only	56	61	61	59	64	61	67	69	66	62	64	63
Total	100	100	100	100	100	100	100	100	100	100	100	100
Number of cases	366	377	364	202	218	189	210	96	226	179	190	115

*Less than 0.5 percent.

TABLE 4-10 (Sheet 2 of 2)

PURCHASES OF SPECIFIC HOUSEHOLD DURABLES, PRICES PAID, AND THE USE OF CREDIT – 1966-1969

(Percentage distribution of purchases)

	Cooking Range				Furniture[b]				Other major appliances[c]			
	1967[a]	1968[a]	1969[a]	1970[a]	1967[a]	1968[a]	1969[a]	1970[a]	1967[a]	1968[a]	1969[a]	1970[a]
Proportion purchasing	5	6	5	6	17	19	17	18	7	10	10	12
Total price paid												
$1–99	22	22	17	16	14	18	8	8	10	11	7	9
$100–199	30	27	27	29	25	20	15	16	46	44	42	35
$200–249	21	18	19	19	7	7	11	8	25	22	20	21
$250–299	9	17	12	11	5	5	6	5	9	11	14	14
$300–399	8	14	20	16	13	15	10	12	5	10	11	9
$400–499	4	2	3	7	8	8	8	7	1	1	3	10
$500 or more	6	0	2	2	28	27	42	44	4	1	3	2
Total	100	100	100	100	100	100	100	100	100	100	100	100
Proportion of purchases involving:												
Credit	33	35	37	37	37	38	36	43	25	31	37	40
Cash only	67	65	63	63	63	62	64	57	75	69	63	60
Total	100	100	100	100	100	100	100	100	100	100	100	100
Number of cases	134	132	127	82	499	466	428	244	225	253	256	161

[a] Families buying two units of an item are counted twice.
[b] All furniture bought during the year, rather than specific purchases.
[c] Clothes dryers, dishwashers, air conditioners.

TABLE 4-11 (Sheet 1 of 2)

TELEVISION OWNERSHIP AND PURCHASES BY INCOME, AGE OF HEAD AND EDUCATION OF HEAD

(Percentage distribution of families)

	Total Family Income						
	Less than $3000	$3000 -4999	$5000 -7499	$7500 -9999	$10,000 -14,999	$15,000 or more	All families
All families	11	15	17	14	23	20	100
Television ownership in early 1971							
No television	14	9	4	4	2	1	5
Black and white television	73	66	57	53	45	31	51
Color television	10	13	23	27	23	22	21
Both black and white and color televisions	3	12	16	16	30	46	23
Total	100	100	100	100	100	100	100
Television purchases during 1970							
Purchased one or more televisions	8	13	13	15	18	21	16

TABLE 4-11 (Sheet 2 of 2)

TELEVISION OWNERSHIP AND PURCHASES BY INCOME, AGE OF HEAD AND EDUCATION OF HEAD

(Percentage distribution of families)

| | Age of Head | | | | | | | Education of Head | | | | | | | | |
	Under 25	25 -34	35 -44	45 -54	55 -64	65 -74	75 or older	0-5 grades	6-8 grades	9-11 grades	12 grades	Completed high school plus non-college training	College no degree	College degree	College advanced degree	All Families
All families	9	19	18	20	15	13	6	7	18	17	17	12	15	10	4	100
Television ownership in early 1971																
No television	11	6	2	5	4	5	6	9	6	7	3	2	4	5	5	5
Black and white television	72	44	49	47	47	57	65	67	59	57	50	44	41	46	41	51
Color television	12	29	20	14	24	19	22	15	20	18	22	21	22	21	25	21
Both black and white and color televisions	5	21	29	34	25	19	7	9	15	18	25	33	33	28	29	23
Total	100	100	100	100	100	100	100	100	100	100	100	100	100	100	100	100
Television purchases during 1970																
Purchased one or more televisions	21	20	20	12	16	9	2	17	13	15	15	20	14	17	16	16

5

FINANCIAL ASSETS

The proportion of American families owning various types of financial assets remained relatively constant in 1971, with the notable exception of the proportion of families holding certificates of deposit. Primarily because of their relative safety and the high yields that they bore during 1970, the proportion of families owning certificates of deposit nearly doubled between 1970 and 1971.

The proportion of families with savings accounts continued an increase which was begun after the Second World War. Early in 1971, nearly two-thirds of all American families had savings accounts, a proportion which came close to the three-quarters of all families with checking accounts. Only 16 percent of all families had no bank account (savings or checking) whatsoever, while an additional 14 percent had less than $200 in the bank (Table 5-2). On the other hand, 21 percent of all families had at least $5,000 in savings and checking accounts and certificates of deposit.

The great increase in holdings of certificates of deposit was most heavily concentrated among families with higher income levels although increases were reported in all but the very lowest income brackets (Table 5-3). Among families earning at least $15,000 a year, the ownership of certificates of deposit increased from 13 to 23 percent. The increase in the ownership of certificates occurred in all age groups. The oldest people, who probably had the greatest desire for security and risk-free assets, increased their holdings of certificates of deposit from 17 to 21 percent.

The ownership of securities, stocks, bonds, and mutual funds, ranged from 5 percent of those families with less than $3,000 income to 68 percent of those families earning at least $25,000 per year. These findings which are shown in Table 5-6, are incomplete because the amounts of securities owned were not ascertained among some families. The size distribution of these holdings also differed greatly by income. Among families with incomes of $25,000 or more, nearly half had holdings of securities valued at more than $10,000.

In 1971, an analysis was made of the total financial assets of each family. These consisted of bank accounts, including certificates of deposit, and securities, consisting of stocks, bonds, and mutual funds. It was found that about one-third of all families had less than $1,000 in financial assets while 7 percent had extensive financial assets, valued at $25,000 or more. (Table 5-7)

Lower income families usually had small amounts of financial assets. For example, nearly half of those families with incomes under $3,000 had no financial assets whatsoever, and another 19 percent had financial assets of less than $500. Less than 1 percent of those families making at least $25,000 a year, however, had under $500 in financial assets, and almost two-thirds of these high income families had at least $25,000 in financial assets.

In terms of age, the holdings of large amounts of liquid assets was usually confined to older families, although the absence of these kinds of assets was noticeable among both young and old families.

TABLE 5-1

PROPORTION OF FAMILIES HOLDING SELECTED
FINANCIAL ASSETS, IN PERCENT

	Early in						
	1951	1960	1963	1968	1969	1970	1971
Savings accounts	47	55	56	64	62	65	66
Certificates of deposit	a	a	a	4.5	4.9	7.7	13.0
Checking accounts	44	60	62	71	72	75	74
Bonds[b]	43	32	26	26	26	28	28
Stocks[c]	9	17	20	23	24	26	27
Number of family units (in millions)	46.3	53.5	36.2	61.2	62.5	64.0	65.1

[a]Not available.

[b]In 1968, and in years before 1968, only government savings bonds. The ownership of other bonds was so uncommon in earlier years that these data are reasonably comparable to those for later years. In 1971, 4 percent of families owned nongovernment bonds.

[c]Includes mutual funds.

TABLE 5-2

LIQUID ASSET HOLDINGS[a] - 1963, 1965, 1968, 1969, 1970, 1971

(Percentage distribution of families)

Amount of liquid assets[b]	1963	1965	1968	1969	1970	1971
None	22	20	19	19	16	16
$1-199	15	17	15	14	14	14
$200-499	14	11	12	12	12	12
$500-1,999	21	21	24	22	22	24
$2,000-4,999	14	14	13	15	15	13
$5,000-9,999	8	9	8	8	9	9
$10,000 or more	6	8	9	10	12	12
Total	100	100	100	100	100	100

---

[a]Liquid assets include savings accounts, certificates of deposit and checking accounts. Before 1971 government savings bonds were also included.

[b]Cases in which the amount of liquid assets were not ascertained are distributed among holders of different amounts of liquid assets.

TABLE 5-3

DISTRIBUTION OF CERTIFICATES OF DEPOSIT - EARLY 1970 AND 1971

(Proportion of each group who owned, in percent)

	Ownership of Certificates	
	Early 1970	Early 1971
All families	8	13
Total family income		
Less than $3,000	5	4
$3,000-4,999	8	12
$5,000-7,499	9	13
$7,500-9,999	6	12
$10,000-14,999	7	11
$15,000 or more	13	23
Age of family head		
Under age 25	2	7
25-34	3	8
35-44	5	8
45-54	7	14
55-64	11	19
Age 65 or older	17	21

TABLE 5-4 (Sheet 1 of 2)

SAVINGS ACCOUNTS[a] BY INCOME, AGE, EDUCATION AND LIFE CYCLE - EARLY 1971

(Percentage distribution of families)

			Savings Accounts			
	None	$1 -499	$500 -1,999	$2,000 -4,999	$5,000 or more	Total
All families	38	15	18	11	18	100
Total family income						
Less than $3,000	68	5	9	12	6	100
$3,000-4,999	54	11	14	4	17	100
$5,000-7,499	46	15	14	9	16	100
$7,500-9,999	43	17	18	9	13	100
$10,000-14,999	26	21	27	12	14	100
$15,000-19,999	13	19	29	15	24	100
$20,000-24,999	15	14	17	18	36	100
$25,000 or more	10	2	6	23	59	100
Age of family head						
Under age 25	44	30	20	5	1	100
25-34	44	19	20	11	6	100
35-44	38	19	26	10	7	100
45-54	35	16	14	12	23	100
55-64	34	7	14	14	31	100
65-74	35	2	14	15	34	100
75 or older	36	*	12	10	42	100
Life cycle stage of family head						
Under age 45						
Unmarried, no children	38	29	16	7	10	100
Married, no children	27	19	32	15	7	100
Married, youngest child under age 6	43	22	22	9	4	100
Married, youngest child age 6 or older	40	22	24	8	6	100
Age 45 or older						
Married, has children	35	17	19	11	18	100
Married, no children, head in labor force	23	9	10	17	41	100
Married, no children, head retired	34	1	15	11	39	100
Unmarried, no children, head in labor force	39	8	26	13	14	100
Unmarried, no children, head retired	45	2	7	15	31	100
Any age						
Unmarried, has children	69	9	9	6	7	100

---
[a]Including certificates of deposit.
*Less than 0.5 percent.

TABLE 5-4 (Sheet 2 of 2)

SAVINGS ACCOUNTS[a] BY INCOME, AGE, EDUCATION AND LIFE CYCLE - EARLY 1971

(Percentage distribution of families)

			Savings Accounts			
	None	$1 -499	$500 -1,999	$2,000 -4,999	$5,000 or more	Total
Education of family head						
0-5 grades	67	*	12	5	16	100
6-8 grades	47	10	13	11	19	100
9-11 grades	48	15	13	9	15	100
12 grades	36	16	18	11	19	100
High school plus non-college training	33	18	21	14	14	100
College, no degree	23	21	22	17	17	100
College, bachelor's degree	21	20	26	11	22	100
College, advanced degree	20	10	30	10	30	100

---

[a]Includes certificates of deposit.

*Less than 0.5 percent.

TABLE 5-5

NUMBER OF SAVINGS ACCOUNTS BY INCOME

(Percentage distribution of families)

	Number of Savings Accounts					
	None	One	Two	Three	Four or more	Total
All families	36	33	17	7	7	100
Total family income						
Less than $3,000	65	27	8	*	*	100
$3,000-4,999	49	33	14	3	1	100
$5,000-7,499	46	31	14	4	5	100
$7,500-9,999	40	36	14	7	3	100
$10,000-14,999	24	41	19	9	7	100
$15,000-19,999	14	34	30	7	15	100
$20,000-24,999	15	25	25	16	19	100
$25,000 or more	10	18	20	18	34	100

---

*Less than 0.5 percent.

TABLE 5-6

OWNERSHIP OF SECURITIES[a] BY INCOME AND AGE - EARLY 1971

(Percentage distribution of families)

		Value of Securities Owned			
	None	$1 -1,999	$2,000 -9,999	$10,000 or more	Total
All families[b]	78	8	7	7	100
Total family income					
Less than $3,000	95	3	2	*	100
$3,000-4,999	92	2	5	1	100
$5,000-7,499	82	8	6	4	100
$7,500-9,999	88	7	3	2	100
$10,000-14,999	76	12	7	5	100
$15,000-19,999	59	13	17	11	100
$20,000-24,999	46	16	18	20	100
$25,000 or more	32	8	11	49	100
Age of family head					
Under age 25	91	6	3	*	100
25-34	80	13	5	2	100
35-44	76	9	9	6	100
45-54	72	8	8	12	100
55-64	75	3	9	13	100
65-74	80	5	9	6	100
75 and over	84	5	7	4	100

---

* Less than 0.5 percent.

[a] Securities include stocks, bonds and mutual funds.

[b] A substantial proportion of families unable to give the amount of securities owned has been omitted. This explains the discrepancy between Tables 5-6 and 5-1.

TABLE 5-7

OWNERSHIP OF FINANCIAL ASSETS[a] BY INCOME AND AGE – EARLY 1971

(Percentage distribution of families)

	None	$1 -499	$500 -999	Value of Financial Assets $1,000 -4,999	$5,000 -9,999	$10,000 -14,999	$15,000 -24,999	$25,000 or more	Total
All families[b]	19	22	10	23	9	5	5	7	100
Total family income									
Less than $3,000	48	19	6	19	4	2	1	1	100
$3,000–4,999	34	27	8	12	6	6	6	1	100
$5,000–7,499	24	27	6	21	9	3	5	5	100
$7,500–9,999	18	32	10	22	6	2	4	6	100
$10,000–14,999	5	23	16	33	11	7	2	3	100
$15,000–19,999	4	11	16	31	20	3	9	6	100
$20,000–24,999	3	3	10	27	12	8	19	18	100
$25,000 or more	*	*	2	9	15	13	7	54	100
Age of family head									
Under age 25	20	43	15	20	2	*	*	*	100
25–34	18	35	11	25	7	2	2	*	100
35–44	16	24	11	31	8	3	3	4	100
45–54	14	19	12	21	10	8	7	9	100
55–64	25	9	9	16	16	3	7	15	100
65–74	19	12	4	25	12	11	10	7	100
75 and over	27	4	7	16	12	6	13	15	100

*Less than 0.5 percent.

[a] Financial assets include checking accounts, savings accounts, certificates of deposit, stocks, bonds and mutual funds.

[b] A substantial proportion of families unable to give the amount of financial assets has been omitted. This explains the discrepancy between Tables 5-7 and 5-2.

APPENDIX TO PART ONE

TABLE I-1

DISTRIBUTION OF FAMILIES' INCOME DURING SIX RECENT YEARS

(Percentage distribution of families)

Income Groups	Families					
	1962	1965	1967	1968	1969	1970
Less than $1,000	4	3	2	3	2	1
$1,000-1,999	9	8	9	7	5	5
$2,000-2,999	9	9	7	7	7	5
$3,000-3,999	8	8	7	7	7	7
$4,000-4,999	10	7	7	7	5	8
$5,000-5,999	12	8	7	6	5	6
$6,000-7,499	14	13	10	11	11	11
$7,500-9,999	16	17	17	17	16	14
$10,000-14,999	12	17	22	23	24	23
$15,000 or more	6	10	11	13	18	20
Total	100	100	100	100	100	100

TABLE I-2

MEAN INCOME OF TOTAL INCOME
WITHIN EACH INCOME DECILE

(Percentage distribution of families)

	Mean Income			
Decile	in 1960	in 1968	in 1969	in 1970
Lowest	$1,200	$1,210	$1,620	$1,650
Second	2,440	2,610	3,120	3,430
Third	3,630	4,080	4,830	4,870
Fourth	4,930	5,570	6,570	6,410
Fifth	6,110	7,090	7,990	7,920
Sixth	7,310	8,540	9,520	9,450
Seventh	8,590	10,110	11,260	11,370
Eighth	10,200	11,850	13,310	13,680
Ninth	12,710	14,270	16,220	17,990
Highest	22,320	26,740	29,790	28,320
Total	$7,940	$9,220	$10,420	$8,620

TABLE I-3

SHARE OF TOTAL INCOMES
WITHIN EACH INCOME DECILE

(Percentage distribution of families)

Decile	Share of Total Income			
	1960	1968	1969	1970
Lowest	1	1	1	2
Second	3	3	3	3
Third	5	4	5	5
Fourth	7	6	6	6
Fifth	8	8	8	7
Sixth	9	9	9	9
Seventh	11	11	11	11
Eighth	13	13	12	13
Ninth	16	15	16	17
Highest	27	30	29	27
Total	100	100	100	100

TABLE I-4

LIMITS OF EACH INCOME DECILE, 1960 to 1970

(Percentage distribution of families)

Decile	Lowest Income						1970 to 1960	1970 to 1969
	1960	1962	1964	1968	1969	1970		
Lowest	-	-	-	-	-	-	-	-
Second	$1,500	$1,650	$1,600	$1,930	$2,400	$2,700	1.80	1.13
Third	2,640	2,800	2,850	3,290	3,900	4,000	1.52	1.03
Fourth	3,700	4,000	4,050	4,800	5,810	5,500	1.49	.95
Fifth	4,600	5,000	5,200	6,300	7,300	7,000	1.52	.96
Sixth	5,500	5,825	6,320	7,750	8,690	8,600	1.56	.99
Seventh	6,275	6,800	7,500	9,290	10,400	10,045	1.60	.97
Eighth	7,200	8,000	8,860	10,900	12,200	12,010	1.67	.98
Ninth	8,590	9,500	10,675	13,000	14,460	15,000	1.75	1.04
Highest	11,090	12,190	13,700	16,200	18,410	20,000	1.80	1.09
Ratio of highest to second decile	7.4	7.4	8.6	8.4	7.6	7.4		
Ratio of ninth to third decile	3.25	3.39	3.75	3.95	3.71	3.75		

PART 2

THE OUTLOOK
FOR
CONSUMER
DEMAND

INTRODUCTION

Since the early 1950s the Survey Research Center has conducted periodic surveys in order to collect data on changes in the attitudes, expectations, and buying inclinations of consumers. Beginning with 1960 the surveys have been conducted at quarterly intervals. A few weeks after receipt of the interviews, the Center issues extensive reports to the survey participants whose contributions make the surveys possible. In addition, brief press releases are published indicating the changes in the Center's Index of Consumer Sentiment and pointing to major reasons for the changes. In monographs entitled *Survey of Consumer Finances*, published by the Center each year from 1960 to 1971, the full quarterly reports have been reproduced. This practice which yields a permanent record of both the data collected, and their interpretation is continued in the present volume. The reports issued in the four quarters of 1971 as well as in the first quarter of 1972 are presented in the following five chapters in the form in which they were issued, except for minor revisions of style and the omission of duplications. The tables issued with each report are presented once, following the five chapters.

What are the purposes of the quarterly surveys? The surveys are based on a theoretical position designated as behavioral or psychological economics. The underlying theory postulates that the human factor is important in economic affairs. Discretionary expenditures, which greatly influence the course of the economy in affluent societies, depend not only on income, prices, interest rates and other traditional market variables, but also on the attitudes of the decision makers. How consumers and businessmen view past developments and what expectations they have reflect their willingness to buy which, together with their ability to buy, determines effective demand. While some autonomy in decision-making by business, especially regarding business investment, has been recognized at earlier times, the proposition that consumers may likewise change their rate of expenditures in a manner different from changes in the income they receive is fairly new. In most general terms, the purpose of the quarterly surveys is to measure changes in consumer willingness to buy and to test the propositions of behavioral economics. Consumer sentiment is assumed to influence primarily people's discretionary money outlays which include expenditures on major durable goods, housing and leisure-time activities, as well as the incurrence of installment debt and additions to financial savings.

The first task of the quarterly surveys is to provide evidence that attitudinal and expectational variables can contribute to an understanding of what has happened in consumer spending during that quarter. The second task is to predict forthcoming developments. Attitudes and expectations provide a basis for predictions because it is assumed that they represent predispositions to action and change prior to the action itself. Predictions represent the best test of new propositions, and an analysis of the circumstances of either fulfillment or nonfulfillment of predictions serves scientific inquiry.

Two types of data are collected. Some questions asked in the quarterly surveys relate to developments which are assumed to be influential at most or all times, such as those relating to the perception and expectation of change in income or prices. The second type of question relates to economic developments at certain times, such as those regarding proposals to change taxes or control prices. Therefore part of the questionnaire used has remained unchanged over ten or twenty years, but these questions have been supplemented in most quarterly surveys by additional questions formulated according to the requirements of a given time. Altogether, 25 to 30 questions are asked in each survey.

A summary measure is derived from five major questions of the first type by constructing an Index of Consumer Sentiment. (Two questions on changes in the personal financial situation, two questions on expectations about the general economic outlook, and one on supply conditions and prices of durable goods are included in the Index with equal weight; the Index is calculated from the frequency of favorable answers minus those of unfavorable answers plus 100.) Yet the Index and its changes represent only a small part of available indications that are used for purposes of prediction. This is the case because (a) there are other unchanging questions as well, (b) there are unique questions, and (c) the major questions are supplemented by questions about people's reasons for their answers.

Beyond finding out how consumer sentiment has changed at a given time—determining whether consumers are more or less optimistic and confident—it is important to ascertain why the changes have occurred. Whatever answers the respondents give, the interviewer asks "Why do you think so?" or "Why do you say so?" The fixed question/free answer interviewing method used by the Survey Research Center yields detailed answers that are noted down by the interviewers verbatim or quasi-verbatim. The replies are quantified by calculating the frequency of references, for instance, to higher or lower incomes or prices at different times.

An understanding of the studies conducted and the reports issued in 1971 may be enhanced by a brief reference to some prior findings. Chart II-1 indicates the movements of the Index of Consumer Sentiment in the two years between February 1969 and February 1971, as well as during two previous recession periods. It is shown in the chart that the Index deteriorated sharply in 1969—the decline began as early as May 1969—pointing toward the recession of 1970 far in advance. In 1970 the Index changed little, remaining at or close to its lowest level. The decline of the Index in 1969 was as rapid as in 1957, prior to the recession of 1958. Recovery set in earlier both in 1958 and in 1967 (following a mini-recession in consumer durable goods) than in 1971. The chart only indicates changes in willingness to buy; changes in consumers' ability to buy were much smaller in 1969-70 than in 1957-58.

To illustrate the necessity of considering more than the movements of the Index alone, the changes of the five Index components are shown in Chart II-2 for the three years between February 1969 and February 1972. The more recent data presented in that chart will be discussed in detail in the following chapters. It will suffice to point out here that the movements of the five Index components differed greatly in 1971. Attitudes toward the personal financial situation changed much less extensively than expectations about business conditions or the evaluation of supply conditions.

The attitudinal and expectational data foretold a slow and sluggish recovery. Even by February 1972, only a part of the deterioration of 1969-70 had been recovered. The factors responsible for the deterioration of consumers' willingness to buy were analyzed in the *1969* and *1970 Survey of Consumer Finances*. A study of the reasons for the slow recovery in 1971 and an analysis of consumer reactions to the price and wage controls introduced in August 1971 comprise the major contents of the following five chapters.

Data collected in five consecutive surveys are presented in the following chapters.

Date	Number of Cases	Type of Interview
February 1971	1,321 family units	Personal interview
May 1971	1,400 family units	Telephone reinterviews
Aug. 23-Sept. 8, 1971	1,230 family units	Telephone reinterviews
Oct. 15-Nov. 20, 1971	1,297 family units	Personal interview
February 1972	1,422 family units	Telephone reinterviews

Interviews conducted over the telephone, rather than by visiting the selected respondents in person, may be completed in a much shorter period than personal interviews, but give rise to some sampling problems and do not necessarily permit a detailed and lengthy probing of respondents. Reinterviews by telephone of a sample previously interviewed in hour-long personal interviews are not subject to these problems. At the end of each personal interview respondents are asked for permission to call them back at a later time and are asked for their telephone numbers. Both requests are granted by practically all respondents who have a telephone. (The telephone reinterviews are weighted for the absence of nontelephone owners and for nonresponse; the changes in the responses of individual respondents are also calculated.) Some data that are difficult to obtain over the telephone, especially about family income, are available from the personal interviews. Usually the respondents recognize the interviewer who had previously visited them and they are willing to discuss the questions asked in great detail, so that the telephone reinterviews last 20 to 30 minutes. Reinterviewing represents a method that is particularly suitable for the determination of changes in opinions and attitudes.

The methods of the surveys are described in detail in Part IV of this volume. To summarize briefly, the Survey Research Center uses carefully worked out techniques of probability sampling and the fixed question/free answer interviewing method. The basic unit of the survey is the family unit that consists of all related people living in the same dwelling unit. (A family unit may consist of a single person; two or more family units may live in the same dwelling unit.) In most cases the head of the family unit, defined as the husband in complete families, is interviewed.

Sample surveys are subject to errors. The Survey Research Center pays particular attention to mitigating two rather damaging kinds of errors, resulting from nonresponse or faulty responses (response error). Sampling errors are relatively large because of the small samples used. Tables on sampling errors appear in Part IV of this book. It may suffice to repeat here that in case of attitudinal variables, the sampling error of a survey value of approximately 50 percent is +1.65 percent when 1350 cases are used (one standard error or 67 percent probability); the sampling error of a difference between such findings in two surveys is 2.0 percent. When the survey value is lower or higher than 50 percent, the sampling error as expressed in percent is smaller. The sampling error of the Index of Consumer Sentiment is 1.2 percent and for differences in two Index values it is 1.3 percent (one standard error in both instances).

6

THE OUTLOOK FOR CONSUMER DEMAND, FEBRUARY 1971

Highlights

Consumer confidence improved somewhat from November 1970 to February 1971, but the gains were small. The average American was still far from being optimistic.

The Index of Consumer Sentiment stood at 78.2 in February 1971, the same level in February 1970, and only a few points above the 75.4 recorded (after adjustment for the auto strike) in the fourth quarter of 1970. Even after this modest recovery, the Index stood no higher than its low point in 1957-58. (It should be remembered that the Index is indicative of the level of consumer willingness to buy and does not reflect the substantial increase in consumer resources over the last decade or two.) Changes in the sentiment of high and low-income families were quite similar during the last three months.

Although this upturn was just barely significant at the 95 percent confidence level, quite substantial improvements did occur in several consumer attitudes which, taken together, signaled a break from the depressed sentiment which persisted through 1970.

Much of the improvement in the Index may be traced to more favorable opinions concerning market conditions for large household durable goods. Relatively low prices and the availability of good buys were cited by 25 percent of all families, compared to 13 percent in November 1970. At the same time, the proportion saying it was a bad time to buy because of high or rising prices, fell from 26 to 19 percent.

Despite widespread awareness that business conditions were worse than they were a year ago, the proportion believing that the economy would improve during the next year increased to 31 percent from 22 percent from November 1970 to February 1971. Greater optimism concerning the outlook for business during the next twelve months or five years was associated with more favorable anticipations concerning unemployment and interest rates. A majority of consumers expected interest rates to decline during the next twelve months. When respondents were asked if they had heard of any changes in business conditions, they cited primarily lower interest rates and optimistic business forecasts.

Contributing to more opimistic expectations about the economy was a rather general feeling on the part of some people that bad times could not last much longer, and that the government would do something to make things better.

Several important factors prevented a stronger recovery in consumer sentiment:

Nearly one-quarter of all respondents said that their family income was lower in 1970 than in 1969. Nearly one-third claimed to be worse off financially than a year ago. Many upper income families gave such reports. This is the only component of the sentiment Index which deals with evaluations of change over the past year, rather than with expectations about the future. It is also the only component which declined. If the Index were based on just the other four of the five components, it would have advanced another two points or so during the three months prior to Feburay 1971.

Second, inflation and unemployment were mentioned as frequently in February 1971 as they were three months previously as reasons why business conditions would not be good during the next year. This was true even though, as mentioned above, an increased proportion expected lower unemployment. Some people had become accustomed to higher prices, as evidenced by a lessened impact of inflation on how people viewed both their financial situation and buying conditions, but there had been no decline in the extent of inflation which consumers expected during the next year.

Finally, to some degree, consumer sentiment continued to be depressed by a general dissatisfaction with the social as well as the economic climate.

The housing market in February 1971 benefited greatly from widespread awareness of lower interest rates and greater credit availability, in combination with considerable pent-up demand carried over from the previous year when mortgage money was in short supply.

Consumers' evaluations of market conditions for cars, despite some improvement toward the end of 1970, remained slightly less favorable in February 1971 than in February 1970, and intentions to buy remained depressed. High car prices were frequently mentioned (29 percent of all respondents) as a reason why 1971 was expected to be a bad time to buy a car.

Recovery from the substantial loss of confidence that characterized the recession of 1970 appeared likely, in the February 1971 survey, to be slow and greatly influenced by the extent to which consumers saw progress in reducing unemployment and inflation.

Retail sales were stimulated in January 1970 and February 1971 by a catch-up in auto sales following the strike, and by widespread sales and discounts of which consumers were very much aware. In February it appeared that further gains might be expected, but the continued low level of sentiment suggested that they would be moderate and that the saving rate would remain fairly high during the next six months.

The Index of Consumer Sentiment

The Survey Research Center's Index of Consumer Sentiment fluctuated within a narrow range (between 75.4 and 78.2) during the twelve months prior to February, 1971 (see Table II-1).* Despite its improvement at the end of 1970, the Index stood at the same low level in February 1971 as it did one year earlier. Nevertheless, it would be a mistake to conclude that there were not significant changes in consumer attitudes during 1970.

The Index is designed to provide a summary measure of changes in consumers' willingness to buy, and is constructed by giving equal weight to five questions which are repeated in each quarterly survey. Significant changes in just one or two components of the Index, or changes among the components in different directions which offset each other, may result in relatively small movements in the total Index. For this reason, and because the Index is based on only five among some 25 or 30 questions included in each survey, the movements of the Index do not give a complete picture of changes in consumer sentiment.

The last survey before February 1971 was conducted in October-November 1970, while the auto strike was in progress. The strike had a substantial impact on consumer sentiment; it created uncertainty and brought about sizable declines in expectations for favorable business conditions during the next twelve months and five years, and a negative attitude as to whether the next twelve months would be a good or a bad time to buy durable goods. Experience with the steel strike in 1959, which was settled midway during the interviewing for one of the Survey Research Center's quarterly surveys, indicated that some of the impact of a major strike on consumers' expectations is temporary, and news of a settlement brings with it some recovery in expectations. Accordingly, it was suggested in the SRC report on the October-November survey that the Index value should properly be adjusted upward three points to 75.4, which is the figure plotted in Chart II-1 and shown in Table II-1. (Corresponding adjustments have *not* been made in the other tables in this report.)

While some adjustment in the October-November Index value was clearly required, it was not possible to determine just how much of the decline in expectations measured during the auto strike was reversed by the news of the

---

*The tables designated as II are to be found in the section entitled "Outlook Charts and Tables," following Chapter 10 (page 137).

strike settlement. It is therefore not known exactly how much consumer sentiment changed during the three months prior to February 1971, after the strike was settled. However, the change over the six months from August 1970 to February 1971 bridges the strike period and indicates no substantial improvement in consumer sentiment.

The improvement in expectations concerning business conditions during the third quarter of 1970 was maintained in the first quarter of 1971; with the decline caused by the strike fully recovered. In addition, there was a substantial improvement in evaluations of market conditions for durable goods, which had not turned up prior to the strike and which were greatly depressed during the strike. In the six months following August 1970, however, there was a sizable deterioration in consumers' evaluation of recent changes in their financial situation, especially among families with incomes of less than $10,000.

Expected Business Conditions

Consumer sentiment is influenced both by how people feel about their own financial situation and by how they feel about business conditions in the country. Usually, attitudes toward business trends fluctuate to a larger extent than those toward personal trends, but the direction of change is frequently similar. During the twelve month period from February 1970 to February 1971, however, there were great differences between the changes in the two kinds of attitudes. A crucial issue to examine in these differences is whether improvements in business expectations occur earlier than changes in personal expectations and thus point to a subsequent further improvement in the Index.

The conclusion appears to be affirmative if there is reason to assume that the factors which brought about the improvement in business expectations will continue to prevail. The February 1971 survey revealed that the recent upturn in business expectations was attributable to two major considerations. The first of these was widespread awareness of lower interest rates, which were viewed as a good sign and generated the expectation that interest rates would decline further. The second factor was the news heard by some people that business conditions might be improving, creating the belief that recovery was in sight and inspiring less pessimistic opinions about the future rate of unemployment. There were indications that the opinion about a recovery in the near future—which was far from universal—was prompted by government announcements rather than by personal experiences. It appeared that if interest rates were to turn up again, or if the rate of unemployment and also the rate of price increases were to fail to decline in the next few months after February, the recovery in business expectations might be precarious.

Consumers were asked about economic news they had heard; the proportion of consumers reporting to have heard such news had increased during 1970, especially among upper income people. They continued to report unfavorable news heard much more frequently than favorable news, and the frequency of reports on bad news was still substantial. But the proportion of people reporting to have heard favorable news increased greatly (Table II-6).

There were hardly any changes in the kind of unfavorable news reported; the drop in employment and increased unemployment, as well as bad business in various industries and references to recession in general, continued to be noted by many people.

In reporting on favorable news, for the first time in two years a sizable number of respondents emphasized that there were signs of recovery or mentioned easier money and lower interest rates. (References to improvement in the stock market were much less frequent.)

Awareness that business conditions had worsened during 1970 remained widespread. As in the previous three quarterly surveys, the majority of consumers said in February 1971 that current business conditions were worse than those of a year ago. An improvement in these opinions, indicative of the notion that business conditions had not worsened toward the end of 1970, was noticeable only among upper income respondents and was rather small (Table II-2).

In contrast, in February 1971, 31 percent of the sample thought that business conditions would be better in February 1972 than they were at present and 17 percent thought that they would be worse. These data represent a substantial improvement in opinion; nine or twelve months previous to February 1971 the proportions were almost reversed. Upper income respondents especially were quite optimistic in predicting an upward turn in business trends (Table II-3).

Some results of these divergent opinions may be seen from answers to the question in which respondents were asked whether in their opinion there would be good times or bad times during the next twelve months. In February, 41 percent answered good times and 35 percent bad times. These proportions are similar to those obtained twelve months before, but represent a more favorable assessment of economic trends than was obtained nine, six, or three months before. Among upper income people the improvement in opinions was more pronounced than among lower income people (Table II-5).

Favorable changes also occurred in people's expectations about business trends during the next five years. Although many more people still expected that in general, bad times rather than good times would prevail, pessimism became less pronounced (Table II-9).

Two specific questions relating to expected changes in unemployment, and especially to expected changes in interest rates, elicited the greatest change in opinion from November 1970 to February 1971. In February, 43 percent of all consumers thought that unemployment would increase during the next twelve months, and 23 percent thought that it would decrease. But a year earlier, in February 1970, the respective percentages were 60 and 8. Again, upper income people were much less pessimistic than lower income people. Among those consumers with an income of $12,500 and over in February 1971, 38 percent expected that unemployment would increase and 30 percent expected it to decrease (Table II-7).

A decline in interest rates during the twelve months from February 1971 to February 1972 was expected by the majority of consumers; only one in seven thought that interest rates would go up. Table II-8 shows that in February 1969 the notion that interest rates would decline was practically non-existent.

In this discussion of the reasons for either pessimistic or somewhat optimistic business expectations, inflation has not been mentioned. The reason for this omission is that attitudes toward price increases changed little during the three months prior to February 1971. In a later description of attitudes toward purchases of durable goods and also toward personal finances, there will be ample opportunity to analyze the perception of the price situation; during the last part of 1970, however, the change in consumer sentiment was not influenced significantly by considerations of inflation. In explaining why the business outlook is unfavorable, respondents mentioned inflation as frequently in February as they did three months earlier, and the extent of expected price increases also remained unchanged (see Table II-11). That the salience of inflation in people's thinking probably declined somewhat, is indicated by the absence of references to inflation in descriptions of news heard. Yet the process of habituation to inflation is slow, and there were no indications of consumers having heard news that the fight against inflation was won or that inflation was slowing down.

Concern with the war in Vietnam and its impact on the domestic economy did not show any decline. In the February 1971 survey respondents were given a list of imaginary headlines which they might see in the next few years and were asked to indicate which of them would, in their opinion, have a great influence on domestic business conditions. Among the news items listed, an end to the Vietnam war and reduction of spending on military equipment were thought to be capable of having great influence on economic trends by the largest proportion of respondents (see Table 6-1 at the end of this chapter).

Three other news items on the list shown to respondents were also mentioned with substantial, although somewhat lower frequency. These were news items about a reduction in taxes, a decline in unemployment, and increased expenditures for fighting pollution. News of a reduction in the rate of price increases was also mentioned frequently as influencing domestic business, but by a slightly lower proportion of persons than the three items just noted.

Two of the imaginary headlines were assigned a relatively small influence on domestic business. These was news of increased racial tensions and an increase in rioting on campuses. Possibly a smaller proportion of people accepted such news as probable than was the case with the other news items.

The inquiry just reported indicated that in the opinion of very many Americans, it is not only economic news regarding taxes, unemployment and prices, but also political and social matters, which cause concern and which are thought to be related to economic trends. The war in Vietnam and pollution are two of the most powerful issues of this nature.

Changes in the Personal Financial Situation

The impact of the recession of 1970 on the American people's income situation was substantial. In the February 1971 survey, respondents' family income in 1970 was determined on the basis of a long list of detailed questions. Respondents were than asked whether their income was higher, lower, or substantially the same as their income had been in 1969. In reply, 49 percent reported higher, and 23 percent lower income. A similar inquiry a year earlier yielded 55 percent with income increases and 16 percent with income decreases (Table 6-2).

The change in the income trend extended not only to those with low incomes in 1970—which group must include most of those poeple who were unemployed during that year—but also to upper income families. The proportion of families making more than $10,000 in 1970 who reported lower incomes in the February 1971 survey than those reported a year earlier was 18 percent as against 10 percent in February 1970.

Families with rising incomes still greatly outnumbered those with declining incomes, but the difference in the size of the two groups became much smaller. It hardly needs to be said that changes in the amount of money income received do not constitute the only consideration which affects people's financial well-being. A joint consideration of the effects of price increases and income changes was available from replies to the question about being better or worse off than a year ago. That question, to be sure, is rather broad, and in evaluating recent changes in their financial situation respondents considered many other factors as well, including changes in their assets or debt, or the relation of what has happened to what they expect to happen. We found that in February 1971, 31 percent professed to be better off and 32 percent claimed they were worse off; in February 1970, 33 percent reported being better off and 28 percent claimed they were worse off (Table II-14). For the first time in many years the proportion saying they were worse off exceeded the proportion saying they were better off. To assess the extent of change over several years it may suffice to point out that during the very good times in 1965, 38 percent said they were better off than they were a year before and 17 percent thought they were worse off.

Again, the change over several years was substantial among upper income families as well. Among those making more than $12,500 in February 1971 the proportion of people who said they were better off exceeded the proportion claiming to be worse off, but not fewer than one-fourth said they were worse off. In 1965 only 7 percent of that group professed to be worse off.

Data on the distribution of income in 1970 are presented in Table 6-3. They indicate that the process toward increased proportions of upper income families and reduced proportions of lower income families, very rapid in previous years, slowed down in 1970. Income expectations changed less radically than reports on past income changes, but the direction of the trend was the same and the deterioration was sizable in expectations as well. In February 1971, 39 percent expected that they would make more that year than in 1970 and 14 percent expected that they would make less. Expectations of reduced income are usually under stated because income declines are frequently unexpected. A year earlier the respective proportions of persons who expected to make more or less in 1970 than in 1969 were 44 and 12 percent. The deterioration of income expectations was not restricted to low and middle-income families. Upper income families also believed that on the whole the unfavorable experience of 1970 would be repeated in 1971 (see Table 6-2).

Related findings, as shown in Table II-15, indicate the proportion of families who expected to be better off and those who expected to be worse off a year from February 1971. The findings were substantially the same as those obtained during every quarter in the twelve months since February 1970. In contrast to business expectations, personal financial expectations did not indicate any recovery.

The reasons given for changes in the personal financial situation were rather similar in February 1971 and in November 1970. The frequency with which respondents referred to income increases or income decreases was substantially the same. Yet spontaneous complaints about inflation as the factor responsible for their being worse off were made by a somewhat smaller proportion of respondents: 19 percent did so in February as against 23 percent in November.

The Demand for Durable Goods

Consumers' evaluations of buying conditions for large household goods became much more favorable during the three months prior to February 1971. These opinions were more favorable than they were one year before. This was the first time a year-to-year improvement had been measured in this attitude since mid-1968. The proportion saying that February 1971 was a good time to buy (42 percent) was larger than the proportion saying that it was a bad time (25 percent). In November 1970, the opposite was true (Table II-20).

Some part of the improvement reflected a seasonal change usual for the first quarter, and in addition the very low reading in October-November could, to some degree, be attributed to the uncertainty caused by the auto strike. But this is by no means the whole explanation; much of the improvement was caused by a large upward shift in the proportion saying that good buys were available. Nearly twice as many respondents (25 percent) gave this reason in February 1971 as they did three months earlier. At the same time, the proportion of respondents saying it was a bad time to buy because prices are high fell from 26 to 19 percent. (Table II-21).

Inflation and the recession were the major factors influencing evaluations of market conditions for household durables during 1970. In the first half of that year, many people said it was a bad time to buy because prices were high, but at the same time many others said that because of slack demand good buys were available. An unusually high proportion of respondents mentioned prices in one or the other context. Toward the end of 1970, concern with high prices continued but at the same time people became less convinced that good buys were available, and so market evaluations deteriorated. Early in 1971, consumers became aware of widespread sales and discounts, and references to good buys were more frequent than complaints about high prices.

It has happened before, particularly in 1958, that consumers have been a stabilizing influence around the lowpoint of a recession because people became accustomed to high prices and aware of good buys due to slack demand. But it was not the expectation of slack times ahead which made for more favorable evaluations of market conditions in February 1971. Quite the opposite was true: among those respondents who expected business conditions to improve during the next year, 54 percent said that it would be a good time to buy large household goods, compared to only 29 percent among those respondents who expect business to deteriorate. The improved optimism concerning both the business outlook and buying conditions, served to reinforce each other.

Opinions about buying conditions for cars also improved greatly during the three months prior to February 1971. However, after making allowance for the large seasonal upturn usual at the start of a new year, and for the impact of the auto strike in the fourth quarter of 1970 when 12 percent of respondents said it was a bad time to buy a car because of the strike, much of the change during the period from November 1970 to February 1971 was accounted for. Unlike evaluations of market conditions for large household goods, opinions about the car market were slightly less favorable in February 1971 than they were one year earlier (see Table II-17). Attitudes toward car prices were to blame. In February 1971 nearly twice as many respondents said the next twelve months would be a bad time to buy a car because prices were too high as those who said it would be a good time because good buys would be available (Table II-18). Possibly these opinions reflected to some extent, a lingering impact of the auto strike, still mentioned by 4 percent of respondents in February 1971.

Intentions to buy a car during the twelve months following February 1971 were hardly changed from one year before, although plans to buy a new car were somewhat less frequent than usual in a February survey (Table II-19). However, an unusually high proportion (48 percent) of those who planned to buy a new car expected to do so before the middle of the year. Potential used car buyers were especially frequent among respondents saying that the next twelve months would be a bad time to buy a car.

Evaluations of market conditions for houses became more favorable during the three months prior to February 1971 as consumers became aware of eased interest rates and credit conditions (Table II-22). Although tight money was still mentioned by 34 percent of all respondents as a reason why this was a bad time to buy, other respondents mentioned low interest rates as a favorable factor in February 1971. The high price of houses continued to be mentioned by many people as an adverse factor (Table II-23). Respondents who said it was a bad time to buy a house still outnumbered those who said it was a good time to buy, 62 percent to 30 percent.

Intentions to buy or build a house during the next one or two years were more frequent in February 1971 than in previous years (Table 6-4). Plans to make additions and repairs to the home were little changed from February 1970, but were somewhat less frequent than in some earlier years.

Table 6-1

Opinions About Influence of Imaginary Future
Headlines on Business Conditions

(Percentage distribution among all families, February 1971)

Imaginary Headlines	Great Influence	Some Influence	Little Influence	Total[f]
Government cuts spending for military equipment	53	31	13	100
Fighting in Vietnam stops	52	31	15	100
Taxes to be lower next year	47	32	17	100
Large government spending to fight air and water pollution	44	31	20	100
Somewhat more people out of work	39	37	21	100
Prices not rising as fast as before	34	43	19	100
Cities report more racial problems	22	30	41	100
Rioting hits campuses	16	27	49	100

[f]Including Don't Know and Not Ascertained answers.

Note: The order in which the news items were presented to respondents was different
        from the one shown in this table.

The question was: "Here are some imaginary headlines you might see in the next few
                    years. We are interested in how the events they describe might
                    influence business. Which of these in your opinion have a
                    great influence, which some influence, and which only a little
                    influence on business conditions?"

Table 6-2

Change in Family Income in Calendar Years[1]

	Past Income Change[2]						Expected Income Change[3]				
	1965 vs. 1964	1967 vs. 1966	1968 vs. 1967	1969 vs. 1968	1970 vs. 1969		1966 vs. 1965	1968 vs. 1967	1969 vs. 1968	1970 vs. 1969	1971 vs. 1970
					A. All Families						
Higher	55%	49%	54%	55%	49%		43%	50%	48%	44%	39%
No change	28	33	30	28	27		45	38	42	43	45
Lower	16	17	15	16	23		8	10	9	12	14
Don't know, not ascertained	1	1	1	1	1		4	2	1	1	2
Total	100%	100%	100%	100%	100%		100%	100%	100%	100%	100%
					B. Families with Incomes of $10,000 and Over						
Higher	70%	50%	71%	72%	61%		50%	56%	57%	49%	48%
No change	17	33	17	17	20		37	32	30	35	36
Lower	13	17	12	10	18		10	10	11	14	14
Don't know, not ascertained	*	*	*	1	1		3	2	2	2	2
Total	100%	100%	100%	100%	100%		100%	100%	100%	100%	100%

*Less than half of one percent.

[1] Data collected in surveys taken in February of each year.

[2] Income in the previous year as compared to income in the year before that. The question asked in February 1971 was: "Was your family's total income higher in 1970 than it was the year before that (1969), or lower or what?"

[3] Income expected for the current year as compared to income in the previous year. The question was: "How do you think your total family income for this year, 1971, will compare with the past year, 1970--will it be higher, about the same, or lower?"

Table 6-3

Distribution of Income Before Taxes

(In percent of family units)

Total Family Money Income	1962	1963	1964	1965	1966	1967	1968	1969	1970*
Under $3000	22	23	21	19	20	19	18	13	11
$3000 - 4999	18	17	16	15	15	14	13	12	14
$5000 - 7499	26	26	23	22	20	18	17	16	17
$7500 - 9999	16	15	17	17	18	17	17	16	14
$10,000 and over	18	19	23	27	27	32	35	43	44
Total	100	100	100	100	100	100	100	100	100

*Based on a somewhat smaller sample than in previous years.

(Family units are defined as people related by blood, marriage, or adoption who are living in the same dwelling unit. Some family units consist of one person.)

Table 6-4

Expressed Intentions About Housing

Intentions to Buy or Build a House	Feb. 1966	Feb. 1967	Feb. 1968	Feb. 1969	Feb. 1970	Feb. 1971
In next 12 months:						
Probably will	5.5%	4.1%	5.6%	5.2%	n.a.	6.2%
Might, undecided	2.7	3.1	2.6	2.8	n.a.	3.0
During the year after that:						
Probably will	2.7	2.7	2.1	1.6	n.a.	3.1
Might, undecided	4.7	5.4	5.4	5.4	n.a.	7.2
Total	15.6%	15.3%	15.7%	15.0%		19.5%

Intentions to Make Additions or Repairs in Next 12 Months						
Probably will		22.9%	23.6%	23.5%	21.7%	20.4%
Might, undecided		7.5	5.1	6.0	5.9	7.3
Total		30.4%	28.7%	29.5%	27.6%	27.7%

n.a.--Not available.

The questions were: "Do you expect to buy or build a house for your own year-round use during the next twelve months?" (IF NO) "How about during the year after that?"
"Do you expect to make any large expenditures for work on this (house and lot/apartment) during the next 12 months -- things like upkeep, additions, or improvements, or painting or decorating?" (EXCLUDE FARM BUILDINGS AND INCOME PROPERTY)

7

THE OUTLOOK FOR CONSUMER DEMAND, MAY 1971

Highlights

Consumer sentiment continued to rise at a moderate rate during the second quarter of 1971. The improvement, which began early in the year, resulted from less pessimistic attitudes concerning trends in the economy and from more favorable opinions about buying conditions for durable goods.

The Survey Research Center's Index of Consumer Sentiment rose to 81.6 in May 1971 from 78.2 in February and 75.4 in November 1970. The Index stood significantly higher than at any time in 1970, but nevertheless remained far below the cyclical peak reached in February 1969. Almost 20 points were lost during 1969 and 1970, so that the six points gained during the two quarters preceding May 1971 recouped only about one-third of the previous decline.

The Index reflects fluctuations in consumers' willingness to buy, but ability to buy is likewise a major factor shaping consumer demand. Gains in real income remained rather frequent during 1969 and most of 1970, softening the impact of greatly worsened sentiment. Therefore the recession was relatively mild. In May 1971, the ability to buy and consumer sentiment were both on a moderate upward trend and served to reinforce each other. Reduced pessimism, rather than increased optimism, appears to be the most appropriate description of what happened between February 1971 and May. The proportion of families expecting bad times during the next twelve months declined in May 1971.

Consumers' evaluations of past trends became somewhat more favorable during the three months prior to May 1971. Not as many people believed that they were financially worse off than a year ago. The proportion saying that

95

business conditions were better than a year ago increased.

Nevertheless, the American people remained well aware of the unfavorable economic developments of the preceding two years. The proportion saying that business was worse than a year ago still exceeded the proportion saying that it was better. And reports of having heard unfavorable news of changes in business conditions still outnumbered reports of favorable news.

Improved business conditions a year from the time of the survey were expected as frequently in May as in February 1971, even though evaluations of current conditions improved in the meantime. Business prospects of the next five years were still judged in a pessimistic manner; this was the only component of the Index which failed to improve during the second quarter of 1971.

The expectation that unemployment would increase during the twelve months following May 1971 still greatly exceeded the expectation that it would decrease.

Evaluations of buying conditions for houses and large household goods became much more favorable during the second quarter of 1971. Opinions about the car market improved to a smaller extent, and were greatly influenced by the awareness of high car prices. Intentions to buy new cars were only moderately higher than they were in May 1970.

What is the explanation for the improvement in consumer sentiment? In May 1971, expectations of relatively small price increases were more frequent, while expectations of large increases were less frequent, than at earlier times. In addition, some people had become habituated to the recession and unemployment, so that the impact of these two problems on people's thinking and feeling had diminished.

The May 1971 survey findings pointed to a slow and gradual growth in consumer demand rather than to a rapid surge. Good news, which would have contributed a stimulus to sizable growth, was not forthcoming.

The Index of Consumer Sentiment

Experience over a twenty-year period has indicated that a change in the Index is of greater significance if it extends over more than a single quarter, if all or more of the Index components move in a consistent direction, if the attitudes of both high and low-income families move in the same direction, and finally, of course, if the change in the Index is relatively large.

An improvement in the Index in one single quarter, as reported in February 1971, might have been suspect because it might have been viewed as only the first leg of a zigzag movement. The May 1971 data eradicate this suspicion.

Two components of the Index were responsible for much of the improvement in the first and second quarters. Expectations about business conditions during the next twelve months and evaluations of buying conditions for large household goods chalked up substantial gains in both February and May of 1971.

A third component, evaluation of the current personal financial situation in comparison to a year ago, posted an increase in May 1971 after continuing to decline in February. It has been noted in the past that this attitude, often a leading indicator at times when sentiment declines, tends to be a coincident or lagging indicator when sentiment recovers. As such, the upturn of this component in May 1971 provided added evidence that a significant improvement in sentiment had occurred.

The other two components of the Index, expectations about the personal financial situation during the next year and expectations about business conditions over the longer run (five years), did not improve during the period from February 1971 to May 1971, and remained at approximately the same low level as in mid-1970. Continued pessimism and uncertainty in these expectations caused the rise in the Index to be less steep in the three to six months preceding May 1971 than it was in some earlier periods of recovery, greatly reducing the chances that there would be a rapid surge in consumers' discretionary spending in the months ahead.

During the three months prior to May 1971 the Index improved to a similar extent among both high and low-income families (Table II-1). Attitudes toward business trends over one year improved somewhat more among upper income families, while perceptions of recent past personal financial trends improved to a greater extent among lower income families.

Expected Business Conditions

An overall evaluation of attitudes toward business conditions was obtained from the responses to the question which asked whether there would be good or bad times in the country during the next twelve months. In many past good years a great majority of consumers gave the answer "good times" to this question. The proportion declined to 34 or 36 percent in 1970. In February 1971 it rose to 41 percent and remained at the same level in May. The frequency of the "bad times" replies—as high as 41 and 38 percent in 1970—fell only slightly (to 35 percent) in February and more sharply to 28 percent in May 1971. Intermediate rather than optimistic answers gained during the second quarter. The decline in pessimistic answers was especially pronounced among high-income people (Table II-5).

It has been repeatedly observed that, on the whole, Americans are well aware of economic trends. Beginning in November 1969, more people spoke of business conditions having deteriorated than of their having improved. In the last three quarters of 1970 the difference of opinion was very large, and in this respect there was no improvement in February 1971. From February to May 1971, evaluations of past economic trends improved significantly. Yet still in May, the proportion of consumers saying that business conditions were worse than a year earlier was higher than the proportion calling business conditions better (Table II-2). The replies to this question over the last two years indicate a widespread awareness that a recession has taken place, followed by an increased realization, still shared only by a minority, of having passed the worst.

Another question in the survey asked respondents whether a year from that time business conditions would be better or worse than they were at present. The answers may only be fully understood if they are compared with those to the previous question (Are business conditions better or worse than they were a year ago?). For example, if a person believes that there has been an improvement in the recent past and then says that a year from now business conditions will be the same as they are today, he is more optimistic than another person who gives the same answer about the future but thinks that recent business conditions have worsened. Therefore the data in Table II-3, which show substantially the same distribution of expectations in May as in February 1971, do not contradict the general picture of improved attitudes toward business.

A comparison of the data presented in Tables II-2 and II-3 indicates that those who already see an improvement in business conditions are most optimistic about the future. As shown in the summary tabulation (II-4), there was a sizable improvement during the three months prior to May 1971 in the proportion of respondents giving answers to the two questions which, taken together, portray an optimistic trend. Even so, the pessimists still outnumbered the optimists. About one-third of all respondents indicated pronounced pessimism by expecting deterioration in business either to continue or to be maintained.

An inquiry about news heard of changes in business conditions turned up somewhat fewer unfavorable reports (drop in employment, layoffs, bad business in certain industries) in May 1971 than it did three months earlier (Table II-6). The decline occurred primarily among families with an income of $12,500 or more. Good news, which usually triggers an upsurge in demand, was still mentioned much less frequently than bad news. Good news did not become more frequent between February and May 1971, but at both times it was reported by a higher proportion of respondents than in either 1969 or 1970.

In February 1971, easier money and declining interest rates were mentioned most often among items of favorable news heard. In May 1971 such reports were less frequent, but an increased number of respondents pointed to an improvement in various industries. References either to prices or the stock market were fairly rare at both times.

More than twice as many people expected unemployment to grow as those who expected it to decline in the twelve months following May 1971, with a substantial minority anticipating unchanged unemployment (Table II-7).

These opinions were somewhat more favorable than those entertained during the worst times of 1969 and 1970, but they clearly indicated that in May 1971 there was no widespread optimism with respect to unemployment, only somewhat less pessimism.

Reduced interest rates were foreseen by a majority of respondents in February 1971. At that time, the turnabout of interest rates represented good news. In May 1971, an increase in interest rates during the next twelve months was expected by as many respondents as anticipated a decrease (Table II-8).

Underlying pessimism, even though less pronounced in May 1971 than a year previous was reflected in people's expectations about the course of business during the next five years. Especially among low and middle-income people, many more expected mostly bad rather than mostly good times during the next few years. Although, it was known from previous surveys that longer run personal financial expectations had remained rather favorable, there were many people who were far from reassured about the future course of the economy. The rise in consumer sentiment in the second quarter of 1971 indicated that some misgivings, aroused for instance by the Vietnam war and social or inner city problems, had become less salient. But the data presented in Table II-9 indicate that there was little confidence in smooth sailing for the economy during the next few years. Upper income people were greatly divided in this respect, lower income people were mostly pessimistic.

Confidence in the economic policies of the government, the belief that the government was making progress in its fight against inflation and unemployment, was not widespread in May 1971. In reply to a direct question, the majority chose the middle alternative, namely, that the government was doing a fair job rather than either a good or a poor job. Yet in May 1971 only 14 percent expressed pronounced confidence by saying that the government was doing a good job, while 28 percent expressed doubts and misgivings by saying that it was doing a poor job. There was little change in these opinions during the six months prior to May 1971 (see Table II-10).

Opinions about the government's economic policies were correlated with expectations about both business conditions and the personal financial situation during the coming year. Among those people who believed that the government was doing a good job in fighting inflation and unemployment, fully 56 percent expected good times during the next twelve months while 17 percent expected bad times. Comparable figures for those who said the government was doing a poor job are 30 percent good times and 41 percent bad times.

Most people who were surveyed in May 1971 expected inflation to continue. The great majority of people who were surveyed gave an estimate of the price increase they expected during the next twelve months; the proportion expecting fairly small price increases went up in the second quarter of 1971.

In May 1971, 37 percent of all respondents spoke of price increases of from 1 to 4 percent during the next twelve months, a higher proportion than at any time during the previous five quarters. Similarly, the proportion expecting price increases of 6 percent or more declined from February to May 1971, but only from 13 to 11 percent (Table II-11). Misgivings about inflation were still widespread, as indicated by complaints about prices in response to questions about the personal financial situation.

Changes in the Personal Financial Situation

The proportion of families saying that they personally were worse off financially than they were a year ago increased over the three years prior to 1971, and reached a high of 32 percent in February 1971. In May 1971, for the first time there was a sizable decline in the proportion, to 27 percent (Table II-14). At the same time, the proportion believing they were better off increased by only 1 percent; the difference was made up by a rise in the "same" category.

In explaining their personal situation, both in May and in February 1971, about 30 percent of all families spontaneously referred to an improvement attributable to higher wages, larger profits, or an increased number of earners in the family. One or two years previously, mention of higher income was somewhat more frequent. The number of families with increases in money income was of course, much larger than 30 percent, but for many families, gains in income do not contribute to a feeling of being better off.

A noteworthy cause of feeling better off was an improved asset position or lower debt. This cause was mentioned by close to 10 percent of all families in each survey conducted during the year and a half preceding May 1971.

According to the responses to a direct question, there was some decline during the six or nine months prior to May 1971 in the proportion of families believing that they were making more money than they were a year ago. Especially among families with incomes of $10,000 or more, income gains were claimed less frequently than they were one or two years prior to the time of the survey. The proportion of those families saying that they had a lower income inched up to 15 percent, more than twice as many as in 1969.

Lower income, primarily because of layoffs and unemployment, made many people feel worse off. Spontaneous references to lower income increased to 18 percent in February, but fell back to 13 percent in May 1971. The other major reason for feeling worse off was inflation. In May almost one out of every four families referred to rising prices or increased expenses as a reason for not feeling better off. There was a rather small decline in these references from February to May 1971.

Expectations of being either better or worse off during the coming year changed to a fairly small extent during the two years prior to the May 1971 survey. The decline in this indicator was relatively small and occurred entirely in the second and third quarters of 1969. During the nine months prior to

May 1971 there was some improvement in the expectations of families with high incomes (Table II-15).

The Demand for Durable Goods

Opinions about market conditions for buying cars and large household durables deteriorated greatly during 1969 and 1970. Many people came to believe that it was wisest to postpone buying big-ticket items whenever that could be done without great inconvenience.

The most obvious reason for these unfavorable attitudes toward buying, and the reason consumers most often gave for its being a bad time to buy, was that of high and rising prices. High interest rates and tight credit were also an important factor. But these were not the only factors contributing to the negative attitudes. Widespread awareness of recession and unemployment, together with uncertainties about other economic and noneconomic problems in society played a major role, especially during 1970. The great improvement in attitudes toward buying conditions in the first two quarters of 1971 provided the clearest evidence that these pessimistic notions diminished in the few months prior to the May 1971 survey.

Evaluations of market conditions for cars became much more favorable during the first two quarters of 1971 among families with both high and low incomes. However, the improvement was not as great as that for large household goods (Table II-17 and II-20). The car data for May 1971 were not much different from those of May 1970, and much less favorable than those in some earlier years. In the May 1971 survey, 38 percent of consumers said that the next twelve months would be a good time to buy a car, while nearly as many (35 percent) said it would be a bad time to buy. Comparable figures for May 1968 were 54 and 18 percent, and those for the really good auto year, 1965, were as favorable as 58 percent and 7 percent.

Most consumers believe that a car is not a luxury, but rather an expensive necessity. Therefore, attitudes toward buying conditions for cars are closely correlated with changes in how consumers perceive car prices. Much of the improvement in the second quarter of 1971 in opinions of buying conditions for cars, may be traced to a decline in the proportion of respondents who mentioned high prices as a reason for its being a bad time to buy a car in the three to six months prior to May 1971. Some, but by no means all, of this decline may be traced to the diminishing impact of the auto strike late in 1970. The strike no longer played a role in May 1971, but still twice as many respondents said that it was a bad time to buy because prices were high as those who said that it was a good time because prices were low (Table II-18).

Further evidence that consumers were very much aware of high car prices is found in the 21 percent of all families who said that it was a good time to buy a car because prices were going still higher, or at least would not be any lower. While this proportion was even higher (31 percent) in May 1968 when it was found that some people planned to buy in advance of expected price increases on the new models, the comparable figure in May 1970 was only 9 percent. Accordingly, it must be concluded that these expectations provided some stimulus to the demand for cars in May 1971 but not as much as in the late spring and summer of 1968.

Consistent with the above findings, intentions to buy new cars recovered from the depressed levels of three and six months prior to May 1971 but only part way. As shown in Table II-19, the proportion of families expecting to buy a new car in the twelve months following May 1971 was higher than the proportion in May 1970, but not as high as the proportions in the few years before that. Intentions to buy used cars were relatively frequent in May 1971 if allowance is made for the fact that used car intentions are usually understated in telephone reinterview surveys.*

Evaluations of market conditions for large household durables showed substantial improvement in February, and again in May 1971. In just six months, most of the deterioration during 1969 and 1970 was recouped (Table II-20). Among families with incomes over $12,500 the data were very nearly as favorable as in May 1969, although still well below May 1968 at which time fully 69 percent of these families said it was a good time to buy large household items.

Evaluations of buying conditions for houses also greatly improved during the three and six months prior to May 1971. For the first time in three years, the proportion saying that it was a good time to buy a house exceeded the proportion saying that it was a bad time. During 1970, unfavorable opinions were three times as frequent as favorable opinions (Table II-22).

---

*The telephone data in this report are adjusted to compensate for the absence of replies from non-telephone owners and for reinterview non-response. Experience has shown that in most respects, the adjusted telephone data are comparable to data from personal interviews with a representative sample of all families. Intentions to buy used cars are a noteworthy exception.

8

THE OUTLOOK FOR CONSUMER DEMAND, SEPTEMBER 1971

Highlights

Consumers' first reaction to the wage-price freeze instituted on August 15, 1971 was overwhelmingly favorable. More than three out of four believed that it was a good thing. A very great proportion expressed satisfaction that the government had taken action to fight inflation and unemployment, and optimism increased somewhat in these areas. Attitudes toward buying a car became much more favorable.

Nevertheless, the Index of Consumer Sentiment was less than one point higher than it was three months prior to September 1971. Among families with incomes above $12,500 the Index actually declined nearly five points. Of the five components of the sentiment Index, two are concerned with respondents' evaluation of trends in their personal financial situation (past and future), and two with their expectations about business conditions (during the next twelve months and five years). Among all families, these attitudes changed very little during the three months preceding September 1971 except for some decline in the proportion saying that they were better off financially than they were a year ago. All four of these components deteriorated among families with incomes above $12,500.

There are three major reasons why these attitudes did not improve:
1. While most consumers (70 percent) believed that some form of controls would persist after the 90 days were up, there was uncertainty about the impact of controls on the personal financial situation and on the economy. Opinions were greatly divided as to whether or not the government would be successful in reducing inflation and unemployment during the next year or two: 39 percent said "yes" and 43 percent said "no." Many of

these answers were qualified by expressions of uncertainty. The strong relationship between these opinions and key measures of consumer sentiment suggested that uncertainty about what would happen impeded the recovery of optimism in September 1971.

2. The improvement in consumer sentiment recorded in the first half of 1971 was moderate because it was *not* attributable to favorable news, but rather to the fact that some people became habituated to inflation and unemployment, so that the impact of these problems on people's thinking and feeling diminished. The announcement of controls was therefore a two-edged sword. Most people regarded it as an important piece of favorable news, but at the same time the controls focused renewed attention on the twin problems of inflation and unemployment.

3. Finally, consumer sentiment was at a low level for a sustained period. In particular, many people had lost faith in the long-run outlook for the economy, and in the ability of the government to solve economic and social problems (poverty, pollution, inner city problems, etc.) which contributed to the general malaise. Under these circumstances, it took *time* for sentiment, and especially the long-run outlook, to recover in response to favorable news.

The five questions which comprise the Index are significant indicators of change in consumers' willingness to buy, but given the circumstances which prevailed in September 1971, it was especially important to take a careful look at the other thirty questions in the survey in order to get a balanced view of the likely impact of the price-wage freeze in the months ahead. Many important determinants of consumer sentiment showed substantial improvement: price expectations, unemployment expectations, opinions about whether it was a good or bad time or buy durable goods, attitudes toward the government's economic policy, and the frequency of mention of favorable news. Accordingly, the sentiment index was expected to improve in the months ahead. But the considerations presented above suggested that the recovery in sentiment might be rather slow and greatly contingent on whether consumers perceived success or failure in the government's economic policy later that year.

Income gains were substantial during several months prior to September 1971. This factor, combined with a moderate recovery in sentiment, was expected to prompt a continued upward trend in retail sales. But a restoration of confidence to pre-recession levels, a sharp drop in the personal savings rate, and a corresponding surge in spending were not in sight. The savings rate was expected to stay fairly high during the 6 months following September 1971, probably above 7 percent.

Opinions about buying conditions for household durables improved greatly earlier in 1971. Attitudes toward buying a car remained by comparison rather unfavorable (mainly because consumers believed car prices to be high) even though a relatively large number of respondents said in May that it was a good time to buy because car prices would go up further in the fall. Under these circumstances, the price freeze and the promised excise tax elimination greatly improved the outlook for auto sales in the fall. If opinions about whether it was a good or a bad time to buy a car were substituted in the Index in place of opinions about buying conditions for large household durables (the fifth component of the Index), the gain in the Index which occurred in September 1971 would have been more substantial:

	Index of Consumer Sentiment	Index with "good or bad time to buy a car"
August 1970	77.1	74.9
February 1971	78.2	75.6
May 1971	81.6	78.4
August-September 1971	82.4	82.0

Attitudes toward buying a house became much more favorable during the first and second quarters of 1971, primarily because of widespread awareness of lower interest rates and more available credit. During the 3 months prior to September 1971 there was some upswing in the proportion saying it was a bad time to buy a house, especially among families with incomes above $12,500.

There was no evidence in the September 1971 survey to suggest that many consumers would react to the price freeze by buying in advance of price increases at the end of the 90-day period. Few people believed that prices would be allowed to advance greatly after 90 days. Of course, a tendency to buy in advance might have been expected to develop later if events were to change these expectations.

The first favorable emotional response of the American people to the new economic policy was important. It has an impact on the second, more carefully considered response. But the rate of improvement in consumer attitudes depended on whether people came to believe that the measures to be announced in the next few weeks after the September 1971 survey would succeed or fail. The chances for success were enhanced by the initial favorable response, but changes in people's attitudes and expectations had to be watched carefully in the months ahead.

Consumer Reaction to the Wage-Price Freeze

In order to fully understand the survey findings concerning the new government economic policies it was essential to keep in mind the consumer mood which existed prior to the President's speech on August 15, 1971.

It should be noted, first, that the recovery in sentiment which occurred in the first half of 1971 was not robust. It did not result so much from the positive impact of favorable news as it did from people becoming accustomed to the unfavorable news. There was little optimism about solving the twin problems of inflation and unemployment.

The persistent severity of these economic problems during all of 1970 and the first half of 1971, contributed greatly to a pervasive lack of faith that we would have good times over the long run. But these were not the only determining factors; noneconomic problems (pollution, racial conflict, crime, urban decay, Vietnam) had an increasingly adverse impact on sentiment during the previous four of five years.

In addition, surveys conducted during the twelve-months prior to September 1971 showed that relatively few people believed that the government was doing a good job in its economic policy with regard to inflation or unemployment. Many consumers, high income as well as low, lost faith in the government's ability or willingness to come to grips with these problems. A strong relationship existed in May 1971 between attitudes toward the government and attitudes toward the outlook for business and personal finances (Table II-10).

More than three out of four respondents expressed approval of the wage-price freeze. Satisfaction with this action was remarkably uniform across income groups. Three kinds of qualifications were expressed, with almost equal frequency: that 90 days was too short a period, that the freeze might not work, and that the freeze discriminated against some segments of the population (especially wage earners and "the little man"). Fully 20 percent of respondents, however, mentioned without being asked, that controls should have been put on sooner.

Opinion of Price-Wage Freeze	All Families	Family income			
		Less than $5000	$5000 -7499	$7500 -9999	$10,000 or more
Good thing	55%	53%	52%	53%	59%
Good thing, with qualifications	21	21	19	25	20
Pro-con	5	3	7	6	6
Bad thing, with qualifications	2	2	2	2	2
Bad thing	10	11	12	10	8
Don't know; not ascertained	7	10	8	4	5
Total	100%	100%	100%	100%	100%

There can be no question but that the freeze represented a very salient development of which people were much aware. A majority of respondents mentioned the freeze *before* the interviewer began to talk about the government's economic policy, in answering questions about the personal financial situation, business conditions or buying conditions for durable goods. The freeze was frequently mentioned as an item of favorable news about recent changes in business conditions, entirely accounting for the increase shown in Table II-6.

Opinions about the government's economic policy became more favorable, with nearly twice as many respondents saying that the government was doing a good job in the August-September as those in May (Table II-10). The improvement was found equally among respondents with high and low incomes. When asked to explain their opinions, many respondents cast their answers in terms of the government *doing* something, or trying to solve the problems. The relationship between attitudes toward the government and attitudes toward the personal financial situation or business conditions remained as strong in August-September as it was in May. But many people entertained serious doubts about whether the government would be successful. In answer to a direct question, 43 percent of the respondents said that there would be little improvement in inflation and unemployment during the coming year or two, while 39 percent thought that the government would meet with some measure of success. Many of the latter answers were qualified by saying that the problems would not be fully solved, or that little progress would be made against unemployment.

As with opinions about whether the government was doing a good job, expectations about whether the government would be successful in reducing inflation and unemployment were strongly related to consumers' expectations about their personal financial situation and about the outlook for business conditions in both the short and long run. Not surprisingly, expectations of future government success were highly correlated with opinions as to whether the government was doing a good job at the time.

Whether government will be successful in reducing inflation and unemployment	Government now doing:		
	A good job	Only fair	A poor job
Successful	35%	14%	9%
Successful, with qualifications	30	23	11
Pro-con	3	2	3
Not successful, with qualifications	7	11	9
Not successful; hardly any improvement	13	35	55
Depends on how price-wage freeze works out (not codable above)	2	3	3
Don't know; not ascertained	10	12	10
Total	100%	100%	100%

The widespread doubt about whether the government would be successful goes far to explain why it was that the somewhat more favorable attitudes toward the government, and the favorable initial reaction to the price-wage freeze, were not translated into improved consumer sentiment. High rates of inflation and unemployment persisted over a long period so that many consumers regarded them as problems which would be difficult to solve.

During the first few weeks after the announcement of the new economic policy on August 15, attitudes and expectations about business conditions were little changed from what they were in May 1971. There was a slight increase in the proportion of consumers expecting conditions to improve during the next 12 months (Table II-3) or saying that times would be good during the next 12 months (Table II-5) or 5 years (Table II-9). Among families with incomes over $12,500, expectations about the longer run outlook became more pessimistic, and less favorable September 1971 than at any time since this question was first asked in 1948.

Unemployment remained a major source of concern to the American people, including many who did not face the threat of unemployment themselves. When asked to say which of the two problems—inflation or unemployment—would have the more serious consequences for the country during the next year or two, unemployment was mentioned more often than inflation, especially by those respondents who doubted that the government's policy would be successful.

More serious consequences for the country during the next year or two	All Families	Government will be: Successful	Government will be: Not successful
Inflation	37%	45%	33%
Unemployment	48	44	52
Both equally serious	9	7	10
Don't know; not ascertained	6	4	5
Total	100%	100%	100%

Expectations about unemployment and inflation during the 12 months following the survey became somewhat less pessimistic than they had been in May 1971. Table II-7 shows some decline in the proportion of consumers who expected unemployment to increase. Nevertheless, these expectations could hardly be termed optimistic. Altogether, 73 percent of all families expected unemployment to either increase or stay the same during the 12 months following September 1971.

When asked whether "prices of the things you buy in general" would go up, go down, or stay the same in the next year or so, many respondents apparently thought of the next few months in which there would be a price freeze. Forty-three percent of the respondents in August-September said that prices would *not* go up, and another 4 percent said that they did not know what would happen to prices. Altogether, 47 percent could not be asked the follow-up question about how large a price increase they expected. (Table II-11).

There are many indications that some respondents answered the question about whether or not prices would go up during the next 12 months without much thought. A few people answered the question by saying "Haven't you heard? Prices *can't* go up now." Many of the people who said that prices would not go up also said later on in the interview that the new economic policy would probably not be successful. Therefore, the data in Table II-11 should not be taken literally to mean that there was a great increase in the proportion of people who believed that inflation was no longer a problem. The data do suggest, however, that there was a sizable group of people who believed that the freeze would keep prices from rising at least in the short run.

Respondents were asked what they thought might happen after the 90 days had passed—whether the price and wage freeze would be extended for a longer period, or whether prices and wages would then be allowed to increase. Fully 54 percent answered by saying simply that the freeze would be extended. An additional 15 percent expected wage and price controls to continue in some form. Only 15 percent thought that prices and wages would be allowed to increase. Among those who believed that some form of controls would continue (but not the freeze) a majority expected that the government program would be successful.

Changes in the Personal Financial Situation

During the three months prior to September 1971 there was a decline in the proportion of families saying that they were better off than they were a year ago (Table II-14). The deterioration was especially noticeable among families with incomes above $12,500; only 32 percent of these families said that they were better off in August-September. This was only a slightly higher percentage than that of families who claimed to be worse off (27 percent). Usually the spread between the two proportions is much larger than five percentage points.

When respondents were asked to tell why they were better or worse off than a year earlier, the most frequently mentioned concerns were income, prices, and the asset or debt position. The following tabulation of these reasons shows less frequently mention of higher income and more frequent mention of lower income in August-September 1971 than one year earlier. Mentions of higher prices were somewhat less frequent in the first half of 1971 than they were during 1970, but the frequency bounced back up in August-September.

	Aug. 1968	Aug-Sept. 1969	Feb. 1970	Aug. 1970	Feb. 1971	May 1971	Aug-Sept. 1971
Better off because of:							
Better pay; higher income	38%	36%	35%	34%	30%	30%	27%
Better asset/debt position	8	8	9	8	9	9	7
Worse off because of:							
Less work; lower income	10%	9%	11%	10%	17%	14%	15%
Higer prices	16	24	23	22	19	17	21
Increased expenses	6	5	6	5	7	3	5

Expectations about being better or worse off a year from the time of the survey did not change greatly among all families during the three months prior to September 1971 (Table II-15). A somewhat higher proportion than usual said in August-September that their situation would not change, an expectation which might for some respondents, have been related to the wage-price freeze. Among families with incomes above $12,500, however, there was a substantial decline since May 1971 in the proportion expecting to be better off a year from the time of the survey.

Several times in the two years prior to this survey, the Survey Research Center has asked a question designed to measure the extent to which consumers feel that their financial situation permits them to make discretionary expenditures. The data suggest that financial pressures were eased somewhat during 1971 for lower income families, but not for those with incomes above $12,500.

Evaluation of Personal Buying Situation	All Families				Income $10,000 or more			
	Oct-Nov. 1969	Apr-May 1970	Oct-Nov. 1970	Aug-Sept. 1971	Oct-Nov. 1969	Apr-May 1970	Oct-Nov. 1970	Aug-Sept. 1971
Good time to buy	27%	30%	27%	33%	44%	40%	41%	41%
Pro-con	2	3	3	3	3	2	4	3
Bad time to buy	67	61	66	59	49	53	50	51
Not ascertained	4	6	4	5	4	5	5	5
Total	100%	100%	100%	100%	100%	100%	100%	100%

The Demand for Durable Goods

Opinions of buying conditions for large household durables improved greatly during the first two quarters of 1971. A further small improvement in August-September returned this component of the Index of Consumer Sentiment close to the level recorded in February 1969, prior to the downturn in consumer attitudes (Table II-20). Much of the improvement was caused by an upward shift in the proportion of consumers saying that good buys were available.

With respect to cars, the change in opinions of buying conditions followed quite a different pattern; the upturn in attitudes during the first two quarters of 1971 was quite modest in comparison to household durables, primarily because many consumers remained aware of high car prices. The demand for cars rose during the first half of the year for three reasons: first, there was a sustained period of catch-up from the auto strike in the fall of 1970. Many would-be purchasers postponed buying a car then, often to some indefinite time in the future, and it took time to attract them back into the showroom. As more and more of these people bought, the high level of sales generated interest in buying on the part of friends and neighbors, some of whom eventually bought. The impact of the strike was probably felt as late as the summer of 1971.

Second, as shown in Table II-18, a substantial proportion of consumers said in May 1971 that it was a good time to buy a car because they expected prices to go higher. This expectation was quite frequent in the spring of 1968 and contributed greatly to sales of new cars in the summer of 1968. In the spring of 1969 it was less frequent, and in April-May 1970 it was quite infrequent. In May 1971 the expectation of rising auto prices was again widespread.

Third, the new small cars were rather favorably received and stimulated interest in buying new cars in general.

In August-September 1971, following the President's speech, opinions of market conditions for cars improved greatly (Table II-17). Because consumers were very conscious of auto prices, circumstances were ripe for a very favorable reaction to both the price freeze and the elimination of the excise taxes, which many consumers expected to be enacted. In addition, there was some further reduction in the proportion of people who said that the next 12 months would be a bad time to buy a car because of high interest rates and tight credit.

Intentions to buy a new car were somewhat more frequent than in May 1971, at which time the proportion planning to buy a new car probably still included a relatively large number of people who had postponed buying a car at an earlier time (Table II-19). Intentions to buy used cars tend to be understated in telephone reinterview surveys.

In summary, the outlook for sales of new cars in the fall of 1971 was more favorable than it would have been if the new economic policies had not been initiated.

Opinions of buying conditions for houses, which improved substantially early in the year as the great majority of consumers became aware of eased credit conditions, became somewhat less favorable in August-September 1971 (Table II-22). This change occurred although a small proportion said that interest rates had gone up during the last few months (13 percent). Most respondents said that interest rates had stayed the same (35 percent) or said that they did not know what the rates were at the time (31 percent). Nineteen percent said that rates had declined.

9

THE OUTLOOK FOR CONSUMER DEMAND, NOVEMBER 1971

Highlights

Consumer sentiment changed little in response to Phase II. Somewhat more optimistic attitudes among families with incomes above $12,500 were balanced by increased pessimism among families with lower incomes. Among both groups, sentiment was not much different from what it was six months prior to November 1971.

Many Americans continued to have doubts about the eventual success of the New Economic Policy. When asked whether the government would be successful in reducing inflation during the next year or two, only 35 percent gave an affirmative answer. Nearly 50 percent said that there would be little improvement.

When asked what had happened to prices since August 15, 37 percent of all respondents said that the prices of the things they buy had increased. A larger proportion, 53 percent, believed that prices had not increased, but even among these people, there were frequent misgivings about future trends: only 42 percent thought that the government would be successful in reducing inflation during the next year or two, and 29 percent expected prices to be "a lot" higher five years from then than they were at the time of the survey.

During the early days of Phase I, SRC found many consumers who were uncertain about how the controls on wages and prices would affect their *own* personal financial situation. In October-November, in answer to a direct question, more respondents believed that they would take a loss (23 percent) than those who expected to come out ahead (14 percent). The majority (52 percent) said that considering everything, the controls would not make much

113

difference, while only 11 percent were unable to answer the question.

The SRC survey conducted in August-September suggested several reasons why sentiment was expected to show some modest improvement in the months ahead: more frequent mentions of favorable news about business conditions, somewhat less unfavorable attitudes toward the government's economic policy, and some improvement in people's expectations about future trends in inflation and unemployment. Among families with incomes above $12,500, there was in fact some improvement between August and November. These families more often said they were better off, had more optimistic expectations about business conditions over the next five years, and had somewhat more favorable attitudes toward the government's economic policy. Among families with lower incomes, however, attitudes toward the personal financial situation and the business outlook were less favorable, apparently because of increasingly pessimitic expectations about whether or not the government's fight against inflation would prove to be successful.

Consumer sentiment had been at a low level for a long time by November 1971. The sharp decline began in the second quarter of 1969 and continued into 1970. Many people lost faith in the long-run outlook for the economy, and in the ability of the government to solve economic and social problems. While the controls were greeted by most consumers as good news, the SRC data which was presented earlier suggested that this sentiment would not be translated promptly into an increase in expenditures, with the single exception of automobile purchases.

Data from the new survey confirmed the earlier findings. Accordingly, our forecast remained the same as it had been for the five quarters prior to November 1971: consumer spending would continue to recover slowly. A surge in discretionary spending, or a marked fall in the rate of personal saving out of income, was still not in sight.

To be sure, there were reasons to believe that there might have been a temporary bulge in retail sales during the Christmas season. There was evidence that some consumers were buying not only cars but also other durables as well in advance of expected price increases. Fully 26 percent of all respondents in October-November 1971 gave future price increases as a reason why November was a good time to buy large household items. To some extent, the demand for cars and other major discretionary items at that time was borrowing from future demand.

Second, as already mentioned, there was a significant improvement in the way upper income families evaluated past changes in their financial situation. Consumers had been saving at a high rate over a prolonged period and had accumulated substantial liquid assets. Under these circumstances, when people felt a *need* to buy something, or when a special occasion came along, they would not deny themselves even if sentiment were low.

Index of Consumer Sentiment

Especially at times when, as in November 1971, new developments have a great impact on consumer sentiment, it is necessary to keep in mind that the Index of Consumer Sentiment was based on just five among some 35 or 40 questions in the November SRC survey. Nevertheless, the Index did provide a good summary measure of changes in sentiment because it focused upon those determinants of willingness to buy which continued to be important.

It has been found in the past that when all five Index components move together in the same direction, there is a great likelihood that a significant change in sentiment has occurred. In October-November 1971 something rather unusual happened: all Index components posted gains among families with incomes above $12,500, but at the same time all components lost ground among families with lower incomes.

Among upper-income families, substantial improvements occurred during the two months prior to November 1971 in the proportion saying that they were better off financially than they were a year ago, and in the proportion expecting that we would have good times in the economy during the next five years. Among lower-income families, both short and long-term expectations about business conditions became less favorable. Changes in the other Index components were rather small.

Consumer Reaction to Wage and Price Controls

The third quarter Survey of Consumer Attitudes, conducted shortly after the introduction of controls, studied people's initial reaction to the New Economic Policy. The fourth-quarter survey was conducted after the announcement of Phase II and after consumers had had some time to think about some of the uncertainties surrounding wage and price controls. It should be noted in this context that the general shape of Phase II did not come as a surprise to most consumers. In August-September fully 69 percent expected price and wage controls to be continued in some form after the ninety days.

During the few months prior to November 1971, opinions about the government's economic policy became somewhat more favorable among families with incomes above $12,500, but somewhat less favorable among families with lower incomes (Table II-10). Considering all families together, there was little change in these opinions, which coincides well with what happened to the Index of Consumer Sentiment.

A strong relationship continued to prevail between attitudes toward government policy on the one hand and attitudes toward the personal financial situation and business conditions on the other hand. Among those who believed the government was doing a poor job, the proportion thinking we would have bad times during the next 12 months was nearly twice as large as the proportion saying that times would be good, and more people believed that business conditions would be worse than those who said that they would be better.

Attitudes toward the job the government was doing were strongly related to expectations about whether the government would be successful in reducing inflation and unemployment, as shown in the following table:

Whether government will be successful-	All Families	In regard to inflation and unemployment, the government is doing:		
		Good job	Only fair	Poor job
In reducing inflation:				
Will be successful	35%	62%	35%	11%
Little improvement expected	12	8	16	8
Will not be successful	36	17	34	68
Depends, pro-con, don't know	17	13	15	13
Total	100%	100%	100%	100%
In reducing unemployment:				
Will be successful	25%	40%	26%	7%
Little improvement expected	11	10	15	8
Will not be successful	50	38	47	72
Depends, pro-con, don't know	14	12	12	13
Total	100%	100%	100%	100%

In August-September respondents were asked one question about whether the government would be successful in reducing inflation and unemployment during the next year or two. In October-November, this was broken into two questions, one asking about inflation and the other about unemployment. The new findings are shown in Tables II-12 and II-13.

While a precise comparison between the two surveys is not possible because of the change in questions, the next tabulation shows somewhat less optimism in November 1971 than there was two months before, that the government would be successful in its economic policy. The findings suggest that families with incomes less than $7500 became rather pessimistic about reducing inflation in the next year or so. More than half of these families expected little improvement.

Consumers who were pessimistic about government success were also

Proportion saying that government will be successful in reducing:	All Families	Less than $5000	Family Income $5000 -7499	$7500 -9999	$10,000 or more
Inflation and unemployment (August-September 1971)	39%	36%	37%	38%	42%
Inflation (October-November 1971)	35%	21%	30%	39%	45%
Unemployment (October-November 1971)	25%	22%	24%	25%	27%

pessimistic in other respects. Expectations about inflation were strongly related not only to personal financial expectations but also to both the short and long-term business outlook, and expectations about unemployment were related not only to the business outlook but also to personal financial expectations. It is interesting to note that long-run expectations about the personal financial situation were more closely related to inflation than unemployment, while long-run expectations about business conditions were equally affected by both inflation and unemployment (Table II-12 and II-13).

These findings support the notion that consumer sentiment was greatly affected by expectations about unemployment. In answer to a direct question about whether inflation or unemployment would have the more serious consequences for the country during the next year or two, more respondents pointed the finger at unemployment than at inflation, as shown in the following table. These data are little changed from August-September 1971.

More serious consequences for the country during the next year or two	All Families	In regard to inflation and unemployment, the government is doing:		
		Good job	Only fair	Poor job
Inflation	40%	47%	41%	35%
Unemployment	47	44	49	51
Both equally serious	8	5	8	11
Don't know; not ascertained	5	4	2	3
Total	100%	100%	100%	100%

It appears that people who thought the government was not doing a good job, or who lacked faith that the government would succeed, tended to believe that unemployment was the more serious problem. Many people did not see how the new economic policy could have any impact on reducing unemployment. In this connection it should be noted that only 15 percent of consumers expected success against *both* inflation and unemployment.

In October-November, respondents were asked whether in their opinion prices had gone up since the freeze was introduced August 15. Not fewer than one-half said that prices had remained unchanged. The proportion was somewhat lower (43 percent) among respondents who said that they had been hurt a great deal by inflation.

Prices since the freeze have-	All Families	Hurt by inflation	
		A great deal	Little
Gone up	37%	45%	33%
Remained unchanged	50	43	54
Gone down	3	1	4
Don't know	10	11	9
Total	100%	100%	100%

The question was: "Since August 15, when the price freeze was introduced, have prices of the things you buy remained unchanged, or have they gone up, or have they gone down?"

Even among those who said that prices had remained unchanged, however, there were many respondents who said that the government would not be successful in curbing inflation, or that prices would rise substantially in the next 12 months or five years. Nevertheless, the following tabulation shows that people who believed that prices had been stable were much more optimistic about their personal financial situation and about business conditions, as well as about inflation.

These findings are reinforced by replies to another question which asked respondents to say whether they would benefit financially or suffer a loss due to the wage and price controls. Those who believed that prices had gone up were much more likely to say that they expected to suffer a financial loss. This was true even though upper-income families ($12,500 and up) were less likely than those families with lower incomes to say that prices had gone up (29 percent versus 43 percent) but somewhat more likely to say that they would suffer a loss from the controls (26 percent versus 21 percent).

How did attitudes toward inflation and unemployment in November 1971 compare with those before August 1971? People's way of thinking about inflation had improved—although primarily among upper income families. The acknowlegement by the majority of price stability during the freeze went along with a sizable proportion who expected lesser price increases in the

	Since the freeze prices have:	
	Gone up	Remained unchanged

Government will be:

Successful in reducing inflation during the next year or two	25%	42%
Not successful	44	32

Prices during the next 12 months:

Will rise 5% or more	35%	26%
Will rise by less	33	33
Will not go up	24	34

Prices 5 years from now will be:

A lot higher	37%	29%
A little higher	31	40
Same or lower	18	19

Personal financial situation in a year will be:

Better than now	25%	38%
Worse	13	43

Business conditions during next 12 months:

Good times	30%	47%
Bad times	33	26

future. Inflationary expectations became less salient among a sizable proportion of Americans.

But trust in the government's ability to manage the economy successfully had not developed, as indicated primarily by the attitudes toward expected trends in unemployment. The proportion believing that unemployment would increase during the next 12 months was somewhat lower in November 1971 than it was in the spring of 1971, but it still greatly exceeded the propor-

Net effect of wage and price controls on the personal financial situation	Families	Since the freeze prices have:	
		Gone up	Remained unchanged
Will benefit	14%	10%	19%
Not much difference	52	46	55
Will suffer a loss	23	34	17
Don't know; not ascertained	11	10	9
Total	100%	100%	100%

tion expecting reduced unemployment (Table II-7). Correspondingly, the 25 percent of respondents who thought the government would succeed in curbing unemployment were dwarfed by the 50 percent who did not expect success in this respect.

In summary, up until November 1971, the impact of the New Economic Policy on the American people's attitudes had been limited. The key to changes in consumer sentiment in the months following November 1971 was whether or not consumers would come to believe that the government's economic policy was working or would work in terms of reducing not only inflation but also unemployment.

Changes in the Personal Financial Situation

During the few months prior to November 1971, there was a substantial increase in the proportion of upper income families saying that they were better off than they were a year ago (Table II-14). However, the attitudes of lower income people toward their financial situation became somewhat less favorable and therefore the improvement for all families was rather modest.

To a great extent the improvement in November 1971 among upper income families only reversed a temporary deterioration in this attitude recorded in August-September. Comparing October-November to May 1971, evaluations of the current financial situation were somewhat improved among upper income families, but unchanged among all families.

Expectations about being better or worse off a year from the time of the survey also improved among upper income families, but the improvement was entirely balanced by less favorable expectations among lower income families (Table II-15). Again, these changes reversed changes which had occurred between May and August-September 1971. Looking at the six months since May, there was little change among either upper or lower income groups.

There were two main facets involved in consumers' attitudes toward their financial situation: income change and price change. Wage and price controls affected both, and the introduction of Phase I suffices to explain the temporary changes in these attitudes in August-September 1971.

More important than the initial reaction of consumers to the wage and price controls was the change in attitudes which was observed after some time had passed. As already noted, the change from May to October-November was not large. Yet there is some evidence that this apparent stability was the net result of less favorable evaluations of income changes and more favorable evaluations of price changes.

On the one hand, the following tabulation shows a much smaller proportion of consumers than in previous years saying that they were making more money at the time of the survey than they were a year before that.

Money income compared to a year ago	All Families				Income $10,000 or more			
	Nov-Dec. 1968	Oct-Nov. 1969	Oct-Nov. 1970	Oct-Nov. 1971	Nov-Dec. 1968	Oct-Nov. 1969	Oct-Nov. 1970	Oct-Nov. 1971
Making more money	47%	50%	51%	41%	66%	69%	67%	56%
Making about the same	40	37	32	39	26	25	23	31
Making less money	13	13	17	19	7	6	10	13
Not ascertained	*	*	*	1	1	*	*	*
Total	100%	100%	100%	100%	100%	100%	100%	100%

*Less than 0.5 percent.

The question was: "Are you people making as much money now as you were a year ago, or more, or less?"

On the other hand, as pointed out in the previous chapter, a substantial proportion of consumers, especially among upper income families, believed that prices had remained unchanged since the introduction of Phase I. Attitudes toward past and expected personal financial situations were much more favorable among these people than among those who believed that prices had gone up in the few months prior to the survey (37 percent). This proportion was much lower than the proportion expecting prices to go up in the 12 months following the survey (60 percent), which in turn was lower than it was before controls were introduced (typically about 75 or 80 percent in recent years—see Table II-11).

How consumers would evaluate price and income trends in the months following the November 1971 survey would play a large role in determining what happened to expectations about the personal financial situation. If more consumers came to expect that the battle against inflation would be won, sentiment would be greatly stimulated.

Net effect of wage and price controls on the personal financial situation	All Families	In reducing inflation, the government will be:	
		Successful	Not successful
Respondent will benefit	14%	21%	9%
Not much difference	52	49	53
Respondent will suffer a loss	23	19	31
Don't know; not ascertained	11	11	7
Total	100%	100%	100%

Expected Business Conditions

In August-September, in the weeks after Phase I was announced, many consumers mentioned wage and price controls or the new economic policy as a favorable item of news affecting business conditions. Two months later, in October-November, such mentions were much less frequent, particularly among lower income respondents. At the same time, unfavorable items of news, mostly about unemployment or declines in specific industries, continued to be mentioned by many respondents, although less frequently than early in 1971 (Table II-6).

Short-run expectations about business conditions became less favorable among lower income families during the last few months prior to November 1971. (Table II-3). But among upper income families, there was some improvement in the opinions about whether business conditions were better or worse than they were a year ago. It was still true, however, that there were more respondents who said "worse" than those who said "better" (Table II-2). However, considering opinions about past and expected business conditions together, respondents expressed their belief in an optimistic trend slightly more often than they did their belief in a pessimistic trend (Table II-4).

Expectations about the trend in unemployment did not change in the few months prior to November 1971, but they did improve substantially over six and twelve months prior to that time. However, in this respect the pessimists still outnumbered the optimists, even among upper income families (Table II-7).

The proportion of upper income respondents expecting good times during the next five years sharply increased, so that for the first time in two years the optimists outnumbered the pessimists (Table II-9). At the same time, these attitudes deteriorated slightly among lower income families. Only 19 percent of families with incomes less than $12,500 said that we would have good times during the coming five years.

There are many reasons, both economic and noneconomic, why long-term expectations for business conditions deteriorated so greatly over the six years prior to November 1971. Lack of faith in the ability of the government to cope with problems of unemployment and inflation was a crucial factor, and in that context it is important to note again that opinions about the government's economic policies and about whether the government can reduce inflation were pessimistic among low-income families.

But there were other reasons why optimism about the long run remained at a low ebb: urban problems, crime, pollution, and so on. Some respondents captured the flavor of these attitudes by saying that "things are out of control in our society." Perhaps it is not surprising that pessimism was more persistent among lower income people, because they were the ones most intimately affected by many of these social problems, as well as by inflation and unemployment.

The Demand for Durable Goods

Cars. Attitudes toward buying a car showed an extraordinary improvement in August-September 1971. In October-November some of this gain had disappeared (Table II-17). The price freeze on the new models and the promised elimination of the excise tax greatly stimulated the belief that it was a good time to buy a car. Altogether, 43 percent of all families, and 48 percent of upper income families mentioned favorable prices in August-September as a reason for buying. In October-November these proportions fell only slightly, to 39 and 45 percent respectively.

A crucial question is the extent to which the high level of auto sales in November 1971, reflected buying in advance of expected price increases, and therefore was borrowing from future demand. There was little direct evidence on this question in the October-November survey, in particular because the question about whether it was a good or a bad time to buy a car referred to "the next 12 months." However, there were indirect indications which suggested that buying in advance was quite substantial.

Opinions of whether it was a good time to buy cars and household durables were strongly related to opinions about whether prices had gone up since the announcement of the wage-price freeze.

Opinion about Buying Conditions	All Families	Since the freeze prices have:	
		Gone up	Remained unchanged
Good time to buy a car	45%	39%	50%
Bad time to buy a car	25	30	22
Good time to buy large household goods	53%	45%	60%
Bad time to buy large household goods	20	27	15

Recalling that the majority of people who thought prices had remained the same during the freeze expected prices to go up during the next year, it is reasonable to conclude that many people felt this pause in the advance of prices represented a good buying opportunity.

Large Household Goods. Opinions of buying conditions for large household goods changed little in the two months prior to November 1971 and remained quite favorable (Table II-20).

Altogether 47 percent of respondents mentioned prices as a reason why it was a good time to buy in October-November 1971. Fully 26 percent said it was a good time to buy before prices went up (Table II-21). Because the question asking whether it was a good or a bad time to buy large household goods referred to the present (rather than to the next 12 months, as is the case with the car question), these data did provide evidence of buying in advance.

Houses. Opinions of buying conditions for houses became somewhat less favorable since August-September 1971 among upper income families (Table II-22), but nevertheless remained more favorable than they had been in May 1971. Among all families, there was little change in these opinions during the six months prior to November 1971. The big improvement over the depressed levels recorded in 1970 occurred between October-November 1970 and May 1971.

While references to tight credit conditions and high interest rates became much less frequent during the last part of 1970 and in 1971, complaints about high prices for houses did not decline to the same extent. In October-November 1971, more respondents said it was a bad time to buy a house because of high prices than because of tight credit and high interest rates (Table II-23).

Interestingly, 18 percent of respondents (22 percent of upper income respondents) said it was a good time to buy because prices might go up further. This suggests that consumers were especially conscious of housing prices at that moment.

Table II-8 shows that there was relatively little change in interest rate expectations during the few months prior to November 1971 except that there was some increase in the proportion of upper income consumers expecting rates to go down.

It was rather difficult for many people to obtain mortgage credit in 1970 and the majority of consumers were aware of that difficulty. In 1971, credit conditions eased greatly, and there was widespread awareness among consumers that this change had occurred. The boom in housing under these circumstances came as no surprise, and there was nothing in the November 1971 survey data to suggest that the boom would not continue into the next year.

10

THE OUTLOOK FOR CONSUMER DEMAND, FEBRUARY 1972

Highlights

During the few months prior to February 1972 there was a substantial improvement in consumers' expectations about what would happen to business conditions and unemployment. The upturn in sentiment was broadly based, but it was most pronounced among middle-income families. Many people believed that some improvement in the economy had already occurred, while many others pointed to the presidential election as a reason why 1972 would be a good year.

The index of Consumer Sentiment stood at 87.5 in February 1972, which is more than five points above the fourth quarter of 1971 and more than twelve points above the recession low reached in 1970. In February 1969, the Index stood at 95.1, much higher than the February 1972 figure; yet more than 60 percent of the decline in the Index during 1969 and early 1970 had been recovered by February 1972.

Attitudes in three areas are determined every quarter by asking several questions regarding each. The improvement in the Index during the 3 months prior to the February 1972 survey was due primarily to a change in attitudes in one area: opinions and expectations about general economic trends. In Feburary 1972, 38 percent of family heads said that business conditions were better than they were a year ago, as compared to 26 percent in November 1971. More than one-half of respondents thought in February that business conditions in the country would be good during the next 12 months, as against less than 40 percent in November. In February, 28 percent thought that unemployment would decline during the next 12 months and the same proportion thought that it would increase; these answers represented a turn toward optimism because in November 1970 only 21 percent spoke of a forthcoming decline and 37 percent spoke of an increase in unemployment.

In the second major area of study, attitudes toward the trend of the personal financial situation, there was little change during the three months prior to February 1972 survey. Compared to 1965-69 personal financial expectations were much more depressed at the time of the survey than were general economic expectations. This was due both to expectations about inflation and to a lesser frequency of reported income gains.

With respect to the third area, the evaluation of supply conditions and prices, in 1971 there was a substantial improvement in the proportion saying that "This is a good time" to buy a car or other durables. During the few months preceding February 1972, the favorable opinions were sustained but there was little further gain.

The upturn in consumer sentiment during the first quarter of 1972 represented a significant break from the depressed attitudes which had persisted over the previous couple of years. The moderate improvement in sentiment in the first half of 1971 resulted primarily from some people having become accustomed to the bad news about inflation and unemployment which had continued over many months, rather than from any significant good news. In contrast, the upturn in sentiment in February 1972 may be traced primarily to good news about economic trends and growing awareness of a recovery in the economy, as well as to a reduction in the frequency of bad news heard. When asked what news they had heard about business conditions, for the first time in several years more respondents mentioned favorable news (32 percent) than unfavorable news (28 percent). In November 1971, favorable news (27 percent) was much less frequently mentioned than unfavorable news (43 percent).

Attitudes toward wage and price controls did not change much during the few months prior to February 1972 insofar as the majority of those with definite opinions continued to believe that the controls would not be successful. But in November 1971 many people expressed uncertainty about the trend in prices and only 37 percent of respondents said that prices in general had risen since controls were introduced. In February 1972 not fewer than 77 percent said that prices had risen and 27 percent even spoke of substantial past price increases. Expectations about the course of prices during the next year, or the next five years, showed only a little improvement compared to February 1971.

While inflationary expectations continued to put a brake on the improvement of consumer sentiment, with respect to willingness to buy cars and other durables, these attitudes had some favorable implications as well. Many respondents said that the present was a good time to buy, before prices went up. But similar considerations and the elimination of the automobile excise tax stimulated automobile buying already in the fall of 1971; therefore in February 1972 consumers had less latitude to translate their price expectations into purchase decisions.

Demand for one-family houses would continue to be stimulated by more favorable attitudes toward buying conditions for houses. In February 1972, 49 percent said it was a good time to buy houses, as against only 29 percent who said it was a bad time. In the second half of 1971, the two percentages were approximately equal.

Opinions about the expected business trend during the next 5 years improved somewhat during the three months prior to February 1972, but were still greatly depressed compared to the opinions that prevailed prior to 1969. Awareness of societal problems—race, poverty, pollution—continued to dampen consumer confidence.

In addition to changes in sentiment, consumers' ability to buy represents an important factor influencing demand. If real incomes were to continue to improve in 1972, the available indications of improved willingness to buy in February 1972 were expected to be reinforced. Therefore, the prospects for the second half of 1972 had to be judged more favorably than they were a few months prior to February 1972.

Yet the findings about longer-range expectations pointed toward a slow rate of improvement and a continued fairly high rate of saving, rather than toward a surge in discretionary spending.

Change in the Index of Consumer Sentiment

Following two quarters of little change, the Index of Consumer Sentiment resumed its upward course in the first quarter of 1972. The more than five-point gain chalked up in February 1972 represented the largest quarter-to-quarter increase since mid-1958.

And yet, all but one point of the gain was due to improvement in just two of the five Index components, namely consumers' expectations about what would happen to business conditions during the next twelve months and five years. The other three components went up only a little or not at all.

At most times, the Index for upper-income families moves rather closely along with that for lower-income families. This was the case, for example, when the Index for all families rose 6.2 points in the first two quarters of 1971 (Table II-1). After that time, however, the changes for upper and lower-income families became divergent.[1] In August-September 1971 the Index for upper-income families fell while that for lower-income families continued to improve. In October-November the upper-income Index gained sharply

---

[1]This divergence is especially pronounced when the upper-income group is defined to include families with before-tax incomes of $12,500 and over (now about 28 percent of all families) rather than $10,000 and over as in previous SRC reports.

while the lower-income Index fell. In February 1972 there was a small improvement among upper-income families, but a sharp improvement among lower-income families.

Changes in the Index components are summarized in the tabulation shown on the next page. In August-September, after the New Economic Policy had been announced, the attitudes of upper-income families became much less favorable with respect to both the personal financial situation and the outlook for short-term as well as long-term business conditions. In October-November there was a sizable improvement in each of the five Index components for upper-income families, especially in the evaluation of recent past changes in the financial situation and in the expectations for business conditions during the next five years. The upturn in these two components was noteworthy because both had been at the recession low point in August-September.

The sharp improvement among upper income families in October-November 1971 was a favorable sign because the attitudes of these families tend to lead the way in periods of business cycle recovery. The February 1972 findings provided an important confirmation for this turn toward optimism. Attitudes of lower-income families improved markedly, especially with respect to expectations for business conditions, both short- and long-term.

On the other hand, for upper income families, the February findings did not show further improvement in attitudes toward the financial situation. However, short-term business expectations posted a substantial gain and the previous improvement in five-year business expectations was sustained.

These changes may be traced in large part to more optimistic expectations about unemployment and less optimistic expectations about inflation, as detailed in the following sections of this report.

Improved Expectations about Business Conditions

During the few months prior to February 1972, a substantial proportion of the American people came to believe that the economy was on the road to recovery. Not only was there increased optimism that business conditions would improve during the next year; in addition many respondents said that the economy had already turned up.

Throughout 1971, the proportion of consumers who believed that business conditions had improved was far smaller than the proportion who saw some deterioration. These attitudes (Table II-2) did not change significantly after the announcement of the New Economic Policy in August 1971. In February 1972, however, a substantial change occurred, with more people seeing improved business conditions (38 percent) than worse conditions (25 percent). Among upper-income families (those with incomes of $12,500 or more), the change was also quite pronounced, with nearly 50 percent saying in February

Change in Index Component from Previous Quarter [1]

	May 1971	Aug-Sept. 1971	Oct-Nov. 1971	Feb. 1972
	All Families			
Change in financial situation:				
From a year ago	+ 6	− 6	+ 5	0
Expected a year from now	+ 1	0	0	+ 4
Expected business conditions:				
During the next 12 months	+ 8	+ 3	− 8	+ 22
During the next 5 years	− 3	+ 2	+ 2	+ 8
Buying conditions for large household goods	+ 11	+ 6	− 1	+ 3
Change in the Index	+ 3.4	+ 0.8	− 0.2	+ 5.3
	Families with Incomes $12,500 or more			
Change in financial situation:				
From a year ago	+ 2	− 14	+ 23	− 8
Expected a year from now	+ 5	− 9	+ 11	0
Expected business conditions:				
During the next 12 months	+ 18	− 12	+ 8	+ 23
During the next 5 years	− 6	− 6	+ 18	− 1
Buying conditions for large household goods	+ 13	+ 4	+ 8	− 3
Change in the Index	+ 4.2	− 4.9	+ 9.5	+ 1.6

[1]Increase in percent of respondents giving a favorable or optimistic answer minus increase in percent giving an unfavorable or pessimistic answer. Therefore a plus sign indicates improvement and a minus sign deterioration in the component.

that business conditions were better than they were a year ago.

As shown in Table II-3, expectations about future change in business conditions had also improved substantially since November 1971, although the upturn was not as great as the upturn of opinions about past trends. Nearly half of all respondents continued to say that business would be neither better nor worse a year from the time of the survey. Yet, considering that many people believed that business had improved already, an expectation of no further change did not imply the degree of pessimism as did the same response in the fall of 1971.

When opinions of both past and future trends are considered together, as in Table II-4, the extent of increased optimism is evident. In November 1971 an optimistic trend was expressed only slightly more frequently than a pessimistic trend. In February 1972, the ratio was more than two to one.

More than half of all respondents, and nearly two-thirds of upper-income respondents believed that we would have good times in the economy during the twelve months following February 1972. These figures represented a substantial increase over November 1971 (Table II-5). These expectations had shown considerable improvement in the first half of 1971, but largely because of the uncertainties about controls they were lower in November than in May 1971.

The first years of the 70's have been eventful with respect to news about the economy. When asked to report on any favorable or unfavorable news they had heard about changes in business conditions during 1970 and 1971, most respondents were able to think of at least one item of news, more often than not an unfavorable one. In October-November 1971, these news items were mostly concerned with the slack economy and unemployment, although inflation was also mentioned frequently. In February 1972, unfavorable news was mentioned much less frequently (Table II-6). Indeed, for the first time in six years, favorable news items were mentioned more frequently than unfavorable items. Among upper-income families, favorable news was mentioned more than twice as frequently as was unfavorable news.

In February 1972, unlike during 1971, the majority of respondents said that they had not heard any news about changes in business conditions. Furthermore, many of the respondents who mentioned favorable news referred to a general improvement in the economy rather than to specific items of favorable news about business or employment. This circumstance suggests that economic matters did not occupy as important a place in consumers' awareness as was the case during the preceding couple of years.

Nevertheless, there was a substantial improvement since November 1971 in expectations about what would happen to unemployment during the next twelve months (Table II-7). In this respect, there was relatively little change in the last three quarters of 1971. Especially toward the end of 1971, and particularly among lower-income respondents, unfavorable expectations about unemployment were an important factor retarding recovery in consumer sentiment. Even in February 1972, however, the proportion expecting an increase in unemployment was as large as the proportion expecting a decline.

An additional factor stimulating consumers' expectations for business conditions in Febtuary 1972 was the forthcoming national election. In years past, SRC had found that a presidential election stimulates sentiment, in part because of the opinion of some people that the incumbent party will do what it can to make the economy prosperous prior to the election, and in part because of the opinion that a new president might be able to solve old problems. The impact of the election this year was somewhat stronger than at the time of previous presidential elections. The elections were spontaneously mentioned as a reason why we would have good times by 13 percent of all families and 19 percent of upper-income families.

One of the important factors contributing to sluggish discretionary spending and a high rate of saving in the few years prior to 1972 was the rather pessimistic expectations about what would happen to business conditions over the long term. Although long-run expectations about business conditions improved significantly during the six months prior to the February 1972 survey, long-run attitudes continued to retard the recovery in consumer sentiment.

Impact of Government Economic Policy

During the twelve months prior to February 1972, changes in consumer sentiment were closely tied to people's attitudes toward the government's economic policies. The upturn in sentiment in the first quarter of 1972 cannot be fully understood except in the context of shifts which occurred in opinions about wage and price controls and expectations of inflation.

In February 1972, the attitudes of upper-income people toward government policy worsened somewhat (Table II-10). Fewer people believed that the government was doing a good job, while the opinion that the government was doing "only fair" had grown larger.

These changes may be understood in the light of what people believed had happened and what they believed would happen to inflation, and to unemployment. With respect to inflation, in November 1971 only 37 percent of all families believed that prices had gone up since controls had been introduced. In February 1972, this proportion more than doubled to 77 percent, including 27 percent who said that prices had gone up substantially, 31 percent who said that they had gone up "just a bit," and the remainder saying that the increase was somewhere in between. In other words, a substantial fraction of respondents in February 1972 believed that the controls had failed to hold back inflation. These attitudes were strongly related to consumer expectations, as shown in the tabulation on the next page.

Not surprisingly, people who believed that prices had risen, substantially in the past six months tended to be skeptical about prospects of slowing down the rate of inflation in the next one or five years. Table II-11 shows that expectations about inflation became slightly less optimistic during the few months preceding February 1972. The proportion anticipating price increases of 5 percent or more rose from 28 to 34 percent.

Despite these data, there are good reasons not to exaggerate the extent to which inflationary expectations dampened consumer sentiment in February 1972. First, five-year price expectations had not changed much since November 1971. Both then and in February 1972, 32 percent of all families expected prices to be a lot higher in five years, while the proportion expecting prices to be a little higher increased only from 35 to 41 percent.

Second, it must be remembered that in November 1971 a rather small proportion of consumers expected the government to be successful in restraining future price increases. For many people, the expected had happened by February 1972.

		Since August 15 prices have gone up:		
Personal financial situation in a year will be:	All Families	Substantially	Something in between	Just a bit
Better	35%	29%	27%	42%
Worse	9	15	11	7
Business conditions during the next 12 months:				
Good times	52%	40%	54%	62%
Bad times	21	30	19	17
Prices five years from now will be:				
A lot higher	32%	45%	35%	27%
A little higher	41	29	37	50
Same or lower	18	16	17	16
Prices during the next 12 months:				
Will rise 5% or more	34%	50%	40%	29%
Will rise by less	36	26	36	44
Will not go up	26	17	21	25
Net effect of wage and price controls on the personal financial situation				
Will benefit	15%	9%	16%	19%
Not much difference	54	48	54	55
Will suffer a loss	23	36	21	20

Third, Table II-12 suggests that the improvement in optimism about what would happen to business conditions occurred mainly among those people who doubted that the government would be successful in controlling inflation. Indeed, for some people, less certainty about what might happen with the controls may have made for greater certainty about what might happen to business conditions. Fewer respondents than in November 1971 mentioned controls as a reason why they did not know whether we would have good or bad times during the next twelve months. Under the circumstances prevailing in February 1972, for some people the expectation of only a halfway good job in controlling inflation might have been preferable to uncertainty.

Fourth, opinions about whether the wage and price controls would mean a net loss or gain to the personal financial situation hardly changed during the three months prior to the February 1972 survey.

Nevertheless, consumer sentiment would have gone up much more rapidly had it not been for the prevailing attitudes toward inflation. Attitudes toward unemployment and awareness of a recovery in the economy provided an upward thrust. Opinions about whether or not the government would be successful in reducing unemployment became more favorable (Table II-13), although expectations of success were frequently qualified.

Changes in attitudes toward the personal financial situation are shown in Tables II-14, II-15, and II-16. It can be seen that, especially among lower-income people, the expectation to be better off a year from now increased slightly. Upper-income people evaluated past changes somewhat less favorably than they did three months prior to the February 1972 survey. This is consistent with the finding that upper-income families tend to look upon inflation as a more serious problem than unemployment, while families with incomes less than $12,500 tend to hold the opposite view.

Attitudes toward personal finances remained at a rather low level, having recovered a smaller fraction of the 1969-70 deterioration than did most other attitudes. There were several reasons for this, in addition to inflation. For one thing, income gains continued to be reported less frequently than in the years before 1970. In February 1972, only 42 percent of all families reported making more money than they made a year earlier. In the late 1960s, the proportion was typically 50 percent or above.

Secondly, consumers continued to be very much aware of high taxes. When asked whether the income taxes the average American would have to pay to the federal government in 1972 would be about the same as those in 1971, or higher, or lower, fully 40 percent said "higher" while only 9 percent said "lower." These percentages differed little among income groups.

The Demand for Durable Goods

Consumer opinions about good or bad times to buy cars and other durables improved substantially in the fall of 1971 and did not change much during the three months prior to February 1972. Attitudes toward buying automobiles had benefited greatly in 1971 from the New Economic Policy (elimination of the excise tax, rollback of previously announced price increases). In February 1972, there were relatively few respondents complaining about auto or appliance prices being too high. On the other hand, the proportion saying that "prices are going higher" remained substantial or even increased. What must, however, be considered is that a good deal of buying in advance had already been done; therefore there was less latitude to do so in the few months following February 1972.

Opinions about how prices in general had moved since August 1971 appeared to influence the evaluation of buying conditions for durable goods. Among respondents who thought that prices of things they buy had risen substantially in the recent past, 39 percent said that the present was a good time to buy a car. Among those who spoke of unchanged prices or small past price increases, the same proportion was 52 percent.

The evaulation of buying conditions for houses was a different story. While these evaluations were much more favorable in 1971 than in 1970, even late in 1971 the proportion saying "This is a bad time to buy a house" was as large as the proportion saying it was a "good time." In February 1972 the latter proportion greatly exceeded the former for the first time in several years. References to tight credit and to high interest rates continued to decline during the three months prior to February 1972. At the same time, the proportion saying that prices would go up in the future rose (Table II-22 and II-23).

Consumer discretionary spending remained sluggish during the first few months of 1972, and the rate of saving out of income remained at a fairly high level. During the fall of 1971 some people bought discretionary items, because, in their opinion, good buys were available, thereby borrowing somewhat from future demand. Incurrence of installment debt increased, but the impact of the recession experience persisted and induced many people to add to their financial reserves.

The crucial question in February 1972 was how fast consumers might be expected to loosen their purse strings. There were a number of factors which point to a continued slow improvement, and a high saving rate, rather than to a surge in discretionary spending:

1) Inflationary expectations continued to put a brake on the improvement in sentiment.
2) Despite some recent improvement, long-term expectations about the economy remained rather unfavorable because awareness of societal problems continued to dampen consumer confidence.
3) The 1971-72 upturn in sentiment was not sharp in comparison with recoveries from previous recessions.

4) Finally, consumer sentiment had been in the doldrums for a very long period, and it might require some time before saving habits could be adjusted to more favorable sentiment.

Nevertheless, it was predicted that if expectations about a recovering economy and reduced unemployment were fulfilled and if income gains were frequent and substantial, consumer demand would be favorably affected. The outlook for discretionary spending later in 1972 was better than it appeared three months prior to February 1972.

OUTLOOK CHARTS AND TABLES

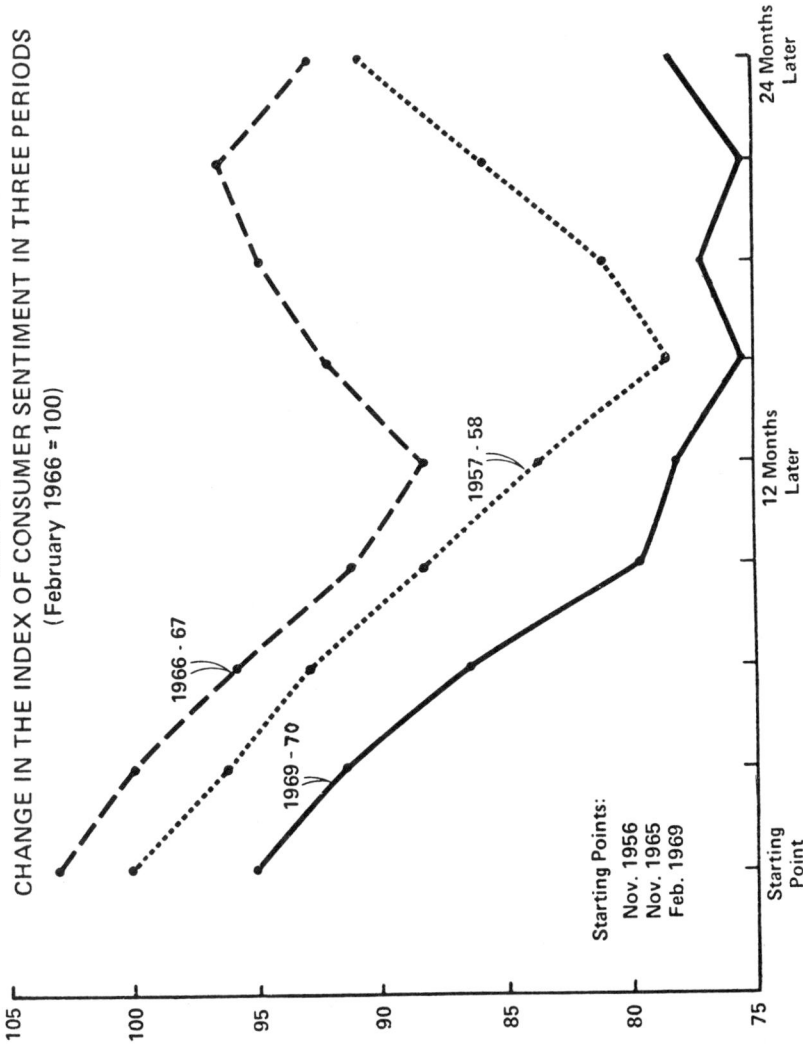

CHART II-1

CHANGE IN THE INDEX OF CONSUMER SENTIMENT IN THREE PERIODS
(February 1966 = 100)

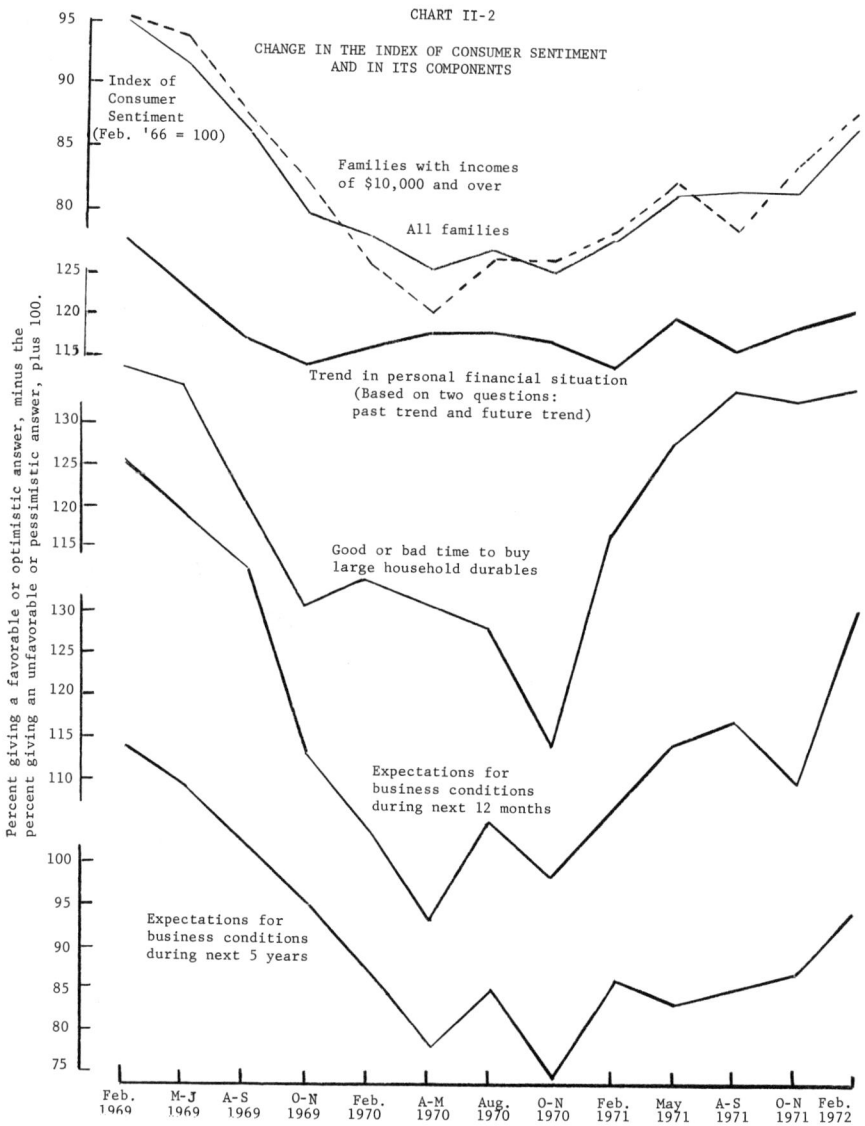

CHART II-2

CHANGE IN THE INDEX OF CONSUMER SENTIMENT
AND IN ITS COMPONENTS

TABLE II-1

Index of Consumer Sentiment

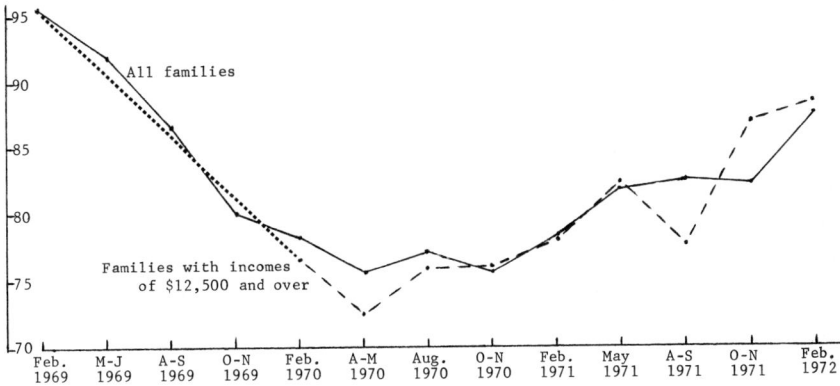

Date of Study	All Families (Feb. 1966 = 100)	Families with Incomes of $10,000 and Over (Feb. 1966 = 100)	Families with Incomes of $12,500 and Over (Feb. 1969 = 95.1)**
February 1969	95.1	95.5	95.1
May-June 1969	91.6	93.9	
Aug-Sept. 1969	86.4	87.5	
Oct-Nov. 1969	79.7	82.3	
February 1970	78.1	75.8	76.4
April-May 1970	75.4	72.1	72.5
August 1970	77.1	76.4	75.9
Oct-Nov. 1970	75.4*	76.4*	75.9*
February 1971	78.2	78.8	78.0
May 1971	81.6	83.0	82.2
Aug-Sept. 1971	82.4	79.2	77.6
Oct-Nov. 1971	82.2	84.6	86.5
February 1972	87.5	88.7	88.1

*Adjusted to allow for temporary impact of the auto strike.

**The base for this upper-income group was set at February 1969 = 95.1 so as to make these data comparable to the Index for all families.

.........No data available for these survey periods.

TABLE II-2

Current Business Conditions in Comparison to Those a Year Ago

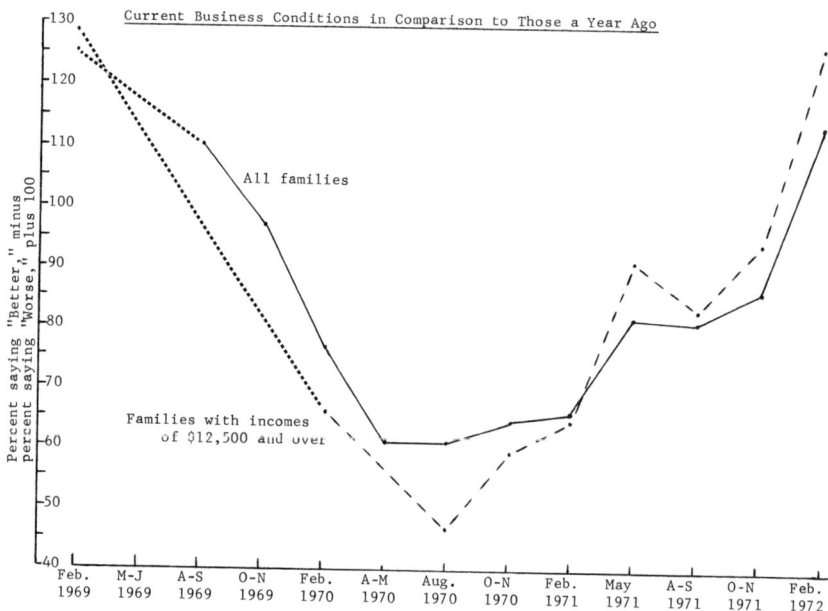

Business Conditions Now Compared to a Year Ago	Nov. 1965	Feb. 1969	Feb. 1970	Apr-May 1970	Aug. 1970	Oct-Nov. 1970	Feb. 1971	May 1971	Aug-Sept. 1971	Oct-Nov. 1971	Feb. 1972
					A. All Families						
Better	54%	36%	21%	16%	15%	18%	18%	26%	24%	26%	38%
About the same	35	50	30	25	29	25	26	28	31	29	34
Worse	6	11	44	55	54	54	52	44	43	40	25
Not ascertained, don't know, depends	5	3	5	4	2	3	4	2	2	5	3
Total	100%	100%	100%	100%	100%	100%	100%	100%	100%	100%	100%
			B.	Families with Incomes of $12,500 and Over							
Better		41%	18%	12%	11%	19%	22%	35%	30%	34%	49%
About the same		44	27	16	24	20	19	21	21	24	27
Worse		13	52	70	64	60	58	43	47	40	23
Not ascertained, don't know, depends		2	3	2	1	1	1	1	2	2	1
Total		100%	100%	100%	100%	100%	100%	100%	100%	100%	100%

The question was: "Would you say that at present business conditions are better or worse than they were a year ago?"

---------- No data available for these survey periods.

TABLE II-3

Expected Change in Business Conditions in Twelve Months

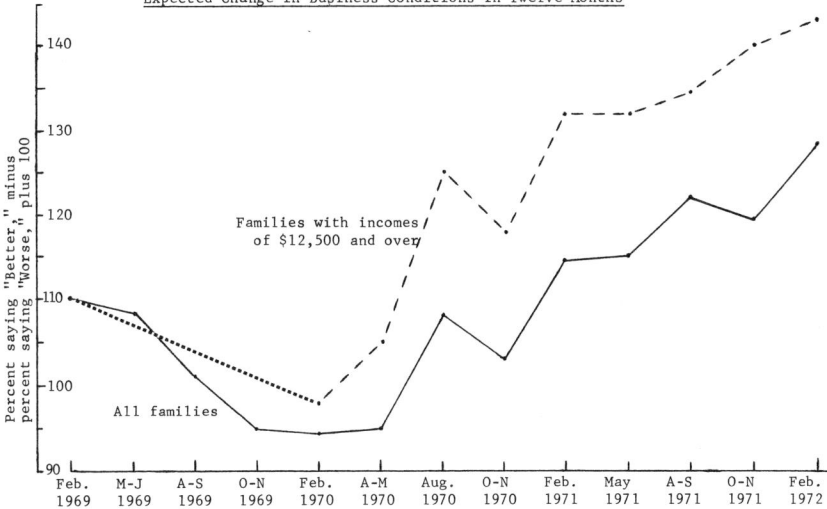

Conditions in 12 Months Compared to Now	Nov. 1965	Feb. 1969	Feb. 1970	Apr-May 1970	Aug. 1970	Oct-Nov. 1970	Feb. 1971	May 1971	Aug-Sept. 1971	Oct-Nov. 1971	Feb. 1972
					A.	All Families					
Better	36%	22%	20%	20%	26%	22%	31%	32%	36%	33%	38%
Same	53	61	49	49	50	52	48	46	45	47	48
Worse	6	12	26	25	18	19	17	18	14	14	10
Don't know, not ascertained	5	5	5	6	6	7	4	4	5	6	4
Total	100%	100%	100%	100%	100%	100%	100%	100%	100%	100%	100%
				B.	Families with Incomes of $12,500 and Over						
Better		23%	23%	29%	39%	32%	45%	44%	46%	49%	50%
Same		60	48	42	43	52	38	41	36	37	39
Worse		13	25	24	14	14	13	12	12	9	7
Don't know, not ascertained		4	4	5	4	2	4	3	6	5	4
Total		100%	100%	100%	100%	100%	100%	100%	100%	100%	100%

The question was: "And how about a year from now, do you expect that in the country as a whole business conditions will be better or worse than they are at present, or just about the same?"

••••••••••No data available for these survey periods.

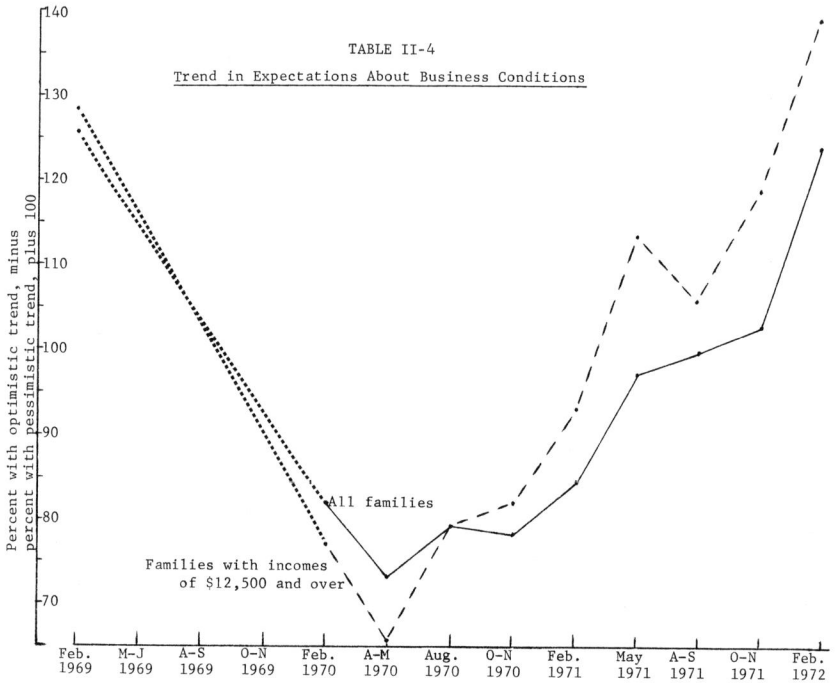

TABLE II-4

Trend in Expectations About Business Conditions

Trend in Business Conditions	Feb. 1969	Feb. 1970	Apr-May 1970	Aug. 1970	Oct-Nov. 1970	Feb. 1971	May 1971	Aug-Sept. 1971	Oct-Nov. 1971	Feb. 1972
					A. All Families					
Optimistic trend*	38%	21%	17%	18%	19%	22%	29%	31%	32%	43
Pessimistic trend	12	39	44	39	41	37	32	31	29	19
				B. Families with Incomes of $12,500 and Over						
Optimistic trend*	42%	19%	14%	15%	23%	25%	40%	36%	42%	54%
Pessimistic trend	14	42	48	36	41	32	27	30	23	15

*Business conditions are better than a year ago and will be the same or better a year from now, or business conditions are the same as a year ago and will be better.

.... No data available for these survey periods.

TABLE II-5

Business Conditions Expected During Next Twelve Months

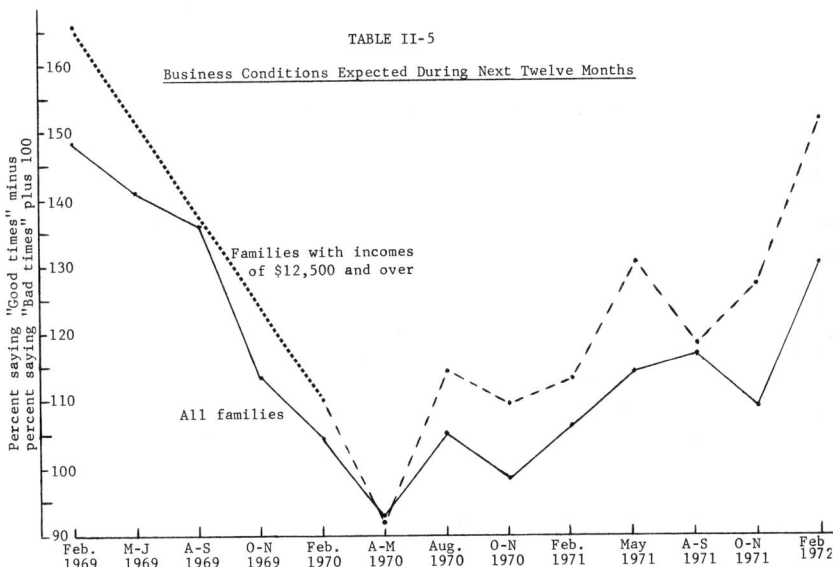

Expected Business Conditions	Nov. 1965	Feb. 1969	Feb. 1970	Apr-May 1970	Aug. 1970	Oct-Nov. 1970	Feb. 1971	May 1971	Aug-Sept. 1971	Oct-Nov. 1971	Feb. 1972
				A.	All	Families					
Good times	71%	62%	40%	34%	39%	36%	41%	42%	45%	39%	52%
Good in some ways, bad in others	4	6	8	9	10	8	8	11	10	8	8
Bad times	8	14	36	41	34	38	35	28	28	30	21
Uncertain	16	17	15	15	15	17	15	17	16	21	16
Not ascertained	1	1	1	1	2	1	1	2	1	2	3
Total	100%	100%	100%	100%	100%	100%	100%	100%	100%	100%	100%
				B.	Families	with	Incomes	of $12,500	and	Over	
Good times		74%	46%	34%	46%	45%	48%	53%	47%	50%	65%
Good in some ways, bad in others		6	6	12	11	9	8	14	11	9	7
Bad times		8	36	42	32	36	35	22	28	23	15
Uncertain		11	11	10	9	10	8	8	12	16	10
Not ascertained		1	1	2	2	*	1	3	2	2	3
Total		100%	100%	100%	100%	100%	100%	100%	100%	100%	100%

*Less than half of one percent.

The question was: "Now turning to business conditions in the country as a whole - do you think that during the next 12 months we'll have good times financially or bad times, or what?"

..........No data available for these survey periods.

TABLE II-6

News Heard of Recent Changes in Business Conditions

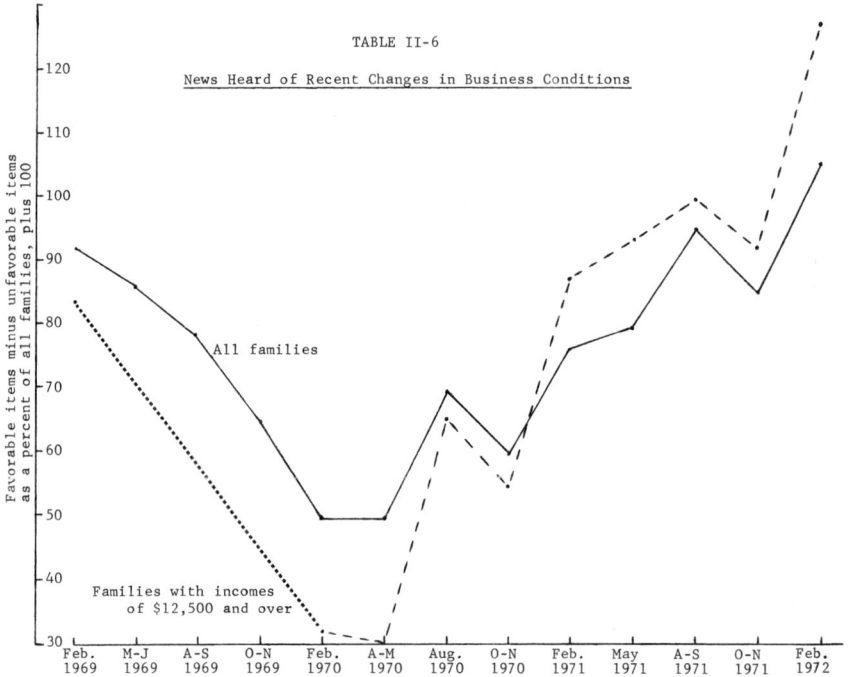

News Heard	Nov. 1965	Feb. 1969	Feb. 1970	Apr- May 1970	Aug. 1970	Oct- Nov. 1970	Feb. 1971	May 1971	Aug- Sept. 1971	Oct- Nov. 1971	Feb. 1972
					A.	All Families					
Favorable news items	29%	16%	9%	10%	16%	17%	28%	26%	36%	27%	32%
Unfavorable news items	13	24	60	61	47	57	52	47	42	43	28
Did not hear any news	66	66	46	42	51	47	41	44	45	46	54
Total	1/	1/	1/	1/	1/	1/	1/	1/	1/	1/	1/
			B.	Families with Incomes of $12,500 and Over							
Favorable news items		21%	14%	13%	24%	25%	45%	45%	48%	45%	52%
Unfavorable news items		38	82	83	59	71	58	52	49	53	25
Did not hear any news		52	28	26	38	32	27	30	34	28	43
Total		1/	1/	1/	1/	1/	1/	1/	1/	1/	1/

$\underline{1/}$Adds to more than 100 percent because some people mentioned two items of news heard. The questions were: "Have you heard of any favorable or unfavorable changes in business conditions during the past few months? What did you hear?"

..........No data available for these survey periods.

TABLE II-7
Expected Change in Unemployment

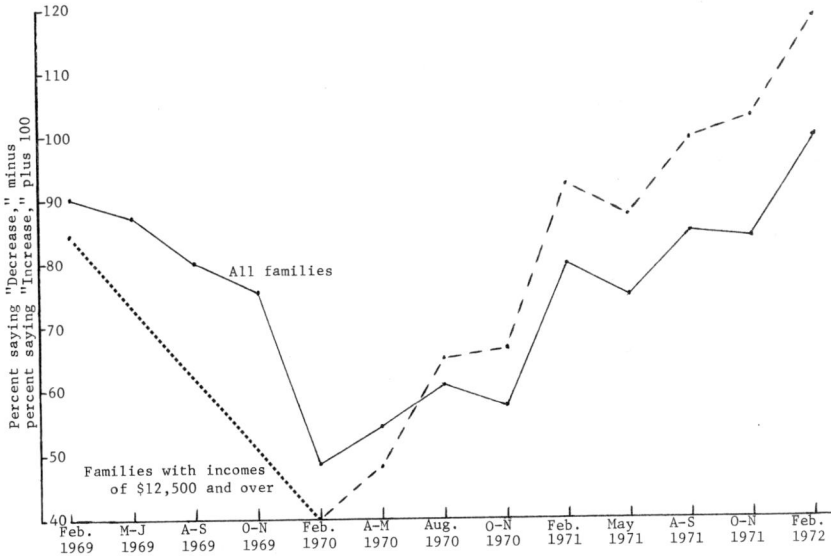

Percent saying "Decrease," minus
percent saying "Increase," plus 100

120
110
100
90
80
70
60
50
40

All families

Families with incomes
of $12,500 and over

	Feb. 1969	M-J 1969	A-S 1969	O-N 1969	Feb. 1970	A-M 1970	Aug. 1970	O-N 1970	Feb. 1971	May 1971	A-S 1971	O-N 1971	Feb. 1972

During the Next 12 Months Unemployment:	Feb. 1966	Feb. 1969	Feb. 1970	Apr- May 1970	Aug. 1970	Oct- Nov. 1970	Feb. 1971	May 1971	Aug- Sept. 1971	Oct- Nov. 1971	Feb. 1972
				A.	All Families						
Will decrease	43%	17%	8%	10%	11%	12%	23%	20%	24%	21%	28%
No change	40	53	29	30	36	29	31	32	34	37	39
Will increase	11	27	60	56	50	55	43	45	39	37	29
Don't know, not ascertained	6	3	3	4	3	4	3	3	3	5	4
Total	100%	100%	100%	100%	100%	100%	100%	100%	100%	100%	100%
				B.	Families with Incomes of $12,500 and Over						
Will decrease	48%	13%	7%	10%	14%	18%	30%	25%	31%	31%	39%
No change	41	55	23	27	35	29	29	35	34	37	37
Will increase	9	29	69	62	49	51	38	38	32	29	21
Don't know, not ascertained	2	3	1	1	2	2	3	2	3	3	3
Total	100%	100%	100%	100%	100%	100%	100%	100%	100%	100%	100%

The question was: "And how about people out of work during the coming 12 months - do
you think that there will be more unemployment than now, about the same, or less?"

.... No data available for these survey periods.

Table II-8

Expected Change in Interest Rates

Interest Rates Will	Feb. 1969	Oct-Nov. 1969	Feb. 1970	Apr-May 1970	Aug. 1970	Oct-Nov. 1970	Feb. 1971	May 1971	Aug-Sept 1971	Oct-Nov. 1971	Feb. 1972
					A. All Families						
Go up	38%	41%	33%	22%	23%	22%	15%	25%	24%	23%	18%
Stay the same	40	31	36	32	40	30	25	38	46	41	48
Go down	5	17	18	31	25	36	51	24	21	22	15
Don't know, not ascertained	17	11	13	15	12	12	9	13	9	14	19
Total	100%	100%	100%	100%	100%	100%	100%	100%	100%	100%	100%
			B. Families with Incomes of $12,500 and Over								
Go up		39%	25%	12%	14%	9%	10%	30%	21%	17%	17%
Stay the same		45	39	35	42	34	24	39	51	49	53
Go down		8	29	43	38	54	62	26	21	28	21
Dont' know, not ascertained		8	7	10	6	3	4	5	7	6	9
Total		100%	100%	100%	100%	100%	100%	100%	100%	100%	100%

The question was: "No one can say for sure, but what do you think will happen to interest rates during the next 12 months?"

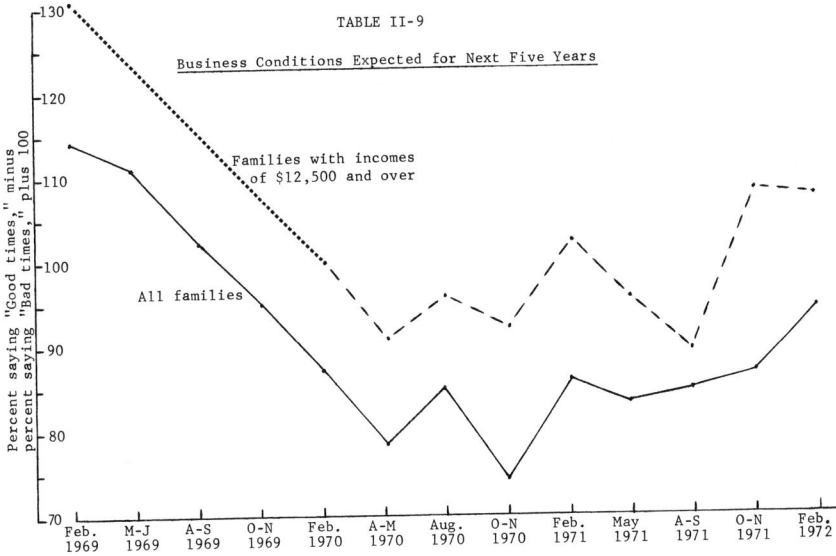

TABLE II-9

Business Conditions Expected for Next Five Years

Expected Business Conditions	Nov. 1965	Feb. 1969	Feb. 1970	Apr- May 1970	Aug. 1970	Oct- Nov. 1970	Feb. 1971	May 1971	Aug- Sept. 1971	Oct- Nov. 1971	Feb. 1972
					A. All Families						
Good times	47%	37%	26%	22%	25%	20%	22%	20%	22%	24%	27%
Uncertain, good and bad	32	31	27	22	26	25	30	27	26	25	24
Bad times	14	23	39	44	40	46	36	37	37	37	30
Not ascertained	7	9	8	12	9	9	12	16	15	14	19
Total	100%	100%	100%	100%	100%	100%	100%	100%	100%	100%	100%
				B. Families with Incomes of $12,500 and Over							
Good times		48%	33%	28%	30%	30%	30%	27%	25%	36%	32%
Uncertain, good and bad		27	28	27	26	21	29	25	25	22	25
Bad times		17	33	37	34	38	28	31	35	27	25
Not ascertained		8	6	8	10	11	13	17	15	15	18
Total		100%	100%	100%	100%	100%	100%	100%	100%	100%	100%

The questions were: "Looking ahead, which would you say is more likely - that in the country as a whole we'll have continuous good times during the next 5 years or so, or that we will have periods of widespread unemployment or depression, or what? (IF DON'T KNOW) On what does it depend in your opinion?"

.... No data available for these survey periods.

Table II-10

Opinions About the Government's Economic Policy

In regard to inflation or unemployment, the government is doing:	A. All Families						B. $12,500 and Over					
	Aug. 1970	Oct-Nov. 1970	May 1971	Aug-Sept 1971	Oct-Nov. 1971	Feb 1972	Aug. 1970	Oct-Nov. 1970	May 1971	Aug-Sept 1971	Oct-Nov. 1971	Feb. 1972
A good job	18%	15%	14%	26%	24%	20%	19%	18%	16%	29%	30%	22%
Only fair	45	47	52	44	46	53	47	53	56	39	46	53
A poor job	26	29	28	24	21	20	27	27	25	27	19	21
Don't know; not ascertained	11	9	6	6	9	7	7	2	3	5	5	4
Total	100%	100%	100%	100%	100%	100%	100%	100%	100%	100%	100%	100%

	C. All Families								
	May 1971			Oct-Nov. 1971			February 1972		
Personal financial situation compared to a year ago	Good job	Only fair	Poor job	Good job	Only fair	Poor job	Good job	Only fair	Poor job
Better off now	39%	37%	23%	39%	33%	24%	39%	31%	21%
Worse off	19	22	36	20	24	40	20	22	40
Expected personal financial situation a year from now									
Better off in a year	40%	38%	29%	39%	34%	24%	46%	36%	28%
Worse off	8	9	17	7	8	15	6	6	18
Business conditions expected during the next 12 months									
Good times	56%	46%	30%	57%	40%	26%	72%	59%	28%
Bad times	17	25	41	15	30	48	8	17	39
Business conditions expected a year from now									
Better in a year	46%	33%	28%	52%	32%	21%	53%	40%	22%
Worse	10	14	27	8	10	27	5	6	24
Business conditions expected during the next 5 years									
Good times	33%	22%	12%	37%	25%	11%	39%	28%	14%
Bad times	28	35	45	24	39	43	19	28	49

The question was: "As to the economic policy of the government - I mean steps taken in regard to inflation or unemployment - would you say the government is doing a good job, only fair, or a poor job?"

Table II-11

Opinions About Extent of Price Increases
Expected During the Next 12 Months

	Feb. 1969	Oct-Nov. 1969	Feb. 1970	Apr-May 1970	Aug. 1970	Oct-Nov. 1970	Feb. 1971	May 1971	Aug-Sept. 1971	Oct-Nov. 1971	Feb. 1972
Prices will go up by:						A. All Families					
1 - 2%	33%	31%	21%	19%	23%	20%	24%	26%	18%	20%	23%
3 - 4%	13	9	11	8	12	10	10	11	8	7	13
5%	23	23	28	30	23	28	28	26	19	22	25
6 - 9%	2	3	4	5	4	4	5	5	3	2	3
10% or more	6	5	9	10	6	8	8	6	5	5	6
Don't know, not ascertained how much prices will increase	6	4	5	6	6	7	5	5	4	4	4
Prices will not go up; not ascertained if will	17	25	22	22	26	23	20	21	43	40	26
Total	100%	100%	100%	100%	100%	100%	100%	100%	100%	100%	100%
Prices will go up by:			B. Families with Incomes of $12,500 and Over								
1 - 2%	29%		21%	17%	19%	19%	21%	25%	15%	22%	25%
3 - 4%	18		14	9	16	17	10	15	12	10	15
5%	32		31	33	30	34	35	30	25	25	28
6 - 9%	3		6	7	7	4	9	7	4	2	4
10% or more	6		7	12	4	7	10	4	5	5	6
Don't know, not ascertained how much prices will increase	1		3	4	2	2	3	3	3	3	2
Prices will not go up; not ascertained if will	11		18	18	22	17	12	16	36	33	20
Total	100%		100%	100%	100%	100%	100%	100%	100%	100%	100%

The questions were: "Talking about prices in general, I mean the prices of the things you buy - do you think they will go up in the next year or so, or go down, or stay where they are now?" (IF WILL GO UP) "How large a price increase do you expect? Of course nobody can know for sure, but would you say that a year from now prices will be about 1 or 2% higher, or 5%, or closer to 10% higher than now, or what?"

Table II-12

Whether the Government Will Be Successful in Reducing Inflation

| | October-November 1971 | | | | | February 1972 | | | | |
| | All Families | Family Income | | | | All Families | Family Income | | | |
Opinion		Under $5000	$5000 -7499	$7500 -9999	$10,000 & over		Under $5000	$5000 -7499	$7500 -9999	$10,000 & over
Government will be successful	19%	10%	15%	23%	26%	14%	12%	16%	13%	16%
Successful, with qualifications	16	11	15	16	19	27	27	26	23	27
Pro-con	1	1	1	1	1	*	*	*	*	1
Not successful; little improvement	48	53	52	45	44	48	48	46	56	48
Depends; don't know; not ascertained	16	25	17	15	10	11	13	12	8	8
Total	100%	100%	100%	100%	100%	100%	100%	100%	100%	100%

| | All Families Oct-Nov. 1971 | | All Families February 1972 | |
	Government will be successful	Not successful; little improvement	Government will be successful	Not successful; little improvement
Expected personal financial situation a year from now				
Better off in a year	41%	28%	42%	33%
Worse off	7	11	7	12
Business conditions expected during the next 12 months				
Good times	55%	31%	67%	45%
Bad times	18	39	12	27
Business conditions expected a year from now				
Better in a year	53%	22%	51%	29%
Worse	6	19	5	14
Business conditions expected during the next 5 years				
Good times	34%	19%	34%	22%
Bad times	23	49	22	40

*Less than half of one percent.
The question was: "During the next year or two, do you think the government will be successful in reducing inflation, or do you expect that there will be little or no improvement?"

Table II-13

Whether the Government Will Be Successful in Reducing Unemployment

| | October-November 1971 | | | | | February 1972 | | | | |
| | | Family Income | | | | | Family Income | | | |
Opinion	All Families	Under $5000	$5000 -7499	$7500 -9999	$10,000 & over	All Families	Under $5000	$5000 -7499	$7500 -9999	$10,000 & over
Government will be successful	15%	13%	15%	16%	16%	13%	12%	13%	12%	15%
Successful, with qualifications	10	9	9	9	11	22	23	22	21	22
Pro-con	1	1	*	2	1	*	*	*	*	*
Not successful; little improvement	61	57	66	64	62	52	49	50	57	54
Depends; don't know; not ascertained	13	20	10	9	10	13	16	15	10	9
Total	100%	100%	100%	100%	100%	100%	100%	100%	100%	100%

| | All Families Oct-Nov. 1971 | | All Families February 1972 | |
	Government will be successful	Not successful; little improvement	Government will be successful	Not successful; little improvement
Expected personal financial situation a year from now				
Better off in a year	37%	30%	42%	33%
Worse off	7	11	5	12
Business conditions expected during the next 12 months				
Good times	55%	35%	69%	45%
Bad times	17	35	10	28
Business conditions expected a year from now				
Better in a year	56%	25%	52%	29%
Worse	8	16	4	14
Business conditions expected during the next 5 years				
Good times	37%	20%	40%	18%
Bad times	20	46	16	43

*Less than half of one percent.
The question was: "During the next year or two, do you think the government will be successful in reducing inflation, or do you expect that there will be little or no improvement?"

TABLE II-14

Current Financial Situation Compared to a Year Ago

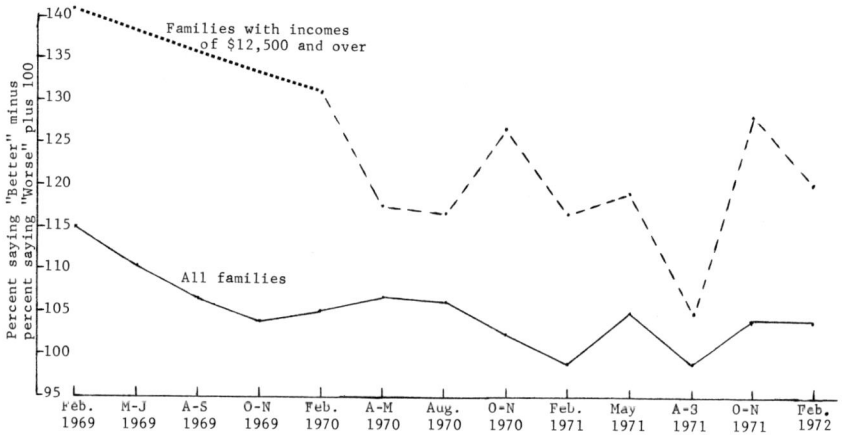

Evaluation of Financial Situation	Nov. 1965	Feb. 1969	Feb. 1970	Apr-May 1970	Aug. 1970	Oct-Nov. 1970	Feb. 1971	May 1971	Aug-Sept. 1971	Oct-Nov. 1971	Feb. 1972
A. All Families											
Better off	38%	35%	33%	33%	32%	31%	31%	32%	27%	31%	30%
Same	44	44	37	39	41	39	36	40	44	41	43
Worse off	17	20	28	26	26	28	32	27	28	27	26
Uncertain	1	1	2	2	1	1	1	1	1	1	1
Not ascertained	*	*	*	*	*	1	*	*	*	*	*
Total	100%	100%	100%	100%	100%	100%	100%	100%	100%	100%	100%
B. Families with Incomes of $12,500 and Over											
Better off		52%	48%	40%	40%	46%	42%	41%	32%	45%	41%
Same		36	34	36	37	34	32	37	40	38	38
Worse off		11	17	22	23	19	25	22	27	17	21
Uncertain		1	1	2	*	1	1	1	1	*	*
Not ascertained		*	*	*	*	*	*	*	*	*	*
Total		100%	100%	100%	100%	100%	100%	100%	100%	100%	100%

*Less than half of one percent.

The question was: "We are interested in how people are getting along financially these days. Would you say that you and your family are better off or worse off financially than you were a year ago?"

·········· No data available for these survey periods.

TABLE II-15

Expected Change in Financial Situation

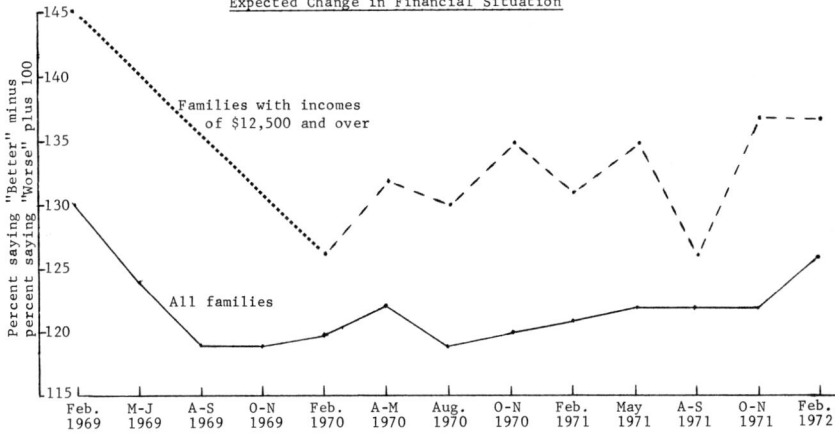

Expected Change in Financial Situation	Nov. 1965	Feb. 1969	Feb. 1970	Apr- May 1970	Aug. 1970	Oct- Nov. 1970	Feb. 1971	May 1971	Aug- Sept. 1971	Oct- Nov. 1971	Feb. 1972
					A. All Families						
Better off	40%	36%	33%	33%	32%	32%	33%	34%	31%	32%	35%
Same	46	48	42	43	42	42	42	40	46	42	44
Worse off	5	6	13	11	13	12	12	12	9	10	9
Uncertain	9	10	11	12	13	13	13	14	14	16	11
Not ascertained	*	*	1	1	*	1	*	*	*	*	1
Total	100%	100%	100%	100%	100%	100%	100%	100%	100%	100%	100%
				B. Families with Incomes of $12,500 and Over							
Better off	50%	38%	42%	39%	43%	41%	45%	36%	43%	44%	
Same	40	39	39	41	37	37	38	41	40	39	
Worse off	5	12	10	9	9	11	10	9	6	7	
Uncertain	5	10	8	11	11	11	7	14	11	10	
Not ascertained	*	1	1	*	*	*	*	*	*	*	
Total	100%	100%	100%	100%	100%	100%	100%	100%	100%	100%	

*Less than half of one percent.

The question was: "Now looking ahead - do you think that a year from now you people will be better off financially, or worse off, or just about the same as now?"

••••••••• No data available for these survey periods.

TABLE II-16

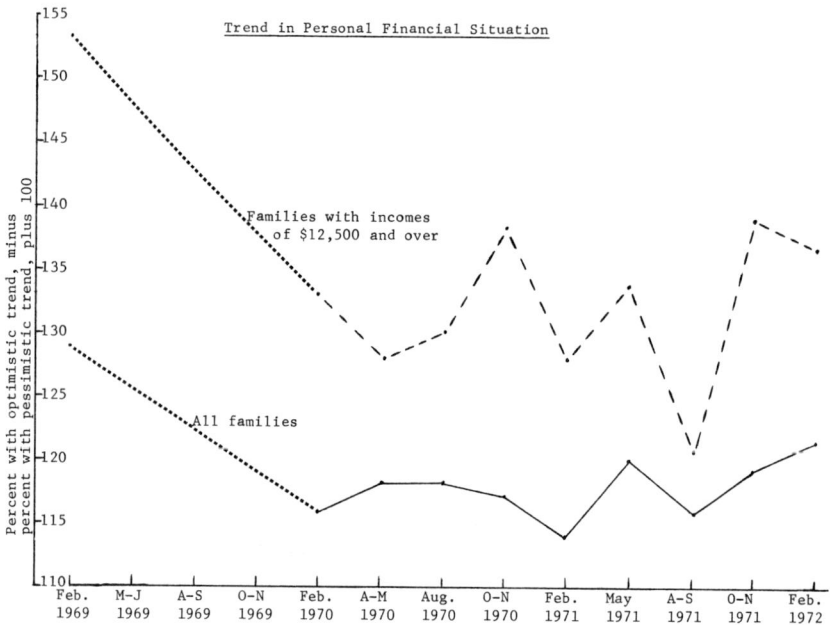

Trend in Personal Financial Situation

Trend in Personal Financial Conditions	Feb. 1969	Feb. 1970	Apr- May 1970	Aug. 1970	Oct- Nov. 1970	Feb. 1971	May 1971	Aug- Sept. 1971	Oct- Nov. 1971	Feb. 1972
					A. All Families					
Optimistic trend*	41%	36%	37%	38%	36%	34%	38%	34%	35%	39%
Pessimistic trend	12	20	19	20	19	20	18	18	16	17
			B.	Families with Incomes of $12,500 and Over						
Optimistic trend*	60	48	45	46	52	44	50	38	51	51
Pessimistic trend	7	15	17	16	14	16	16	17	12	14

*Financial situation is better than a year ago and will be the same or better a year from now, or financial situation is the same as a year ago and will be better.

For questions, see Tables   and

.........No data available for these survey periods.

TABLE II-17

Buying Conditions for Cars

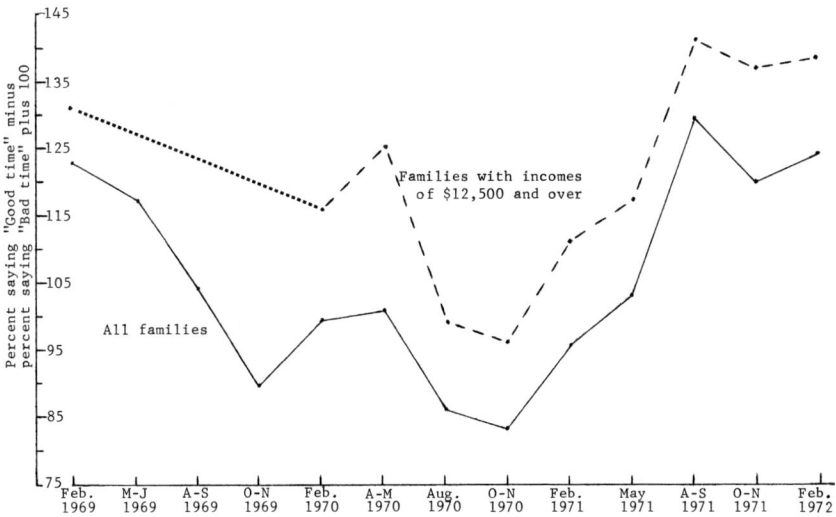

Opinion of Buying Conditions for Cars	Feb. 1969	Feb. 1970	Apr-May 1970	Aug. 1970	Oct-Nov. 1970	Feb. 1971	May 1971	Aug-Sept. 1971	Oct-Nov. 1971	Feb. 1972
					A. All Families					
Good time to buy	44%	35%	35%	29%	24%	33%	38%	51%	45%	46%
Uncertain, depends	35	29	31	28	30	30	27	27	30	32
Bad time to buy	21	36	34	43	46	37	35	22	25	22
Total	100%	100%	100%	100%	100%	100%	100%	100%	100%	100%
				B. Families with Incomes of $12,500 and Over						
Good time to buy	50%	47%	49%	36%	37%	44%	47%	60%	58%	57%
Uncertain, depends	31	22	27	27	22	23	23	21	21	24
Bad time to buy	19	31	24	37	41	33	30	19	21	19
Total	100%	100%	100%	100%	100%	100%	100%	100%	100%	100%

The question was: "Speaking now of the automobile market - do you think the next 12 months or so will be a good time or a bad time to buy a car?"

..........No data available for these survey periods.

Table II-18

Selected Reasons for Opinions
About Buying Conditions for Cars

	Feb. 1969	Oct-Nov. 1969	Feb. 1970	Apr-May 1970	Aug. 1970	Oct-Nov. 1970	Feb. 1971	May 1971	Aug-Sept. 1971	Oct-Nov. 1971	Feb. 1972
					A. All Families						
Good time to buy because:											
Prices are low; good buys available	12%	6%	25%	25%	13%	10%	15%	10%	29%	22%	16%
Prices are going higher; won't come down	20	19	10	9	12	15	16	21	14	17	24
Bad time to buy because:											
Prices are high; going up	16	29	24	23	22	34	29	22	17	21	17
Credit is tight; high interest rates	7	12	15	14	20	9	9	8	3	2	2
Strike	0	*	*	*	2	12	4	1	*	*	*
					B. Families with Incomes of $12,500 and Over						
Good time to buy because:											
Prices are low; good buys available	17%		37%	43%	20%	17%	21%	16%	36%	27%	18%
Prices are going higher; won't come down	22		10	10	15	19	21	23	14	21	29
Bad time to buy because:											
Prices are high; going up	13		19	13	17	30	36	17	13	16	14
Credit is tight; high interest rates	9		16	15	18	7	6	6	2	2	2
Strike	0		0	0	2	14	4	1	*	0	*

*Less than half of one percent.

Responses to the query "Why do you say so?" following the question noted in Table I-17.

Table II-19

Intentions to Buy Cars During Next 12 Months

(Percentage of family units)

Surveys conducted in:	All Cars	New Cars	Used Cars
February			
1967	17.3	9.7	7.6
1968	17.2	9.0	8.2
1969	17.5	9.2	8.3
1970	16.8	9.6	7.2
1971	17.0	8.2	8.8
May			
1967	19.4	10.8	8.6
1968*	17.5	10.5	7.0
1969	19.0	11.1	7.9
1970	15.3	8.1	7.2
1971*	16.7	9.5	7.2
August			
1967*	15.7	8.8	6.9
1968	17.4	10.7	6.7
1969	18.1	9.5	8.6
1970*	15.7	10.1	5.6
1971*	16.2	10.2	6.0
November			
1967	19.5	10.1	9.4
1968	20.8	12.3	8.5
1969	16.0	9.3	6.7
1970	14.6	7.9	6.7
1971	15.1	8.0	7.1

*
Reinterview surveys by telephone.

Notes: Family units reporting that they would or probably would buy, plus one-half of those who said they might buy during the next 12 months.

"Uncertain whether new or used" apportioned equally between new and used cars.

Due to increase in the population, the base rises by approximately 2 percent from one year to the next.

The question was: "Do you or anyone else in the family living here expect to buy a car during the next 12 months?"

TABLE II-20

Buying Conditions for Large Household Goods

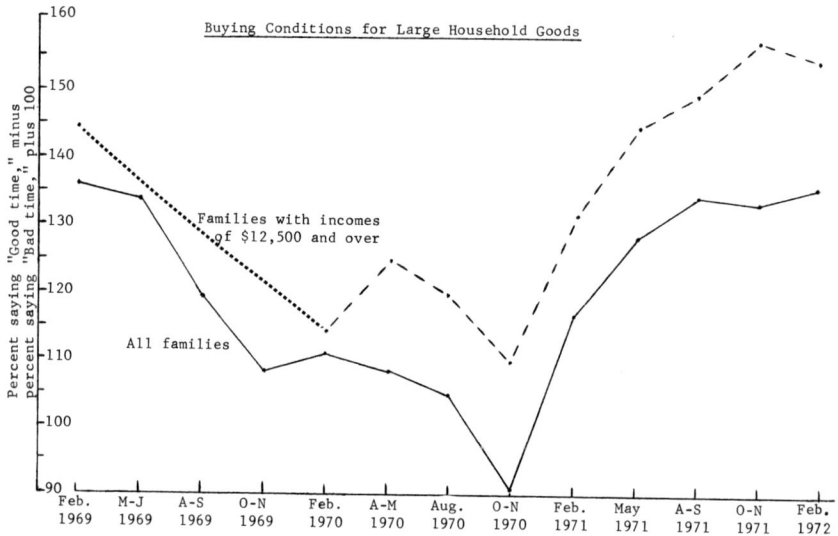

Opinion of Buying Conditions for Large Household Goods	Nov. 1965	Feb. 1969	Feb. 1970	Apr- May 1970	Aug. 1970	Oct- Nov. 1970	Feb. 1971	May 1971	Aug- Sept. 1971	Oct- Nov. 1971	Feb. 1972
				A.		All Families					
Good time to buy	55%	51%	39%	37%	34%	32%	42%	46%	52%	53%	52%
Uncertain, depends	34	34	33	34	37	27	33	36	30	27	33
Bad time to buy	11	15	28	29	29	41	25	18	18	20	15
Total	100%	100%	100%	100%	100%	100%	100%	100%	100%	100%	100%
			B.	Families with Incomes of $12,500 and Over							
Good time to buy		56%	39%	45%	40%	41%	50%	57%	62%	67%	63%
Uncertain, depends		32	36	35	40	28	32	31	25	23	28
Bad time to buy		12	25	20	20	31	18	12	13	10	9
Total		100%	100%	100%	100%	100%	100%	100%	100%	100%	100%

The question was: "About the things people buy for their houses - I mean furniture, house furnishings, refrigerator, stove, television, and things like that. In general, do you think now is a good or a bad time to buy such large household items?"

.... No data available for these survey periods.

Table II-21

Selected Reasons for Opinions
About Buying Conditions for Large Household Goods

	Feb. 1969	Oct-Nov. 1969	Feb. 1970	Apr-May 1970	Oct-Nov. 1970	Feb. 1971	Oct-Nov. 1971	Feb. 1972
			A.	All Families				
Good time to buy because:								
Prices are low; good buys available	17%	11%	22%	18%	13%	25%	21%	26%
Prices are going higher; won't come down	22	20	14	15	18	17	26	24
Bad time to buy because:								
Prices are high; going up	12	23	24	19	26	19	14	14
Credit is tight; high interest rates	5	9	14	13	13	10	2	3
		B.	Families with Incomes of $12,500 and Over					
Good time to buy because:								
Prices are low; good buys available	18%		26%	24%	18%	33%	25%	30%
Prices are going higher; won't come down	25		15	18	26	21	32	29
Bad time to buy because:								
Prices are high; going up	8		20	13	14	15	5	9
Credit is tight; high interest rates	8		15	13	13	9	3	2

Responses to the query "Why do you say so?" following the question noted in Table I-20.

TABLE II-22

Buying Conditions for Houses

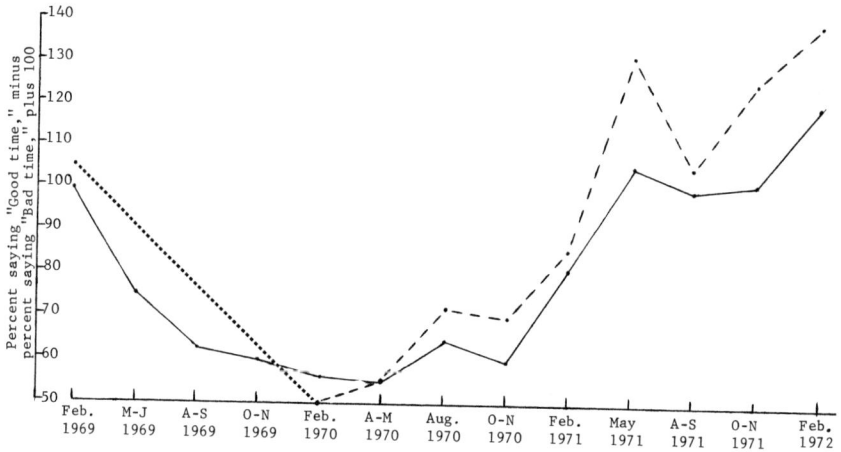

Opinion of Buying Conditions for Houses	Nov. 1965	Feb. 1969	Feb. 1970	Apr-May 1970	Aug. 1970	Oct-Nov. 1970	Feb. 1971	May 1971	Aug-Sept. 1971	Oct-Nov. 1971	Feb. 1972
					A.	All Families					
Good time to buy	51%	38%	21%	18%	23%	20%	32%	43%	41%	41%	49%
Uncertain, depends	30	22	14	18	18	20	17	20	17	19	22
Bad time to buy	19	40	65	64	59	60	51	37	42	40	29
Total	100%	100%	100%	100%	100%	100%	100%	100%	100%	100%	100%
				B.	Families with Incomes of $12,500 and Over						
Good time to buy		44%	20%	19%	28%	27%	37%	60%	45%	57%	63%
Uncertain, depends		16	10	17	16	16	12	12	16	11	13
Bad time to buy		40	70	64	56	57	51	28	39	32	24
Total		100%	100%	100%	100%	100%	100%	100%	100%	100%	100%

The question was: "Generally speaking, do you think now is a good time or a bad time
to buy a house?"

·········· No data available for these survey periods.

TABLE II-23

Selected Reasons for Opinions
About Buying Conditions for Houses

Reasons for Evaluation of Market Conditions for Houses:	Feb. 1969	Oct-Nov. 1969	Feb. 1970	Apr-May 1970	Oct-Nov. 1970	Feb. 1971	Oct-Nov. 1971	Feb. 1972
			A.	All	Families			
Good time to buy because:								
Prices are low; good buys available	3%	1%	4%	4%	7%	7%	8%	7%
Prices won't come down; are going higher	21	13	10	9	9	12	18	21
Credit will be tighter later; interest rates will go up	5	3	3	2	2	2	2	3
Interest rates are low	1	a/	a/	1	1	9	11	13
Bad time to buy because:								
Prices are high; may fall later	21	31	29	29	26	24	24	18
Credit is tight; interest rates high	23	46	56	53	48	34	19	14
Interest rates will come down later	a/	1	*	1	3	4	3	2
	B.	Families	with	Incomes	of $12,500	and	Over	
Good time to buy because:								
Prices are low; good buys available	2%		3%	5%	12%	10%	10%	9%
Prices won't come down; are going higher	29		8	11	13	14	25	25
Credit will be tighter later; interest rates will go up	8		4	1	1	2	3	6
Interest rates are low	1		0	*	2	13	16	21
Bad time to buy because:								
Prices are high; may fall later	16		25	24	19	24	23	13
Credit is tight; interest rates high	35		75	63	52	38	19	14
Interest rates will come down later	a/		*	2	5	5	3	3

*Less than half of one percent.
a Not coded separately.
Responses to the query: "Why do you say so?" following question noted in TABLE II-22.

11

CHANGE IN LONGER-RANGE
ATTITUDES AND SAVING

The attitudinal data collected each quarter by the Suvey Research Center consist primarily of short-range consumer attitudes. Changes in these attitudes are indicative of changes in consumers' willingness to make discretionary expenditures and are relevant for an assessment of economic trends in the six to twelve-month period following each survey. In addition, the Survey Research Center occasionally collects data on longer-range attitudes which likewise contribute to an understanding of economic behavior. Chapter 13 in the volume *1970 Survey of Consumer Finances* contains the attitudinal data obtained in November 1970; the first part of this report presents similar data collected in November 1971.

In addition, information on attitudes toward saving and various forms of saving is included in this report. No doubt, changes in these attitudes are influenced by developments in the recent past and may not persist over long periods. Nevertheless, they have longer-range implications than data on the subjective evaluation of buying conditions or on expectations about the next twelve months.

Longer-Range Personal Financial Attitudes

Two questions have been asked repeatedly in the last few years on personal financial progress during the last four years and expectations about personal financial trends during the next four years. The answers to these questions, in contrast to attitudes about developments during the past twelve months and expectations about developments in the next twelve months, showed a rather small decline immediately before and during the recession of 1970. By November 1971 the four-year data had recovered their level of 1968 (Table II-1).

Of particular importance is the combination of the two questions which indicates the proportion of families who both experienced and expected an improvement. The bottom part of Table 11-1 shows that in response to these questions there were only minor changes during the few years prior to November 1971. Yet the proportion of those who expressed uncertainty, as indicated in the "Don't know" row of the table, was much higher in 1971 than in 1968. Additional information available in the surveys makes it seem probable that concern with, and apprehension about inflation and unemployment made some people uncertain regarding the trend of their personal financial situation.

From 1970 to 1971 the increase in the proportion of those respondents who said they were better off than four years ago as well as of those who expected to be better off in four years was most pronounced in the top income group (annual income of $15,000 or more, see Table 11-2). The attitudes of the very young—under 25 years of age—showed a deterioration from 1970 to 1971 (Table 11-3).

The trend of longer-range personal financial expectations differed sharply from that of business expectations. As reported each quarter, people's expectations about the economic outlook during the next five years slumped sharply between 1968 and 1971; following the low point reached in May 1971, the recovery in these expectations was minor. (It may suffice to mention here that in November 1965, 47 percent of family heads expected continuous good times to prevail during the next five years; in February 1969 the proportion was 37 percent, in May 1971; 20 percent, and in February 1972, 27 percent.) Concern about Vietnam as well as about societal problems (race, poverty, the environment, etc.) were found to influence people's general economic outlook.

Wishes and Desires

While questions about buying intentions relate to the relatively near future and their answers depend not only on people's needs and wants but also on their opinions about supply conditions and prices, questions about things people would *like* to buy have implications for a longer period. In November 1971 a somewhat smaller proportion of family heads expressed wishes to buy goods, commodities or services than did family heads a year earlier. The decline was largest among those with more than $15,000 income, but extended to several other income as well as age groups (Table 11-4).

The decline in the frequency with which automobiles and other durable goods were mentioned among unfulfilled wishes was insignificant; the proportion mentioning wishes relating to their homes declined somewhat more. On the other hand, wishes regarding travel, vacations, and leisure-time activities were mentioned by somewhat more people in November 1971 than they were a year earlier. This was particularly true of the middle-income groups and of young people (Tables 11-5 and 11-6).

Attitudes Toward Saving

It is useful to distinguish two major components of the considerations which are included under the heading "personal saving" in government statistics. One component relates to installment buying (incurrence and repayment of debt) and the other to changes in liquid asset holdings (in banks and securities). Changes in the incurrence of new debt depend on people's willingness to purchase durable goods as well as on their attitudes toward debt. In the second half of 1971 there was an increase in the purchases of automobiles and the incurrence of installment debt (the latter being a negative item in personal saving), while "financial saving" stayed at a very high level.

Financial saving, that is, the net amount put into banks (or savings associations, certificates of deposit), stocks and bonds, may be expected to be smaller in a period of economic recovery than during a recession because some purchases of durables are financed by drawing on liquid asset holdings rather than, or in addition to, borrowing. On the other hand, the following considerations point toward a continuation of relatively high rates of financial saving in the first few years following a recession. First, income gains are commonly used both to increase expenditures and amounts saved; in a period of recovery income increases are more frequent and larger than during a recession. Second, for quite a while after a recession, people continue to be concerned with the possibility of rainy days to come and therefore may feel a pronounced need to increase their savings or reserve funds.

In November 1971 a question was asked about the saving performance during the preceding twelve months, a period of high rates of saving. To a general question about changes in savings or reserve funds, a very substantial proportion of respondents always answered that their savings had remained unchanged. Many people had practically no savings and others neglected small additions, especially when they resulted from accrued interest. The proportions reporting large or typical additions to savings were about the same in 1971 as in 1970. An indication of higher rates of saving was obtained from families with $15,000 income or more, who are the largest savers. In this group there was an increase in the proportion who saved unusually large amounts and a decrease in the proportion who reduced their savings by unusually large amounts (Table 11-7). Additions to savings were reported more frequently in 1971 than earlier in some age groups; the amount of savings increased among those people 45 to 54 years of age, in which group saving is normally relatively high (Table 11-8).

Attitudes Toward Saving Media

Frequently in the past the Survey Research Center has asked a question about the "wisest place" to save: in the respondent's opinion, should new savings be put in a bank, into stocks, or into real estate? Many respondents replied by mentioning two preferred forms of saving. Banks, primarily savings accounts, have always received the highest frequency of mention. Putting new savings in real estate has also been a fairly popular choice for several years.

In November 1971 the preference for saving in banks was much more pronounced than in September 1969 and the preference for putting money into stocks was much less frequent (Table 11-9). These changes prevailed in most income and age groups. It appears that many people were aware that investment in stocks had not proved to be a safeguard against inflation in 1969-71. At the same time, confidence in savings accounts did not suffer, despite the acceleration of inflation.

When respondents were asked why they chose banks as the wisest place to save, safety of deposits in banks was always mentioned as the primary reason. Yet references to safety were made less frequently in November 1971 than in August 1969. The frequency of references to high interest rates did not change during the two years prior to November 1971. More frequent however, were respondents' references to a lack of alternatives to saving in banks. Respondents also spoke in 1971 of having no time or not enough money to consider other forms of saving besides banks. (Such references are included under "Other reasons" in Tables 11-10 and 11-12.) Respondents with an annual income between $3,000 and $10,000 spoke most frequently of the absence of alternatives to putting money into savings accounts.

Among reasons mentioned for putting money into common stocks, the desire for capital gains continued to be mentioned frequently. The opinion that stocks represented a hedge against inflation was mentioned in November 1971 much less frequently than it was two years earlier. The extent of stock ownership did not change substantially during the twelve months prior to November 1971 when 27 percent of all family units reported ownership of stocks and/or mutual funds shares. Only among those respondents with more than $15,000 income did many more than one-half own stocks.

Table 11-1

Evaluation of Past and Expected Changes
in the Personal Financial Situation

(Over the past 4 years and the next 4 years)

	All Families			Families with Incomes of $10,000 or More		
	Aug. 1968	Oct-Nov. 1970	Oct-Nov. 1971	Aug. 1968	Oct-Nov. 1970	Oct-Nov. 1971
A. Better or Worse Off than 4 Years Ago						
Better	53%	50%	53%	71%	68%	70%
Same	23	21	21	17	15	14
Worse	21	25	22	11	14	13
Don't know	3	4	4	1	3	3
Total	100%	100%	100%	100%	100%	100%
B. Better or Worse Off 4 Years from Now						
Better	43%	42%	45%	55%	54%	57%
Same	28	23	19	20	20	17
Worse	8	12	8	8	9	6
Don't know	21	23	28	17	17	20
Total	100%	100%	100%	100%	100%	100%
C. Combination of Past and Future						
Better-better	31%	29%	29%	44%	43%	43%
Better-same or Same-better	15	12	14	18	16	16
Better-worse or Worse-better	9	10	11	9	9	11
Same-same	10	8	7	5	5	3
Same-worse or Worse-same	8	9	5	4	5	4
Worse-worse	3	6	3	2	3	1
Don't know	24	26	31	18	19	22
Total	100%	100%	100%	100%	100%	100%
Number of cases	1320	1402	1297	308	510	537

For questions, see Table 11-3.

Table 11-2

Evaluation of Past and Expected Changes in the
Personal Financial Situation, by Income Groups

	Family Income					
	Under $3000	$3000 -4999	$5000 -7499	$7500 -9999	$10,000 -14,999	$15,000 and over
Better off than 4 years ago						
Oct-Nov. 1971	26%	30%	51%	57%	67%	74%
Oct-Nov. 1970	24	32	49	55	68	68
Will be better off in 4 years						
Oct-Nov. 1971	24	30	42	50	54	63
Oct-Nov. 1970	25	26	42	50	54	55
Combination of past and future						
Better-better, Oct-Nov. 1971	9	10	27	34	37	50
Better-better, Oct-Nov. 1970	10	13	28	34	42	43
Number of families						
Oct-Nov. 1971	190	171	186	166	315	222
Oct-Nov. 1970	229	186	226	204	319	191

For questions, see Table 11-3.

Table 11-3

Evaluation of Past and Expected Changes in the
Personal Financial Situation, by Age Groups

	Age					
	Under 25	25-34	35-44	45-54	55-64	Over 65
Better off than 4 years ago						
Oct-Nov. 1971	55%	71%	66%	55%	43%	23%
Oct-Nov. 1970	63	69	62	53	42	17
Will be better off in 4 years						
Oct-Nov. 1971	80	73	60	43	20	6
Oct-Nov. 1970	78	69	52	42	21	5
Combination of past and future						
Better-better, Oct-Nov. 1971	43	56	40	30	12	2
Better-better, Oct-Nov. 1970	50	53	37	26	15	2
Number of families						
Oct-Nov. 1971	91	242	252	281	209	219
Oct-Nov. 1970	148	258	237	279	199	277

The questions were: "Now thinking back four years (to this time in 1967), would you say that you (and your family) are better off or worse off than you were then?" "And four years from now, do you expect that you (and your family) will be better off, worse off, or just about the same as now?"

Table 11-4

Percentage of Families Expressing Wishes
in Various Income and Age Groups

Express Wishes	Income						Families
	Under $3000	$3000 -4999	$5000 -7499	$7500 -9999	$10,000 -14,999	$15,000 and over	
Oct–Nov. 1971	60%	53%	61%	54%	51%	35%	51%
Oct–Nov. 1970	54	52	62	65	55	54	56

Express Wishes	Age						All Families
	Under 25	25–34	35–44	45–54	55–64	Over 65	
Oct–Nov. 1971	76	69	54	50	42	28	51
Oct–Nov. 1970	74	75	62	58	46	30	56

For question, see Table 11-6.

Table 11-5

Percentage of Families Expressing
Various Types of Wishes, by Income Groups

Wishes Expressed for:	Income						All Families
	Under $3000	$3000 -4999	$5000 -7499	$7500 -9999	$10,000 -14,999	$15,000 and over	
Percentage of Families Expressing Wishes, Oct–Nov. 1971 [†]							
Automobile	11%	11%	16%	5%	11%	5%	10%
Furniture and appliances	33	33	34	31	22	13	26
Housing: additions and repairs	21	22	22	25	24	14	21
Other wishes[*]	20	12	19	16	15	18	17
Savings, assets	3	2	1	4	1	2	2
Change in Percentage Expressing Wishes Since Oct–Nov. 1970							
Automobile	-5	0	0	-7	1	0	-2
Furniture and appliances	10	3	3	0	-8	-10	-1
Housing: additions and repairs	-1	0	-8	-12	-2	-13	-6
Other wishes[*]	4	6	8	6	5	-5	4
Savings, assets	0	-1	-2	1	-2	-2	-1

[*]Wishes for travel, vacation, other leisure-time pursuits, and smaller consumption goods.

[†]The columns do not add to 100% because: (a) the category of people having no wishes has been omitted. This value can be computed from Table 4 by subtracting those values from 100; (b) people who expressed wishes were allowed to mention two specific wishes. The percentages in Table 5 refer to the percentage of families who mentioned a particular wish in either one of their two allowed mentions.

The first of these factors has the effect of making columns add to less than 100%, while the second factor will make columns add to more than 100%. The columns in fact add to less than 100% because the first factor dominates over the second.

For questions, see Table 11-6.

Table 11-6

Percentage of Families Expressing Various Types of Wishes
in Oct-Nov. 1971 and Changes from a Year Ago, by Age Groups

Wishes Expressed for:	Age						All Families
	Under 25	25-34	35-44	45-54	55-64	Over 65	
	Percentage of Families Expressing Wishes, Oct-Nov. 1971[+]						
Automobile	22%	12%	9%	11%	8%	3%	10%
Furniture and appliances	51	35	26	24	19	15	26
Housing: additions and repairs	25	32	25	18	17	9	21
Other wishes[*]	27	23	21	17	11	9	17
Savings, assets	1	3	2	2	?	5	2
	Change in Percentage Expressing Wishes Since Oct-Nov. 1970						
Automobile	0	-3	-5	0	-2	-2	-2
Furniture and appliances	17	-4	-5	-4	-3	3	-1
Housing: additions and repairs	-17	-13	0	-7	-6	1	-6
Other wishes[*]	14	10	2	3	2	-1	4
Savings, assets	-2	-1	-2	-2	-2	3	-1

[*] Wishes for travel, vacation, other leisure-time pursuits, and other consumption goods.

[+] The columns do not add to 100% because: (a) the category of people having no wishes has been omitted. This value can be computed from Table 4 by subtracting those values from 100; (b) people who expressed wishes were allowed to mention two specific wishes. The percentages in Table 6 refer to the percentage of families who mentioned a particular wish in either one of their two allowed mentions.

The first of these factors has the effect of making columns add to less than 100%, while the second factor will make columns add to more than 100%. The columns in fact add to less than 100% because the first factor dominates the second.

The questions were: "About your <u>wishes</u>: Are there any particular things you (and your family) would <u>like</u> to buy or to spend money on, or do you have most of the things you want?" (IF EXPRESSED WISHES) "What things do you have in mind?" "Anything else?"

Table 11-7

Opinions about Change in Savings
and Reserve Funds During the Last 12 Months

Opinion about Change in Savings and Reserve Funds	All Families		Families with Incomes of $15,000 or More	
	Feb-Mar. 1970	Oct-Nov. 1971	Feb-Mar. 1970	Oct-Nov. 1971
Added unusually large amount	5%	5%	7%	9%
Added typical amount	20	19	36	38
Added less than usual	2	1	3	3
Total additions	27	25	46	50
Savings and reserves unchanged	49	47	33	31
Reduced unusually large amount	13	13	14	10
Reduced typical amount	7	6	5	4
Reduced less than usual	1	1	-	1
Total reductions	21	20	19	15
Don't know	3	8	2	4
	100%	100%	100%	100%
Number of families	2576	1297	472	249

For questions, see Table 11-8.

Table 11-8

Opinions About Change in Savings and Reserve Funds
During the Last 12 Months, by Age and Income Groups

Opinion about Change in Savings and Reserves	Income						All Families
	Under $3000	$3000 -4999	$5000 -7499	$7500 -9999	$10,000 -14,999	$15,000 and over	
Oct-Nov. 1971							
Added	7%	13%	21%	26%	33%	50%	25%
Reduced	16	22	27	23	25	15	20
Feb-Mar. 1970							
Added	13	14	20	25	33	46	27
Reduced	19	20	20	23	23	19	21

	Age						All Families
	Under 25	25-34	35-44	45-54	55-64	Over 65	
Oct-Nov. 1971							
Added	21	35	27	29	24	20	25
Reduced	32	21	25	23	19	14	20
Feb-Mar. 1970							
Added	24	30	30	24	30	22	27
Reduced	33	25	20	22	20	13	21

The questions were:
"Considering all your savings and reserve funds in banks, savings associations, bonds, stocks or mutual fund shares – during the past 12 months have
you added to them, reduced them, or have they remained about the same?"
(IF ADDED OR REDUCED) "Was this an unusually large (increase/decrease) or
was it rather typical?"

Table 11-9

Opinions about Wisest Place to Invest Oct-Nov. 1971
and Change from Aug-Sept. 1969, by Income Groups

Opinion about Wisest Place to Invest	Income						All Families
	Under $3000	$3000 -4999	$5000 -7499	$7500 -9999	$10,000 -14,999	$15,000 and over	

Opinions, Oct-Nov. 1971[f]

Banks	51%	60%	53%	46%	44%	34%	47%
Bonds	25	16	21	19	19	15	19
Stocks	3	8	7	8	13	17	10
Real estate	17	20	25	35	38	46	32
Consumer goods, vacation	2	1	3	1	1	-	1
Don't know	4	2	2	4	4	3	3
Number of families	190	171	186	166	315	249	1297

Change in Opinions Since Aug-Sept. 1969

Banks	-3	17	10	18	14	17	9
Bonds	-1	-6	0	-2	4	3	-1
Stocks	-1	-1	-5	-5	-10	-14	-5
Real estate	4	-8	-4	-6	-2	8	1
Consumer goods, vacation	2	0	-2	0	0	0	1
Don't know	-3	-4	-5	-3	-1	-8	-3
Number of families	243	226	310	247	313	167	1557

[f]Columns may add to more than 100% since in some cases people answered banks and bonds, and such answers were treated as favoring both banks and bonds.

The questions were: "Suppose you had some new savings. What would be the wisest thing to do with the money - put it in a checking account or savings account, buy a government savings bond, invest in real estate, buy common stock, or what?" "Why do you make that choice?"

Table 11-10

Reasons for Choosing Banks as Wisest Place to Invest
Oct-Nov. 1971, and Change from Aug-Sept. 1969, by Income Groups

Reasons for Feeling Banks Are Wisest	Income						All Families
	Under $3000	$3000 -4999	$5000 -7499	$7500 -9999	$10,000 -14,999	$15,000 and over	
	Advantages of Investment in Banks Oct-Nov. 1971[/]						
Safety	38%	38%	39%	39%	42%	43%	39%
High rate of return	18	30	26	26	29	32	27
Banks offer liquidity	34	29	24	32	22	19	26
Capital gains	-	1	4	4	4	7	3
Hedge against inflation	-	-	-	-	1	1	-
Other	24	24	30	29	22	13	25
Number of families	98	103	99	77	139	75	611
	Change in Opinions Since Aug-Sept. 1969						
Safety	-10	-17	-5	-12	-9	-7	-10
High rate of return	-1	0	-7	-6	1	12	-1
Banks offer liquidity	8	6	-3	8	-2	-1	2
Capital gains	-2	-1	2	0	0	1	1
Hedge against inflation	0	0	-1	0	1	-4	0
Other	3	11	16	14	4	-9	8
Number of families	132	97	133	71	94	36	589

[/]Columns may not add to 100% because some categories of answers proved uninteresting and were omitted, or respondents were allowed to mention up to two reasons for preferring banks.

Table 11-11

Opinions About Wisest Place to Invest Oct-Nov. 1971,
and Change from Aug-Sept. 1969, by Age Groups

	Age						All
	Under 25	25-34	35-44	45-54	55-64	Over 65	Families
Opinions Oct-Nov. 1971 [/]							
Banks	52%	43%	36%	51%	48%	57%	47%
Bonds	12	10	17	20	24	29	19
Stocks	10	10	14	12	7	5	10
Real estate	40	43	41	31	25	14	32
Consumer goods, vacation	-	3	-	-	1	1	1
Don't know	1	2	4	2	6	5	3
Number of families	91	242	252	281	209	219	1297
Change in Opinions Since Aug-Sept. 1969							
Banks	11	12	9	14	4	7	9
Bonds	0	-3	6	-4	-2	0	-1
Stocks	-3	-8	-4	-5	-7	-3	-5
Real estate	5	1	-4	-1	3	2	1
Consumer goods, vacation	0	1	0	0	1	1	1
Don't know	-4	-4	-2	-4	-2	-4	-3
Number of families	120	287	297	304	241	305	1557

/Columns may add to more than 100% since in some cases people answered <u>banks</u> and <u>bonds</u>, and such answers were treated as favoring both banks and bonds.

Table 11-12

Reasons for Choosing Banks as Wisest Place to Invest
Oct-Nov. 1971, and Change from Aug-Sept. 1969, by Age Groups

Reasons for Feeling Banks Are Wisest	Age						All Families
	Under 25	25-34	35-44	45-54	55-64	Over 65	
	Oct-Nov. 1971[f]						
Safety	32%	32%	43%	37%	41%	47%	39%
High rate of return	21	22	23	30	38	25	27
Banks offer liquidity	42	33	25	20	24	24	26
Capital gains	2	3	3	7	3	1	3
Hedge against inflation	-	-	1	1	-	-	-
Other	25	37	25	27	20	24	27
Number of families	47	105	91	142	100	124	611
	Change in Opinions Since Aug-Sept. 1969						
Safety	-3	-14	-5	-11	-13	-7	-10
High rate of return	-22	-2	-7	-1	15	-2	-1
Banks offer liquidity	12	7	-1	-4	2	1	2
Capital gains	0	0	-2	4	1	0	1
Hedge against inflation	0	-1	0	0	0	0	0
Other	5	18	15	11	1	10	10
Number of families	49	91	80	112	105	150	589

[f]Columns may not add to 100% because some categories of answers proved uninteresting and were omitted, or respondents were allowed to mention up to two reasons for preferring banks.

PART 3

CONTRIBUTED PAPERS

12

"COGNITIVE PROCESSES IN LEARNING: REACTIONS TO INFLATION AND CHANGE IN TAXES."

George Katona *

During the last decade or two, following a period of neglect, psychologists have resumed their concern with cognitive studies. The major concern of these studies, expressed in earlier times as the acquisition of knowledge and its use, has been formulated more recently as the encoding and processing of information, organized for long-term use.

The principal feature which distinguishes the analysis presented in this paper from earlier studies is the subject matter. Rather than continuing the traditional studies of problem solving, or observing cognitive processes in children, the author is concerned with the question of how adults learn about such problems as inflation, price and wage control, or change in taxes, and how they use the knowledge which they have acquired. Instead of analyzing individual learning, the author studies the process of social learning, of change over time in the attitudes and behavior of many people, resulting from the impact of new information. Social learning is defined here as the acquisition of new attitudes and behavior patterns by masses of people.

This analysis of the process of learning makes use of studies which were conducted several decades ago by Max Wertheimer and other Gestalt psychologists including this author, as well as of more recent investigations carried out primarily by Herbert A. Simon and Jerome S. Bruner.

A concern with the process of learning does not imply a neglect of stimuli

*A grant from The Ford Foundation made possible the studies which are reported in this paper.

and responses. Yet, in the studies discussed in this paper, it is often not a simple matter to identify the stimulus in a precise manner. In two instances the stimulus or the circumstances precipitating the subsequent learning experience, may be pinpointed unequivocally. One summer evening in 1962, President Kennedy surprised his audience by proposing in a television speech that income taxes be cut substantially and on a Sunday evening in August, 1971, President Nixon unexpectedly announced the introduction of a wage and price freeze.

In the two other instances which are discussed, the stimuli were much less specific. In 1966, some non-government experts proposed a tax increase (surcharge to the income tax), and during the following year or two the number of Americans who had heard of the possibility of a tax increase rose greatly. In 1969 the rate of inflation accelerated; some people became aware of the more rapid increase in the prices of goods and services purchased early in 1969, and many more became aware of increases during the next six months.

The difference between the specific and non-specific stimuli, however, is not of major importance. In all instances, people received information continuously over prolonged periods. Even in the instances of the tax cut and the wage-price freeze, the stimuli continued to impinge on the American people over extended periods following the first news.

The response to the information received may be divided into an attitudinal and an overt response (action). In all four instances mentioned there was evidence that many people acquired new attitudes and expectations. Furthermore, they changed their overt behavior by spending or saving more or less than at earlier times. Objective indicators of consumer response are available in the form of a change in consumers' discretionary expenditures or in the number of automobiles purchased. The establishment of a connection between the "stimuli" and the "responses," however, constitutes a difficult problem. The major objective of this paper is to describe and analyze those variables which intervene between stimuli and responses, in the hope that this will contribute to establishing a connection.

Personal interviews conducted with representative samples of the population were the source of the material used in the studies in this paper. Data were collected both before and after certain new developments had taken place so that it was possible to make use of "natural experiments." The collection of "before data" was made possible by conducting surveys on peoples' economic attitudes and expectations as well as on certain aspects of their spending and saving behavior at quarterly intervals for more than ten years. Most surveys were conducted with new samples drawn every quarter, but reinterviews with identical respondents were also conducted frequently.[1]

---

[1] The purposes and methods, as well as the findings of the quarterly surveys conducted by the Survey Research Center of The University of Michigan under the direction of the author, are reported in annual monographs entitled *1970 Survey of Consumer Finances, 1969 Survey, 1968 Survey, etc.*

For the purpose of analyzing the learning process, the survey method has some distinct disadvantages. The time spent with each respondent is limited, in most cases, to 30 minutes. The questions are established in advance and cannot be changed by the interviewer in accordance with specific circumstances which might arise during an individual interview. New techniques, however, have been developed to alleviate these drawbacks. The Survey Research Center uses the fixed question-free answer interviewing method and supplements the questions asked with nondirective probes; the answers to these probes are recorded verbatim.

The quarterly surveys yielded four types of data which are used in this study:

1. Time series of consumer attitudes and expectations, consisting of answers obtained to such questions as the following: are you financially better or worse off than a year ago and four years ago? do you expect to be better or worse off during the next year and in several years? is it a good or bad time to buy houses, automobiles, other durable goods? what are your opinions about recent changes in business conditions and expectations about business trends during the next year and the next 5 years? The most important of these data are summarized in an index of Consumer Sentiment, published at quarterly intervals.

2. Whatever the answers to the questions listed under point 1, respondents were asked "Why do you say so?" Time series are available of the reasons given, for instance, for being or not being better off; the frequency of spontaneous references to changes in prices, incomes, etc., is tabulated.

3. Respondents were asked in each survey whether they had heard any news of favorable or unfavorable changes in business conditions during the last few months. Those who answered "yes" to this question, the great majority, were asked, "What have you heard?" Some respondents appeared to be unable to report any news; the answers of the others were tabulated (a) according to the subject matter mentioned, and (b) as to whether the news reported was favorable or unfavorable.

4. In addition to questions which were used in unchanged form over several years, specific questions were formulated for each survey regarding new developments (e.g., government policies, taxes, stock market movements, as well as political news, international problems and social problems). For some of this information, of course, "before data" are not available.

The survey data are of a quantitative nature (averages, frequency distributions, correlation coefficients, etc.,) as transcribed for computer use. In addition, reading the original interviews helps the investigator, who may use them to find out how people have expressed themselves.

Nevertheless, the available data are incomplete and do not yield adequate information for a full-scale analysis of the learning process of individuals. With respect to an analysis of changes in collective attitudes and the process of social learning, the situation is different. It is the basic assumption of these studies that social learning is simpler and more selective than individual learning.

The distinction between macro and micro data, widely used by economists, is relevant for psychological studies as well. Macro data consist of information on the attitudes and behavior of broad aggregates, primarily of all people or all consumers in the country, while micro data relate to the attitudes and behavior of individuals.[2]

Obviously, it is the individual who thinks, learns and feels. Data on changes in opinions, attitudes and expectations can only be collected from individuals. Such data must be aggregated in order to provide information which is suitable for the purposes of economics; economics as a discipline is concerned with what happens to the economy, or broad parts of the economy, and not to individuals. Economics is concerned with an increase or decrease in the total number of cars bought during a given period, but not specifically with the question of whether or not the individual John Smith bought or will buy a car.

The macro model of behavior is much simpler than the micro model. Extensive differences among individuals as well as great variations in the information acquired by individuals, may be neglected when changes in the attitudes of all consumers and when social learning are studied. What many people learn at a given time represents only a small part of what individuals learn. This discrepancy is not attributable simply to idiosyncratic elements in the acquisition of information by individuals. More importantly, similarities in the information transmitted and in the information to which people have access relate only to certain parts of the information received by individuals. Mutual reinforcement among many people extends only to selective rather than to all features of environmental change. A unifying characteristic of social learning consists of the affective connotation of what is learned. Practically everyone in a country may learn at a given time that the economic news is good or bad, that business trends are favorable or unfavorable, pointing to an upswing or a downswing. At the same time, the knowledge of manifold details about what has or will become better or worse varies from individual to individual, depending upon the individual's prior knowledge, his personal experience, and the group to which he belongs.[3]

---

[2]For a more extensive discussion of macro versus micro data, see Katona, 1972.

[3]It should also be noted that survey data on changes in collective behavior and group attitudes are more reliable than survey data relating to individuals. The latter are subject to greater reporting errors and may even be influenced by changes in the mood of the person questioned. Errors and biases of individual data may cancel out when data from many respondents are aggregated.

The Results of the Learning Process

There are two major problems which may be distinguished in the psychology of learning, although the information which is germane to each of these problems is interrelated. One problem, the one most commonly analyzed in past studies, concerns the results of learning; the other concerns the process of learning. Although the major purpose of this paper is to provide information on the second problem, the first area of concern will involve an examination of what has been learned by the American people about economics. This will include information on economic policies as well as information on changes in attitudes and changes in rates of spending and saving.[4]

The quarterly surveys conducted by the Survey Research Center are the source of information on changes in consumer opinions, attitudes, and expectations. Information on changes in consumer spending and saving behavior is taken from economic statistics published by various federal bureaus on components of the GNP. In both of these areas, aggregate or macro data are provided, represented primarily by changes in the attitudes and purchases of all American consumers following the impact of various "stimuli" which impinged on them during the periods studies.

1. The tax cut of 1964. During the first 12 months following President Kennedy's proposals for a tax cut in the summer of 1962, people's attitudes and behavior did not change significantly. Surveys indicated that a very large proportion of Americans had heard of the proposal, but even in 1963, 45 percent of a representative sample of household heads thought that the proposed law would not be passed, and 27 percent thought that it would be passed (the rest were uncertain). Most respondents in the first group thought that what was proposed, namely, to reduce government revenues by approximately 10 billion dollars at a time when there were heavy deficits and the need for an increase in a variety of government expenditures, would be impractical and therefore, would not be done. The opinions of the masses changed slowly. Only toward the end of 1963 and early in 1964 did the majority of people (60 percent) express the opinion that the tax cut law would be passed by Congress. At the same time, the majority (52 percent) acquired the belief that the law would have a favorable impact on the economy. (A year earlier this proportion was under 25 percent.)

While prior to the end of 1963 changes in consumer expenditures could not be related to the discussion of the tax cut, the situation was different between December, 1963 and March, 1964. During this period, before anyone had received any tax benefits, consumer expenditures on durable goods and the

---

[4]Quantitative data have been presented in Katona and Mueller on the tax cut of 1964, in the 1967, 1968, 1969 and 1970 volumes of *Survey of Consumer Finances,* and in Katona et al. on later developments. In the following sections which describe the four instances studied, data which were presented in earlier publications are summarized.

incurrence of installment debt increased significantly, primarily among families with favorable attitudes toward the tax cut. (In this group 17.4 percent expressed an intention to buy a car; those with unfavorable attitudes, only 11.0 percent expressed the same intention.)

Congress passed the law in February, 1964, and starting in March, tax withholdings were reduced so that after-tax incomes increased. In April and May a substantial proportion of people (more than one-third) expressed disappointment about the size of their personal gain, which appeared insignificant compared to their expectation. In the second half of 1964 and early in 1965, however, consumer attitudes improved substantially (the Index of Consumer Sentiment rose by 4 percentage points) and consumer spending increased greatly. An analysis of reports by panel members served to justify the conclusion that these changes were stimulated both by opinions about the effect of the tax cut and by widespread large increases in income earned.

2. The tax surcharge of 1968. Public discussion of the need to increase income taxes began in 1966. In 1967, close to 80 percent of all household heads had heard of the threat of having to pay higher taxes. They believed that the tax increase would affect both their own finances and general economic conditions adversely (two-thirds cited the latter problem). These beliefs contributed to pessimism and restraint in discretionary expenditures. (The Index of Consumer Sentiment was much lower in 1967, after recovery from a mini-recession, than in 1965.) Again, opinions changed slowly and gradually; in November 1967, four times as many people with definite opinions thought that the surcharge would have bad effects on the economy as those people who thought it would have good effects. By May 1968, the proportions were equal. These findings, together with data on other perceived reasons for optimism (the reduction of bombing in North Vietnam, for instance), made it possible to conclude that the major retarding effect of the surcharge had already taken place in anticipation of the tax increase, rather than occurring during the following few months when disposable incomes would actually be reduced (*1968 Survey of Consumer Finances,* p. 179). Shortly after the surcharge was enacted in the summer of 1968, it was viewed by the majority of taxpayers as having only an insignificant effect on their personal finances. In the second half of 1968, consumer expenditures increased, so that the intended effect of the tax increase, to reduce consumer demand and the inflationary pressure on the economy, did not take place.

3. Acceleration of inflation in 1969-71. The Consumer Price Index advanced by less than 2 percent a year in 1964 and 1965, and by less than 3 percent a year in 1966 and 1967, but it rose by close to 6 percent a year in 1969 and 1970. The first findings on consumer awareness of the acceleration of inflation were obtained in a survey which was conducted in February, 1969. At that time, only 60 percent of the large proportion of family heads who reported making more money than they did a year ago, said that they were better off, as opposed to 75 to 80 percent in the previous years. In June 1969, complaints about inflation and expectations of sizable price increases became more frequent and the Index of Consumer Sentiment fell sharply, particularly among those who did complain about inflation. In August 1969, one-fourth of all American family heads said that they were worse off than they were the year before because of rising prices. (This was by far the highest proportion found in 15 years of study.) By that time, a very sharp deterioration had occurred in consumer sentiment, which could be attributed both to an awareness of inflation and to fears of recession and unemployment. (These findings made it possible to preduct that a recession would occur, as it actually did in 1970.) [5]

That inflation was viewed as something unfavorable and depressed consumer sentiment was shown several times in earlier periods as well. But in 1969 and 1970, there were also new findings on opinions and attitudes toward inflation. First, people's price expectations remained rather conservative. In 1970, when the cost of living index rose by 6 percent per annum and the prices of numerous goods and services which were purchased by consumers increased to a much larger extent, only about one-fifth of Americans expected prices to advance by 6 percent or more during the following twelve months, while four-fifths expected smaller price increases. At the same time, most people thought that in five years prices would be higher than they would be a year hence, and that in ten years they would be still higher.

In 1969 and 1970, less than one-third of Americans said that they were hurt much by inflation; more than one-half said that they were hurt "a little," and almost one-eighth said that they were not hurt at all. A substantial proportion of people thought that increases in income helped to compensate for the damage caused by rising prices.

Furthermore, in reply to a question in which survey respondents were asked whether they or their families bought anything during the past few months because they thought it would cost more later, only 12 percent of family heads answered "Yes," while 88 percent answered "No." The question was intentionally formulated so that it was easy to give an affirmative answer, but the reply suggested by the economic theory of rationality, that they were buying in advance in order to beat inflation, was not given by most people. When the small proportion of respondents who said they had brought something in advance were asked what they had purchased, they

---

[5]The Index of Consumer Sentiment declined from a high point of 95.1 in February 1969, to 91.6 in May, 86.4 in August, and 79.7 in November 1969. The recession low of 75.4 was reported in May 1970. The recession set in toward the beginning of 1970 or, at the earliest, toward the end of the year 1969. Incomes continued to grow in 1969, counterbalancing to some extent the deterioration in sentiment. For quantitative data, see the chart on page 152 of *1970 Survey of Consumer Finances*.

spoke of occasional purchases of a variety of small items.[6]

Finally, the year 1970, in which prices advanced most rapidly and complaints about inflation were most frequent, was characterized by record savings and a low rate of discretionary purchases by consumers. The bulk of the amounts saved were deposited in various kinds of savings accounts (in banks and saving associations, including certificates of deposit) in spite of many people's knowledge that these deposits were not protected against inflation.

4. Price and wage controls after August 1971. The announcement by President Nixon of a wage and price freeze and other drastic economic measures in August 1971, came as a surprise to most Americans. In the first half of 1971, however, when people were asked whether the government was doing a good job or a poor job in economic matters, the distribution of answers was much less favorable at that time than during the preceding years; close to one-half of the respondents added spontaneously that the government was doing nothing or far too little to fight unemployment and inflation. Late in August and early in September, people expressed approval of the new measures; more than three out of every four Americans said that the wage-price freeze was a good thing. Nevertheless, the favorable news had little impact on consumers' willingness to buy. Consumer expectations about economic trends and consumer demand improved only moderately.[7] This condition may be explained by the finding that wage controls created widespread uncertainty about prospective increases in income. In addition, many people thought that the new economic policies would not be successful.

In the fourth quarter of 1971, during Phase II of the wage and price controls, consumers' opinions, attitudes, and expectations remained similar to those expressed in their initial responses. In November 1971, 35 percent of a representative sample thought that the government would be successful and 48 percent thought that it would not be successful in slowing down inflation; 25 percent expected success and not fewer than 60 percent did not expect success in reducing unemployment.[8]

While toward the end of 1971 there was some progress in curtailing inflationary expectations, opinions about the probable trend of the economy over

---

[6]Prior to publicly announced price increases on new auto models, there was some advance buying of cars in the summer of 1971 during the price freeze (August to November, 1971), which cancelled those price advances.

[7]Opinions about buying conditions for automobiles and for one-family houses represented an exception. The lifting of the auto excise tax and the price rollback on new cars, as well as news about a more ample money supply, changed consumer attitudes toward cars and houses and increased the demand for them.

[8]The two pairs of percentages do not add to 100 because a sizable proportion professed not to have an opinion in both instances.

the next few years remained rather unfavorable. In the course of the year 1971, the Survey Research Center's Index of Consumer Sentiment recovered only one-third of its substantial deterioration of 1969-70. The change in attitudes corresponded with a slow and gradual, rather than with a sudden and substantial, increase in the rate of consumer demand.

Now that selected changes in consumer attitudes and behavior which occurred in recent years have been described, it is appropriate to summarize the findings from the point of view of social learning. What was learned in the four instances studied? What cognitions did masses of Amercians acquire following the tax cut, the surcharge, accelerated inflation, wage-price controls?

    a. Millions of people learned in 1964 that a massive tax cut might be of help not only to individual taxpayers, but also to the entire economy. An association was formed between a tax cut and expected improvement of business conditions. (This association did not prevail prior to 1963, in contrast to the association between a tax cut and expected improvement in personal financial conditions.) The new belief system was acquired slowly and gradually.[9]

    b. What was learned about the impact of a tax cut propagated a belief in the adverse effect of tax increases on the economy. Nevertheless, in the course of two years, many people acquired the opinion that a small tax increase might be "to the good," because it might help to redress the economic imbalance.

    c. The American people learned: (a) that they were living in an inflationary age in which price increases were continuous; (b) that price increases would be slow and gradual, and would not involve a collapse of the value of the dollar and therefore, (c) it would be unwise to withdraw money from the bank in order to beat inflation by hoarding goods, but on the contrary, (d) thrift would continue to have its rewards and contribute to personal security.

    From the economist's point of view, these survey findings may be summarized by saying that millions of people acquired an understanding of radical differences between creeping and runaway inflation. Needless to say, these expressions were unknown to the masses, who also did not know that at times of runaway inflation, people historically stocked

---

[9]The new opinions may hardly be viewed as expert knowledge. Old beliefs about the analogy between private finances or budgets and government finances persisted. Many people, knowing that they themselves and business firms were not in a position to spend more than they took in over long periods, did not acquire the notion proposed by theories of functional finance, that government finances are a different matter. People continued to believe that government deficits were bad. They did not learn in 1964-65 that under certain conditions a substantial tax cut might not even reduce government receipts.

up and transformed their financial assets into goods.[10]

d. Long before the advent of wage-price controls, the American people believed that the government had great power over the national economy. When, in 1971, the government introduced radical new policies, however, people's reactions were divided, with more people doubting than believing in the government's success. In the case of the tax cut, there was a crystallization of opinions, but this was not the case with respect to the effects of the wage-price controls, at least in the first 9 months after their introduction.

The results of learning have just been described in terms of the acquisition of new beliefs, attitudes and expectations. These acquisitions in turn, had a strong impact on actions, especially on discretionary expenditures and on the amounts saved by consumers. The rate of change in some major forms of discretionary expenditures, as shown in Table 12-1, indicates substantial fluctuations which are in accord with earlier changes in consumer sentiment.

Expenditures on durable goods increased greatly following the tax cut; their rate of growth was smaller during the discussion of a possible tax increase, but not in the year of the introduction of the surcharge (1968). In 1969, after the acceleration of inflation, there was a turn toward a much smaller rate of growth, and in 1970, a recession set in. The number of cars bought shows still greater fluctuations, with large increases in 1965 and 1968, and sizable declines in 1966, 1967 and 1970. (The reduction in 1970 was due partly to an extended strike in the General Motors plants.) Obviously, there were many factors which contributed to these changes, reinforcing the changes in consumer attitudes and willingness to buy. Psychological and economic factors (e.g., change in money supply and in income received) were interacting but a strong psychological influence is demonstrable.

---

[10]What most people learned about inflation again differed greatly from what experts thought, and the experts were far from unanimous. People's opinions about the causes of inflation remained rudimentary and imprecise.

Table 12-1

Changes in Discretionary Expenditures and in Consumer Sentiment

Year	Expenditures on Consumer Durable Goods in Constant Dollars 1	Number of New Passenger Cars Bought* 2	Index of Consumer Sentiment 3
	Annual change in percent		Change in percentage points**
1964	+ 2.4	+ 3.9	+ 5.7
1965	+12.9	+14.8	+ 4.3
1966	+ 7.7	- 4.3	-10.7
1967	+ 1.7	- 7.6	+ 6.8
1968	+11.7	+15.8	- 2.5***
1969	+ 4.3	- 0.1	- 5.1
1970	- 2.8	-12.3	- 8.5

*Data on change in 1964, 1965 and 1966: domestic cars only.

**The change, adjusted for population growth, is presented from the summer of the preceding year to the summer of the year stated in the row, rather than from one calendar year to the next, as is done in Columns 1 and 2. Even this form of dating does not account fully for the finding that attitudes usually change earlier than expenditure or purchase rates. (For instance, the improvement of the Index in 1967 is related to changes in 1968 in the first two columns.) The changes in the Index are presented here for the purpose of indicating changes in direction. The theoretical model postulates that both changes in willingness to buy (indicated by the Index) and changes in ability to buy (in income, assets) influence the changes in the amounts of discretionary expenditures. Measures of ability to buy, not presented in the table, showed an improvement especially during the mini-recession of 1966-67 and also in 1969.

***Plus 2.8 percentage points in the second half of 1968.

Source of Columns 1 and 2: U.S. Department of Commerce and Council of Economic Advisers to the President. Column 3: Survey Research Center.

The Process of Learning

Three successive stages involved in the learning process may be distinguished:

A. The emergence or recognition of a problem.

B. The acquisition and processing of information.

C. Problem solution and theory formation.

Although the three stages will be studied separately, occasionally one stage may be fairly insignificant, and solutions or theories may appear long before the second stage has been completed.

A. Problem Recognition Little information is available on problem emergence and recognition from the traditional problem-solving experiments in which the experimenter presents his subjects with something explicitly designated as a problem and the subjects are externally motivated to solve it. In contrast, in the instances studied in this paper, the emergence of a problem or a crossroad situation was found to be far from automatic following the impact of new stimuli. Inertia and old established habits appeared to exert a strong influence toward classifying the new stimuli as familiar ones, so that old response patterns remained applicable and people were not motivated to deliberate and choose.

There were widespread individual differences regarding the recognition of problems. For many people, frequent repetition of the new stimuli, that is, of the information conveyed, was called for, and the information had to be presented in a variety of ways and reinforced by word of mouth before people recognized that something new had occurred and created a problem with which they were personally involved. We found that for some people it took a fairly long time before they heard a new piece of information; for other people, even after they received the information, they did not find it puzzling or feel that it concerned them personally; for still other people, several aspects of the information were distinguished, some of which appeared familiar and others of which seemed puzzling, but the latter were suppressed.

The beginning of the process of social learning, then is not necessarily instantaneous following the receipt of new information. It often took several weeks and even several months until many people became aware of some questions such as: Is the new development good or bad? If so, for whom? What will happen next? Should I personally do something? If so, what?

The recognition of a problem was slow with respect to the acceleration of inflation in 1969 (instance 3). Toward the beginning of that year a few survey respondents said, in essence, that prices were rising much faster than before, which was greatly disturbing to them; other respondents indicated an awareness of somewhat more rapid price increases, but showed no concern; others appeared to have noticed nothing new. It took six months of a variety of experiences with prices and with information received until the majority of Americans became personally concerned.

The tax increase proposal (instance 2) did not appear puzzling to the majority of people who had heard of it in 1966 and in 1967. They registered it as unfavorable news for themselves as taxpayers as well as for the economy, having classified the information as the opposite of a tax cut which was known to have beneficial effects.

President Kennedy's tax cut proposal (instance 1) was promptly recognized as something new by those who had heard of it. But the information was dealt with simply as impractical, as purely political, or even as impossible, and therefore was not viewed as a matter of personal concern. A year or more passed before many people began to recognize the existence of a pressing problem.

The announcement of the wage-price freeze (instance 4) was seen immediately as a major departure from past practices, with a potential impact on personal finances and on the entire economy. But for many people there was no problem. Some viewed the new information as representing a long-delayed necessary action which would work; others viewed the measures as ineffective, or of only short-run importance, which would not call for a change in behavior. Still others, of course, recognized a problem rather quickly.

Awareness of a problem does not necessarily lead to desiring and searching for additional information. In some cases, definite answers to the questions which were raised emerged almost at the same time as the problem. This was often the case with respect to the affective connotation of the new situation. For instance, the tax surcharge was viewed as bad right away, even by many people who were puzzled about it having been proposed soon after the tax cut and advocated as something good for the country. Whenever a difference emerged between beneficial or harmful effects for oneself and for the country, there was a tendency to recognize the problem.

The question "What will happen next?" commonly emerged earlier than the question "Should I do anything myself?" A response involving prompt action immediately following the recognition of a problem, was observed only rarely.

B. Information Processing In problem-solving experiments, the recognition of a problem is followed by a process which has been commonly described either as trial and error or as rational deliberation, consisting of listing possible alternative courses of action and weighing their appropriateness. In contrast, the process of social learning as observed in the four instances may be characterized as:

1) serial processing of information received, supplemented by 2) selective search for information, usually leading to a 3) clarification of the problem, and resulting either in 4) shortcuts representing a temporary, superficial solution, or alternatively in 5) uncertainty and growing uneasiness.

In all instances, people were subjected to a series of repeated bits of information following the initial news; this involved frequent repetition of the original news, often in greatly elaborated form and by persons viewed as authorities or experts over the TV, radio and in print. Concerned people among survey respondents also reported having discussed the matter with friends or colleagues, and these reports often indicated the recognition of a problem. While information flows serially, its apprehension and processing is highly selective. People usually listened to news which was in line with their initial perceptions and expectations. The selection of information depended to a large extent on the groups to which the listener belonged.

The selectivity of information which was sought after and received was rather obvious in the case of the wage-price freeze. Trade union members and, more generally, low-income people primarily reported unfavorable information they had heard about the impact of the wage freeze. Businessmen and upper income people were usually those who had heard and looked for information about price controls. Similarly, upper income people and Republicans were those who reported unfavorable information about Kennedy's tax proposal most frequently.

In response to the survey question about news heard recently on economic matters, many respondents started out by saying "I have heard of the price freeze" or about "plans to increase taxes," but often they continued in a much less objective manner "and I told that . . ." Survey protocols provide ample evidence (1) about the frequency and importance of information received by word of mouth, through discussions with friends, neighbors and colleagues and (2) about an emotional factor which is present in these discussions. What people talked about was seldom the factual details of the new situation, but rather whether the new developments were good or bad, how they would work out, and what they meant to them. These matters, rarely discussed in the public media, constituted a major part of the information processing.

The outcome of the initial stages of information processing is either a clarification of a problem or a superficial solution. The first type of outcome involves a disclosure of gaps in the information, of missing links and question marks. The other type of outcome involves an apparent closure, usually in the form of a superficial subsumption of the new information under familiar rubrics.

A major indicator for the first outcome is an increase in "Don't Know" statements, especially on the part of better-educated respondents. In contrast to uninformed people whose initial response was frequently a "Don't Know," upper income respondents appeared to know the answer in the first few months after learning of the tax cut proposal. But as time went by, these people grew increasingly puzzled. When asked what they thought of a tax cut some replied, "Formerly, I thought that it was merely a proposal to get votes; now I don't know; many good people say that it would help the economy." They responded similarly with respect to inflation: "A few months ago I was not much concerned, although my wife complained about rising prices; now I don't know; prices are rising so fast that something must be done, but it is now at all clear what could or should be done." (In both quotations we have paraphrased a variety of reports found in interview transcripts.)

As the problem became more acute for some people, motivating them to search further, other people arrived at easy solutions. Only part of the available information appears to have been utilized when some respondents reported, "Experts say that the tax cut will make for more purchasing power (for larger consumer demand) so that business conditions will improve." Or when questioned about inflation, some responded, "The government will do something to slow down price increases" while others stated that, "The government can't do anything; there will be unemployment and bad times, and prices will continue to go up." In numerous answers of this type there were few indications of curiosity, or even of uncertainty. People reported definite expectations about good or bad consequences.

But shortcut solutions may be unstable because new information continues to be received. In some cases, the new information is shrugged off; in other cases, the serial information processing is resumed. The process of social learning continues until the great majority of people acquire a uniform belief system in which there are no gaps or question marks.

This uniformity of opinion among the majority of people which constitutes the final solution of a problem, is an unexpected finding. In the instances of the tax cut and the surcharge, the process of social learning continued until this uniformity occurred. In the spring and summer of 1964, some people thought that the tax cut was rather insignificant, while others believed that it would stimulate economic recovery. The opinions and attitudes of the first group continued to change under the impact of new information received, until in the fall of 1964, they resembled those of the second group. Late in 1964, close to three-fourths of a representative sample spoke exclusively of the beneficial effects of the tax cut. The change was similar in response to the surcharge: in the summer and fall of 1968, there was a general agreement that it had only insignificant adverse effects on personal finances and that it was acceptable with respect to general economic trends.

But other conditions have also been observed. Early in 1971, there was a general agreement that inflation was bad and that something ought to be done to slow it down. There was no agreement, however, about what should or could be done and no indications of a willingness to make personal sacrifices. There was some habituation to inflation: the information was no longer new, and the frequency of complaints diminished. Yet the opinions remained rather unstable; in the absence of a solution to a problem, it might be assumed that the process of learning would continue. But it was, in fact, interrupted by a new development: the introduction of the wage-price freeze in August 1971.

At this time the author is in a position to study changes in responses to these controls over a nine-month period only. During this time span, the problem was not solved. To some extent, a dichotomy of opinions arose; some people expected the new policies to be successful, and others thought that they would fail. It is reasonable to assume that information processing will continue for this problem.

C. Theory Formation An analysis of the final stage of the learning process, the solution of the problem, sheds additional light on information processing. The information which is received is not just serially registered; it is organized so that it represents a step toward the solution. Problem solving constitutes a continuous process of reorganization which ends when all of the pieces fall into place. One may reach this end point when he is in agreement with others in his sphere of contact (face-to-face group), and feels that he is in agreement with most others in the country. Another indication of a solution is a uniformity of affective connotations. As long as one feels that a new development is partly good and partly bad, tension persists. The same condition exists when the development seems beneficial (or harmful) to oneself but harmful (or beneficial) to the country. The resolution of contradictory effects represents an important part of a cognitive solution.

The expression theory may be used to describe the end result. The emergence or formation of theoretical notions constitutes the most satisfactory conclusion of the process. It is not enough that question marks disappear; new schemata must emerge which integrate various pieces of information, and enable the individual to cope easily with additional information. This is the traditional function of a theory, to integrate what is known, and at the same time to go beyond the available data by providing the means to answer other questions which may arise.

The schemata or theories which are constructed in the process of social learning are rather simple. Numerous complexities, puzzling or contradictory in earlier stages, disappear. Clarity results from the simplification and even the suppression of information. This process is, to some extent, analogous to the major stages of theory formation in science, which are abstraction and generalization. However, the analogy between the theories formed by the American people concerning tax changes or inflation and scientific theories is far from complete because in the first case the simplification was usually accomplished by forming superficial theories. The shortcuts which were used disregarded complexities rather than integrated them; satisfaction with the final conclusion was achieved by overlooking various aspects of the problem. Naturally, there were great individual differences in this respect, but what emerged as the result of social learning, which has been subject to mutual reinforcement, must be characterized as containing a few unifying generalizations rather than representing an all-encompassing theory. The answers given in the previous section of this paper about what has been learned may all be viewed as oversimplified and even one-sided theories.

The absence of a solution creates uncertainty and usually results in a "wait-and-see" attitude. Problem solution, on the other hand, results in action, because definite expectations arise and induce many people to change their spending-saving behavior. The emerging theory provides answers to questions about what will happen and about what the individual himself should do.

It follows from this description of the learning process that social learning is usually slow and gradual. For some individuals, sudden reorganization may occur through the emergence of new insights within a very short time.

But usually, long periods of time are required for information processing and the mutual reinforcement of beliefs.

The response is not necessarily slow, however, when measured on a macro-economic scale. If many people remain totally inactive, but a small proportion of people step up or reduce, their purchases of durable goods on the installment plan, for example, the rate of debt incurrence will increase or decrease in the aggregate.

The reorganization process in the case of the tax surcharge is one example of this effect. The new information was first subsumed under the old theory which postulated that a tax increase is bad for oneself as well as for the economy; therefore, some people reduced their discretionary expenditures, which declined in the aggregate. When, much later, there was an understanding that the surcharge would help the economy, many people stepped up their discretionary expenditures.

Background and Consequences

The preceding analysis of the learning process was not interrupted by references to psychological literature, but the author must acknowledge three strains of thought which have influenced his examination of cognitive processes. The first of these consist of the propositions of Gestalt psychology as developed by Max Wertheimer. Wertheimer conceptualized the thought process as well as the learning process as a transition from a starting situation to an end situation: $S1 \longrightarrow S2$. In the course of the transition, a reorganization takes place, consisting of "arriving at required relations" and of "finding the place of an item in a system."[11] The process of "fitting or not fitting" parts within a whole goes on until "closure" is attained, characterized by "praegnanz," that is, an organization which is as simple as possible.

The discovery of inner relations is contrasted to the acquisition of blind connections: "The very first idea of Gestalt psychology involved the confrontation of sensible structures with senseless aggregates."[12] This author carried out a series of experiments more than thirty years ago, in which some subjects learned to solve problems by understanding what was required, and others solved them by memorizing the steps leading to the solution. He showed that the application of newly acquired knowledge to related problems (transfer of training) was common and extensive in the first case, but not in the second case. "Learning by understanding" occurred not only when a person succeeded in solving a problem without help, but also when he received a

---

[11] The expressions placed in quotation marks in this paragraph are taken from and are explained in Wertheimer, 1959.

[12] Quoted from page vi of the Preface written by Wertheimer for Katona, 1940. That book is referred to in the following sentences.

series of appropriate suggestions from the experimenter. What was called "help" in the early studies is analogous to "information received" in this paper: some of the information which was presented to the subjects of the experiments "fit" and represented help in reorganizing the situation in a way which produced closure.

It was recognized in the early studies that the process of learning often did not conform to the ideal case. Wertheimer discussed "shortcut closure processes" in which "the subject fell victim to a seductive simplification." Between the two extremes of acquisition of blind connections and discovery of the best solution, there exists a middle stage which this author frequently found in his studies for this paper.

Herbert Simon proposed an "information processing theory of human thinking." The expressions, "serial information processing" and "selective search" were borrowed from Simon's analysis for use in this paper.[13] What Simon and his collaborators describe as the "progressive deepening strategy" or the "search strategy" in their problem-solving experiments, appeared of lesser importance in the learning process studied in this paper than the serial receipt of information and its "organization into simple schemas," a process which was also observed in their experiments.

While the role of cognitive maps as well as of hypotheses in problem solving and learning has been emphasized for several decades, it was from Jerome Bruner that the author borrowed the use of the concepts theory and theory formation, as the designation of the final stage of the learning process. "Theory is a way to state tersely what one knows without the burden of detail," writes Bruner, and he offers the broad generalization that "man creates theories before he creates tools" (p. 17). Instead of a "gradual accretion of associations," the "child learns to make predictions," Bruner concludes, and shows that expectancies are derived from stored theories. Cognition is found to be, for the most part, "an active process creating order." It is not emphasized by Bruner, but it follows from his assumption of theories constructed by small children, that the theories represent superficial, shortcut belief systems rather than elaborate and systematic integrations of knowledge.

The implications of the analysis of the learning process presented in this paper have a bearing on three important problems. The oldest of these concerns the appropriateness of the concept of *rationality* as postulated by economists in their theories of economic behavior. Problem-solving behavior may be assumed to resemble rational behavior, provided that the latter is defined simply as deliberating and weighing the consequences of alternative choices before arriving at a decision. But the economists' concept of rationality, as elaborated in the nineteenth century as well as quite recently, goes

---

[13]See primarily Herbert A. Simon and Allen Newell, 1971, although other books and papers by these authors are relevant as well.

beyond this definition. It includes (a) the listing of all the conceivable consequences of all actions in the order of the person's preference for them, (b) the transitivity of choices and their consistency over time, and (c) choosing the alternative which maximizes a person's utility or satisfaction.[14] These postulates differ substantially from the results of our analysis of the antecedents of economic decision making.

One difference concerns the assumed ubiquitousness of rational behavior, in contrast to the finding that problem solving and genuine decision-making represent a relatively rate occurrence. The latter occur only in response to major new stimuli; the emergence of problems which supplant habitual behavior does not occur frequently. A second difference is reflected by the malleability of observed behavior, in contrast to the assumed rigidity of the rational choice. Learning represents an adaptation to the requirements of a changed situation. Finally, in addition to the power of inertia and habits, there is widespread use of old-established stereotypes and simple theories, because shortcut solutions forestall the necessity for an extensive search and the weighing of numerous alternatives.

If the economists' theory of rationality is meant to be normative rather than descriptive, to show what should be done rather than what takes place, the principal argument against the theory is that it impedes research into what is actually going on. Economists who assume that economic behavior is or ought to be rational, frequently overlook the need to study what actually happens, even in instances when businessmen and consumers do make new decisions. The same argument applies to the problem of maximization: if it is postulated that everyone consistently tries or ought to try to arrive at the choice which appears optimal for him, research on changes in motives and on differences in the motivational patterns of decision makers is forestalled.

A second problem worth discussing concerns the relation of the findings presented in this paper to the theory of *dissonance.* In essence, Leon Festinger and others postulate that we are motivated to resolve doubt and to establish noncontradictory belief systems. This postulate is related to the process of fitting items of information into consistent wholes, and of transforming nonfitting parts into fitting ones. Yet Festinger provides much more specific conclusions than are implied by our references to missing links and question marks when he defines dissonance as the presence of two cognitions from which obverse consequences follow. The lack of understanding and the recognition of a problem found in our analysis of the early states of the learning process can hardly be identified with the presence of dissonant cognitions.

In later stages of the learning process, many people cope with dissonant

---

[14]The major features of the economists' concepts have been summarized here very briefly because the author devoted a paper to this topic many years ago. (Katona, 1953.)

beliefs. The tax cut experience may perhaps be expressed in terms of the dissonance theory: people saw the tax cut as good for themselves and bad for the country, and finally resolved the contradiction by learning that in fact the tax cut was also good for the country. The surcharge experience was different: the problem arose when people became aware that something was advocated which had nothing but adverse consequences; they eventually learned that it was good for the country and therefore the "dissonance," the fact that a tax increase is bad for the taxpayer, was tolerated. It appears that an integrated belief system sometimes does contain dissonant elements. One basic finding of psychological economics states that most people desire both to spend and to save, to raise their standard of living by acquiring more goods and to increase their security by acquiring larger reserve funds. Since by definition, saving is not spending, it appears that people wish to do A and non-A at the same time. Yet surveys which have been conducted over many years have failed to disclose any feeling of dissonance in this condition. Without perceiving any problem, many people proceeded to do what they wanted to do, using part of their income increases to spend more and part of them to save more. Similarly, it was found in 1969-70 that most Americans had pessimistic short-run expectations but they also had optimistic expectations about personal fortunes in five or ten years, and they did not notice any contradiction in these beliefs. The integration of these beliefs could not accurately be termed an instance of overcoming dissonance, because people were not aware of any conflict and the process was not progressive.

The third and last problem area is usually discussed under the heading *information overload*. The quantity of scientific information which has been produced, and therefore the amount of information with which scholars must cope, has increased greatly during the last few decades. People are generally subjected nowadays to a much larger number of items of information than in earlier times. It has been argued that there are limits to the amount and variety of information which people can tolerate. According to the extreme formulation presented by Alvin Toffler, the American people are subjected to overstimulation and overchoice, creating a "future shock," that is, a distress which results from overloading their adaptive system and their decision-making processes.

Portions of this paper may be recalled which apparently support this argument. While technological change and even social change appear to have been rapid during the last few decades, social learning was slow, and adaptation to changes in the environment must have become more difficult than in earlier times. But is this problem the same as the problem of information overload? The latter problem is derived from the finding that the organism can apprehend, retain and use only a limited number of bits of information. Therefore, as our analysis shows, people order and organize the variety of information impinging on them into a limited number of schemata or theories. In contrast to Toffler's description of "glutting a person with more information than he can process," people find means to cope with complex material. Sensible learning represents the process of creating order, by integrating manifold detailed items of information into a few major, and often far too simple, schemata. The resulting theories are oversimplified, perhaps to their advantage rather than to their detriment.

References

Bruner, J. S. *The Relevance of Education.* New York: W. W. Norton and Co., 1971.

Festinger, L. *A Theory of Cognitive Dissonance.* Stanford: Stanford University Press, 1957.

Katona, G. *Organizing and Memorizing.* New York: Columbia University Press, 1940 (second printing, 1949; reprinted by Hafner Publishing Company, 1967).

Katona, G. "Rational Behavior and Economic Behavior," *Psychological Review,* LX (1953), 307-318.

Katona, G., & Mueller, E. *Consumer Response to Income Increases.* Washington, D.C.: The Brookings Institution, 1968.

Katona, G., et al. *1970 Survey of Consumer Finances* (1969, 1968, etc.). Monographs published annually by the Institute for Social Research, Ann Arbor, Michigan, 1971 (1970, 1969, etc.).

Katona, G., Strumpel, B. and Zahn, E. *Aspirations and Affluence.* New York: McGraw-Hill, 1971.

Katona, G. "Theory of Expectations," to be published in Morgan, J. N., Strumpel, B., and Zohn, E., (Eds.). *Human Behavior in Economic Affairs: Essays in Honor of Goerge Katona.* Amsterdam, Holland: Elsevier, 1972.

Simon, H. A., and Newell, A. "Human Problem Solving," *American Psychologist,* XXVI (1971), 145-159.

Toffler, A. *Future Shock.* New York: Random House, 1970.

Wertheimer, M. *Productive Thinking* (2nd edition). New York: Harper Bros., 1959.

13

"TRENDS IN INTER-FAMILY TRANSFERS."*

Nancy A. Baerwaldt, James N. Morgan

Introduction

Basically, a civilization consists of individuals who make arrangements to facilitate survival. Some individuals can produce what they need for survival, or produce enough commodities or services that can be exchanged in the market for his (or her) own survival. But children and the aged cannot do that, nor can some people in the intermediate ages. Any civilization must therefore provide some mechanism for transferring resources to its dependent members.

Indeed, from the beginning such transfers were absolutely vital to support the women who were bearing children, since a child is not an article of commerce which can be sold to reward its producer, except in slavery situations in which the mother is also a slave. (Some economists argued that producing more slaves was more profitable in pre-Civil War days than using purchased slaves to grow and harvest cotton.) The original mechanisms for this distribution were the nuclear family, the extended family, and the tribe. More highly developed civilizations extend the process to larger agglomerations, up to the "nation state," and even the United Nations (or national foreign aid programs).

One can argue that there is a non-market exchange, particularly within a family, of affection in return for the intra-family material resource transfers.

*The research reported here was performed by the Survey Research Center at the University of Michigan under contract (OEO-4180) from the Office of Economic Opportunity.

A great deal of consumer research has used the family as the basic unit because most of the transfers made without recompense are made within the
family, and most of the family's outside dealings are market transactions.
But we are in the midst of a period of history in which responsibility for the
dependent members of society is being shifted increasingly from the
individual family to larger sets of people. The laws which make people financially responsible for their indigent relatives are not widely enforced and they
are gradually being abandoned. Private philanthropy is being replaced by
various government transfer mechanisms such as social security and welfare.

In view of these changes, it is no longer accurate to describe the distribution of well-being on a family basis; the family is no longer a stable unit. There
are still some extended families taking care of their own members, but there
is an increasing number of families who are breaking up, and we are not very
effective in making families responsible for the children they helped to produce.

It is more sensible then, to start with a sample of individuals, ask what
each one is producing that is marketable, and estimate the extent to which
the individual is providing for other family members on balance, or is being
subsidized by them.[1] The analysis which follows is set in the context of the
American family.

Interfamily Transfers

Even the twentieth-century family extends beyond the nuclear unit to
include relatives in other units or institutions. In 1960, two-thirds of heads of
families opposed having their relatives live with them, yet two-thirds also felt
that relatives should be responsible for old people in need. (Morgan et al., pp.
158, 275.) Ten years later, however, fewer than 40 percent of heads of families

---

[1]The data set is a Survey Research Center panel of about 5,000 families interviewed once each
year since 1968. Two selections were made, one was a representative cross section of 3,000
families, and the other was a subsample of about 1,900 families interviewed previously by the
Census for the Office of Economic Opportunity. This subsample was limited to families whose
income was under twice the poverty line; the head of the family was under 60 years of age, and
the family gave permission to the Census to release the information it supplied to OEO. Interviewers were instructed to make every effort to interview the Head of the household, usually the
husband or main wage earner. In some cases, where it was impossible to interview the head, the
wife or some other adult was the interviewee.

As panel members moved from their original family to form their own units, they too were interviewed and added to the sample as newly-formed units. In the first year of data collection by
the Survey Research Center, Census sample families were paid $5 for their participation, and in
subsequent waves all families were paid. The data were weighted to take account of nonresponse
and the oversampling of those with low incomes. Records exist for both families and individuals,
so that the unit of analysis can be either. Most of the results reported here use the individual as
the analysis unit.

felt that they would have to support their relatives if they had more money.[2]

This small percentage might be expected if families were already supporting family members outside the nuclear unit. Table 13-1 and 13-2 indicate however, that on the average, contributions to dependents outside the family were low, averaging between one and two percent of the total family income (Table 13-1, column 5). With respect to the dollar amounts of contributions to outside dependents, there is some variation according to income decile, with those at the highest decile contributing an average of $500 to dependents outside the family, often dependent children in college. The distribution of help received from relatives according to age is U-shaped, with more help received by young families and those headed by someone with an aged head, than by families with a middle-aged head (Table 13-2, column 3). Predictably, contributions made to members outside the family have an inverted U-shaped distribution, with families headed by middle-aged persons more likely to be helping relatives than either their older or younger counterparts (Table 13-2, column 5). There is, of course, some bias in the reporting of interfamily transfers, since the average reported received is lower than the reported donations. Because the amounts are small, the bias that exists is also negligible when compared to total income.

Although Tables 13-1 and 13-2 indicate that interfamily transfers do little to alter income distribution in this country, they also show a surprising amount of transfers from sources outside the family other than relatives, even among families whose income is in the higher deciles, although the net effect of such transfers is redistributional. The Lorenz coefficient of inequality is .426 for total money income, including receipts from transfers (0 = Perfect equality, 1 = Perfect inequality), but when transfer income is excluded, the coefficient rises to .672. Donations and receipt of income in the form of free help may be hypothesized to supersede monetary contributions in importance, especially among low-income families. Although the study described in this paper has only a minimal amount of data on time contributions, what data there are do not lend support to this hypothesis. When asked if they spent more than forty hours helping friends or relatives in the preceding year, almost two-thirds of family heads at low-income levels reported helping individuals outside the family. There was some variation in the pattern of helping relatives by age of head, varying from about 60 percent of the young heads who helped relatives to 20 percent for the oldest heads of families. But there did not seem to be a greater donation of time among low-income families, even though the cost of an hour of their time is lower than that of a high-income person.

The above observations indicate that the pattern of giving and receiving

---

[2]The question was: "Would you feel you had to help your parents or other relatives (more) if you had more money?"

time and money between families is a small and probably irregular form of transfer income in this society. This does not mean that the current transfer system is not important; it is. But the non-family systems, both public and private, do the most to alleviate inequalities in the distribution of income.

Table 13-3 shows that pattern of increase in business and government transfers from 1950-1970 and provides estimates of interfamily and intrafamily transfers, and private philanthropy. There was a large increase over the twenty-year period in government transfers, attributable to the broader coverage under various types of social insurance. Although estimates of interfamily transfers for 1950 are not available, we can hypothesize that the more than fourfold increase in business and government transfers was either the result or cause of the fairly small amount of interfamily transfers. Although private philanthropy may be a means for providing aid to society's dependents, that amount is also small. Furthermore, it is activity engaged in mostly by high-income families and it is not used to support individuals.

Our attention is therefore turned to the 313.2 billion dollars of intrafamily transfers, an amount more than three times that of all other types of transfers in 1970. This is the amount, estimated from our data set as described in this paper, that is transferred within the family from those earning more than they consume, to those consuming more than they earn, using several definitions of income and consumption allocation rules.

Income Measures

Several variants of income have been used,
1) money income
2) money income + imputed rent + free rent
3) money income + value of housework
4) money income + imputed rent + free rent + value of housework
5) money income + imputed rent + free rent - (estimated federal income taxes + cost of journey to work of head and wife + union dues of head + cost of child care if wife or single head works).

The first definition is simple; the money income of an individual is simply the sum of his annual income from labor, money earnings received from assets he might own, as well as transfers from outside the family. It should be noted though, that the data are coded in such a way that the capital and transfer income accruing to the wife of the head cannot be separated from that of the head's, and therefore capital and transfer income received by the wife is necessarily allocated to the head. This not true for the wife's income from work, nor does this distortion exist for family members other than the head or wife.

The second definition merely adds imputed rent and free rent to the head's income. Free rent accrues only if the family lives in a house rent-free, and its amount is the estimated annual rental value of the dwelling. Imputed rent is calculated for homeowners as six percent of net equity in the home. The rationale for including it as the head's income is that in most cases, he is the owner and hence the income from the equity accrues to him.

The third definition adds the value of housework services to money income, derived by multiplying the hourly market value of housework by the number of hours of housework done by the head and wife. Housework done by family members other than the head and wife is not included. Hourly wage rates vary as follows:

	Region		
City Size	South	Northeast	West, North Central
12 largest metropolitan areas	$2.00	$2.50	$2.00
All others	1.50	2.00	2.00

These amounts were derived empirically as ascertaining the average wage of wives and female heads engaged in similar occupations. Region and city size proved to be the most powerful predictors of the wage rate. Income earned in this way was attributed to the person doing the work. Table 13-13 presents a comparison of results valuing housework hours at opportunity cost and the market wage.

The fourth definition merely adds together money income, imputed and free rent, and the value of housework. The fifth definition adjusts the fourth definition by subtracting from income the costs of earning that income, including costs of the journey to work of the head and wife, the cost of child care if the wife or single head of the family works, union dues of the head, and the estimated amount of federal income taxes paid by the family.

Allocation of Income

If we ask what benefit each individual receives from living with others, or what net contribution he makes, this requires some assumptions about who *consumes* the family income. It also requires distinguishing what an individual would gain or lose from moving out, from what the rest of the family would gain or lose. There are economies of scale and joint consumption in a family, so that the person who moves out is likely to lose more than the family gains on the consumption side. Clearly, then, it is far more difficult to measure what the family loses or gains by the addition or departure of one marginal member than to measure what the individual gains or loses.

Of course, what it might require for an individual to be able to leave and form his own unit may be less than what he was consuming as part of a larger family, but it is instructive to look at the data. Given the uncertainty about how one might allocate the total family consumption (and saving) to its members, we provide three allocations, one simply on a per capita basis (equally divided), the second in proportion to the physical requirements as they differ by age and sex (using food requirements); the third method also allocates consumption in proportion to physical requirements, but in addition allows for saving. In practice, there is a savings component only if total family *money* income is greater than two times the federal poverty line ("Orshansky Ratio").[3] Below that income level, all income is allocated to consumption. For income above two times the Orshansky ratio, an arbitrary amount is allocated to consumption and saving. An example of this method of allocating consumption, which assumes a saving rate of 33 percent of income above twice the Orshansky ratio is:

C_i = consumption of individual

Φ = Orshansky poverty line income for family

Y = total family income

$$C_i = \frac{\text{Individual Food Need}}{\text{Family Food Need}} \times (2\Phi + 2/3 \, [Y - 2\Phi]).$$

As the example shows, income is still allocated according to food needs until an amount equal to twice the Orshansky poverty level is reached; then two-thirds of the difference between total income and twice the poverty line is allocated to consumption in that same manner, and one-third of the difference is assumed to be saving. This one-third saving rate is probably high. Individual saving is calculated as follows:

C = consumption of family

S_i = saving of individual

Y_i = individual income

$$S_i = Y_i \times \left(\frac{Y\text{-}C}{Y}\right)$$

Therefore, net contribution of the individual to the family is $Y_i - C_i - S_i$. Imbedded in this saving function is the assumption that every individual who has some income in a family where the total family income is greater than two times the Orshansky poverty line, saves the same percent of his income that every other family member saves. This means that saving occurs for all family members who have some income, even those who consume more than they earn. This assumption may have some factual basis; a son or daughter who earns $500 may be allowed to keep a certain percentage of what he makes for himself, even though his annual consumption requirements may exceed this sum.

Additional considerations leap to mind with these allocation rules: the extra consumption of the working members, to whom rights in the accumulated savings are given, etc. Our impression is that reasonable adjustments

---

[3]See *A Panel Study of Income Dynamics, 1968-1971 Interviewing Years*, pp. 169-170 for a description of how these family needs measures were derived.

for such things would make relatively little difference, and it is not even easy to decide which of many "reasonable" adjustments to make. Working requires transportation, but this is commonly by car, whose overhead cost is fixed in most families.

An example of how allocation according to food needs is carried out in practice is shown in Table 13-4. The weekly food needs of the individual divided by the total need for the family is assumed to be the fraction of the family's income the individual consumes. Each individual's income, minus his share of that income consumed then equals his net contribution to the family. In the example, which is probably typical, the net contribution of the main earner is positive while that of the wife and child is negative.

Who Houses Relatives

Before investigating intrafamily transfers, it is worthwhile to assess the changes that have occurred over a ten-year period in the family's tendency to house relatives other than the head, wife, and minor children. If a dependent moves in with relatives, he will consume housing, food and other services in proportion to his needs. As Table 13-3 indicates, the value of what he receives from living with relatives will in all probability be greater than what he would have received from this unit were he living apart from it, and because of economies of scale, the host unit would provide a given amount of service to the dependent at a cheaper cost than if he lived alone.

To examine differences across time in the percentage of families who house relatives, a regression was run on 1970 data replicating a similar 1960 analysis, using the Multiple Classification Algorithm (Andrews et al.). This regression's unique feature is that it converts each explanatory classification into a set of dummy variables, which assume the value of one if an individual belongs to a subclass and zero if he does not. In this case, the dependent variable is also a dummy variable and assumes the value of one when there are individuals in the household other than head, wife, or minor children, otherwise it assumes a zero value. Children of the head aged eighteen or older in the household were included in the definition of relatives being housed, since they are adults and are ordinarily capable of self-support. In 1960 the overall percentage of families who housed relatives was seventeen, while in 1970, it was twenty.

Background, demographic, and attitudinal predictors were used in the two analyses. The thirteen predictors which were used in 1970 are listed below; those used in 1960 were very similar, and when the identical predictor was not available, a similar one was substituted.

Age of Head
Whether children under age 18 in family
Education of Head
Race of Head

Sex and marital status of Head
Taxable income of Head and Wife
Whether individuals not in family who are dependent on Head
Number of siblings of Head
Region where Head grew up
Church attendance of Head
Head's attitude toward helping relatives
Size of place where Head grew up
Geographic mobility of Head

The above classifications are associated with both ability and willingness to care for relatives, as well as with the likelihood of having dependent relatives. The middle-aged are more likely to have aged relatives and are probably more able to care for them than are other age groups. The presence of children under age 18 in the family is hypothesized to dissuade families from caring for any more relatives. Financial ability to provide for relatives is indicated by taxable income and education, the latter representing past or potential income. Race is a proxy for cultural differences in the family's living arrangements. Presumably, married couples would not want additional relatives in the household, while single heads of families might. Families who are already supporting others not in the family are probably less likely than other families to be able to support additional relatives within their own household. The variables: number of siblings; region where grew up; church attendance; and size of place where grew up; are background factors that may affect the family's willingness to accept additional relatives. For example, if the head of the family has moved from place to place, then he is probably less likely to be close to relatives, and therefore less likely to provide housing for them.

The thirteen explanatory classifications were able to account for twelve percent of the variance in the 1960 analysis, while they accounted for fifteen percent of the variance in 1970. Details for three of the more interesting predictors, age of head, race, and taxable income of head and wife, are shown next (Tables 13-5 through 13-7). The details for age of head shows that middle-aged heads of families, those age 45-54, are more likely to house relatives than are their older or younger counterparts. The detail according to race, Table 13-6, has been included because of the dramatic increase between 1960 and 1970 in the percentage of non-white families who house other relatives, even after adjustment for other variables. One can only speculate as to the reason for this increase. Perhaps it is a broad cultural change, or perhaps housing discrimination in places where there has been in-migration of non-whites prevents them from acquiring sufficient housing. The detail for taxable income shows the inconclusiveness of income as a determinant of whether the family houses additional relatives. Perhaps the income of the host family is not as great a factor in providing housing as is the need or desire of the individual wanting the housing. It also may be that reasons for housing relatives may differ according to income level; those families with lower incomes may choose to have an extra household member because he contributes to the total family resources, while those with middle to high income may have to house the extra person because he has few resources of his own.[4]

Intra-Family Transfers: Estimates of Amounts

Table 13-8 shows the distribution of individual income before and after consumption. Income is defined here as money plus value of housework plus value of imputed rent, and consumption is allocated in proportion to needs. Judging from this table it is obvious that most children and relatives other than the head or wife are net receivers of the family's resources, while the head is the most important contributor. The median income of both children and other relatives is close to zero before consumption is allocated, but after redistribution it is above $2,000 in these two groups. Almost nine out of ten of the children in the family are completely financially dependent, while about two-thirds of other individuals are also completely dependent. From this tabulation, it appears that need is the main factor which prompts dependents (other than children) to move in with their relatives.

Using the same definition of income and the same allocation procedure, Table 13-9 shows the means according to age, sex, and relation to head. Since there is no saving included in this allocation rule, the "After Contribution" column in Table 13-8 is equivalent to the "Consumption" column in Table 13-9. The ten groups were derived from an Automatic Interaction Detector analysis which forms subgroups by examining the potential reduction in overall error variance achieved by using that classification (Sonquist et al., pp. 1-28). This is done by examining the means of the dependent variable against each explanatory classification. In each case, the best way to use that explanatory classification with respect to the variance explained, was to divide the sample into two parts. The dependent variable which was used to form the ten groups was the net contribution to the family. There was some deviation from the groups formed in that analysis so that the groups would be symmetrical.

Table 13-9 shows that on the average, all heads of families are net contributors to the family, even those aged 65 or older. The income for male heads peaks at middle age and then falls. The composition of income changes as well; older heads have a larger share from income in kind (housework) and income from assets acquired in the past (imputed rent). Even though income

---

[4]Data from the 1968 Survey of the Aged indicate that aged individuals with incomes under $1,500 are more likely to live with their relatives than are those with higher incomes, and widows and widowers are more likely than married couples to live with relatives. (Murray, p. 9).

peaks at middle age for male heads, their consumption does not peak until they reach the 55-64 age group. This indicates that male heads are supporting larger families between the ages of 35 and 54 than they are past age 55, since their average net contribution is highest in the 35-54 age group than in any other. The income for female heads is lower than that of their male counterparts, and more than a quarter of it comes from nonmonetary sources, especially housework. For wives, the income is lower than it is for heads, but this does not necessarily mean that they spent fewer hours working than did the heads; housework is valued on the average at only $2 per hour, but the market rate and the average valuation indicates that wives spend an average of 1,500 hours on housework annually. Despite the substantial number of hours spent on housework by wives over age 45, they are still net receivers of the family's resources.

Means and national estimates of aggregates for the four definitions of income, and three allocation rules are presented in Tables 13-10 and 13-11. It should be noted that while the aggregate amount presented are based on CPS population estimates, the sample size of about 17,000 individuals is relatively small and has been subject to panel losses. The data were over-sampled among low-income families so that optimal estimates could be made for the subpopulation, but aggregates are dominated by higher income individuals who were not over-sampled, so that the effective number of individuals is somewhat smaller than 17,000. Table 13-10 allocates consumption equally among all family members, while allocation is in proportion to food needs in Table 13-11. The net contribution rises for heads of families if imputed rent is added to money income, since the head is assumed to have equity in the house and has a larger income relative to other family members. The contribution of the male head falls to a level below that for money income alone when income is defined as money income plus housework, since his income is only slightly higher because his wife is doing a substantial amount of housework. Correspondingly, a greater contribution is made by the wife when the value of housework is included in income. The net contribution becomes more and more negative for family members other than the head and wife as income includes more and more components, since there is more and more available for consumption. Allocation according to physical needs (Table 13-11) results in a lower contribution by the head since his consumption requirements are higher relative to other family members; the net contributions are also less negative for family members other than the head or wife because of their relatively low needs, while the contributions for wives under 45 are more negative (less positive) when consumption is allocated according to needs. The reverse is true for older wives, their net contribution is less negative when consumption is allocated according to needs for all definitions of income, indicating that they have lower needs relative to other family members.

Table 13-12 separates the net aggregations into two groups: net receivers of the family's resources and net givers. (They do not quite add to the same total and the two totals do not equate because of complexities in the data.) Over four-fifths of the aggregate resources contributed to the family are from heads, both male and female. The percent of female heads who are givers is about the same as for males, but the amounts are smaller because they have lower incomes. A far lower percentage of wives than female heads are contributors. Wives under forty-five are generally members of families with children, and they do only a small amount of some work outside the household, but large amounts of housework to produce income in excess of their consumption requirements. Wives who are age 45 or older have fewer children; they do less housework, and are less likely to work than younger wives, so that they contribute less, but still consume relative to their needs. By far the largest recipient group is made up of individuals other than the head or wife. They constitute 46 percent of all individuals in families, but they consume about four-fifths of the amount received by the net receivers, while almost none of them make net contributions to the family's resources.

Valuation of Housework Time

The hours of housework performed by heads and wives have been valued at market cost, the price one would pay to hire outside help. An alternative approach is to value the hours according to opportunity cost, the foregone earnings of labor which these people might offer on the market. Conceptually, these two approaches are very different and they yield different empirical results.

Wage rates for both calculation procedures were derived empirically from the survey data. The market wage was determined by what wives and female heads in the sample earned doing housework, the opportunity wage was determined by a similar analysis of all wives and female heads who were in the labor force. Opportunity cost wage rates (see Table 13-14) were calculated separately for wives and female heads; education and size of the area were the most powerful variables. (Education of the head was actually used as a proxy for the education of the head was actually used as a proxy for the education of his wife.)

In most cases, opportunity rates were higher than market wage rates for housework. The new valuations of housework and the new average income levels are shown in the tabulation below. The average income increase for older female heads and wives was lower than that for their younger counterparts both because they have fewer years of education and because they perform fewer hours of housework.

	Housework Valued at Market Cost	Housework Valued at Opportunity Cost	Increase in Income	New Average Individual Income
Female Head				
Under age 45	$1803	$2274	$+471	$7445
Age 45 or older	1829	2193	+364	6729
Wife				
Under age 45	3412	4457	+1045	6397
Age 45 or older	3000	3804	+804	5274

The next tabulation gives the net aggregation of the amounts donated by givers, the first column is the same as in Table 13-12 and the second contains the result if housework for female heads and wives is valued at opportunity cost rather than at the market wage rate. The aggregate amount transferred rises from $320 billion to $398 billion. This result is not intuitively obvious and depends in part on the type of family composition that predominates in the population. Imagine, for example a family consisting of a husband and wife who have equal consumption needs; the head of the family has a money income of $6000 and the wife performs housework whose market value is $2000.

	Income	Consumption Needs
Head	$6000	.5
Wife	2000	.5
	$8000	1.0

	Consumption	−	Income	=	Net Subsidy
Head (½ x 8000)	4000	−	6000	=	−2000
Wife (½ x 8000)	4000	−	2000	=	+2000

The net subsidy for either the giver or the receiver in the above example is $2000. Now assume that the wife's housework is valued at opportunity cost; the value of her housework rises to $4000. The net subsidy falls from $2000 to $1000.

	Consumption	−	Income	=	Net Subsidy
				=	
Head (½ x 10,000)	5000	−	6000	=	−1000
Wife (½ x 10,000)	5000	−	4000	=	+1000

The aggregation of either the amounts received by net recipients or the amounts given by net donators will result in a lower aggregate net subsidy if most of the families have compositions similar to the one above. But in most families where the wife or female head does substantial amounts of housework, there are several children, most of whom are recipients of the family's income; the net donation in these cases will rise when housework is valued at the opportunity rather than the market wage.

	Income	Consumption Needs
Head	$6000	.2
Wife	2000	.2
Child	0	.2
Child	0	.2
Child	0	.2
	$8000	1.0

	Consumption	−	Income	=	Net Subsidy
Head	1600		6000		−4400
Wife	1600		2000		− 400
Child	1600		0		+1600
Child	1600		0		+1600
Child	1600		0		+1600

The recipients receive a net amount of $4800 under these conditions. Now assume, as in the first example, that housework is valued at opportunity cost. The picture changes as follows:

	Consumption	−	Income	=	Net Subsidy
Head	2000		6000		4000
Wife	2000		4000		−2000
Child	2000		0		+2000
Child	2000		0		+2000
Child	2000		0		+2000

Opportunity cost valuation of housework increases the wife's income in the same manner as in the previous example, but the net subsidy of the givers or receivers rises instead of falls, after the revaluation of the wife's housework, because most subsidies go to children.

Change in Family Composition

If there is relatively little interfamily transfer of resources, but a substantial amount of resource transfer within the family, then changes in family composition can have substantial effects on the well-being of individuals in the family, and on the reported distribution of family income and family well-being. The data from this panel study do reveal a substantial amount of change in family composition over a three year period. In early 1971, fewer than half the families in the panel contained exactly the same members that they had in 1968.

Some of these changes were caused simply by progression through a normal family life cycle, although the timing or even the changes themselves (having another child) were often affected by environmental conditions: income, employment, housing. Other changes, such as adult relatives of the head or the wife moving in or out of the family, divorce or death, are less predictable, but they may also be affected by environmental forces (or governmental policy). Clearly, these kinds of changes have a substantial impact or intrafamily transfers, and on the distribution of well-being. Data from this study also show that for very young married couples, the unemployment rate in the area has a direct bearing on the probability of having a child; for somewhat older married couples, family income relative to needs appears to be the most powerful determinant of the birth rate. Single men seem more likely to get married when they earn more, and for older families, crowded housing seems to lead to (or at least to speed up) the departure of children who leave home to form new families. It may be not only the birth rate then, that is subject to environmental influence, but also the composition of families, since the latter is such a crucial determinant of the well-being of the individuals in these families.

References

Andrews, F. M., et al. *Multiple Classification Analysis.* Ann Arbor: Institute for Social Research, 1967.

Institute for Social Research. *A Panel Study of Income Dynamics, 1968-1971 Interviewing Years.* Ann Arbor: 1971.

Morgan, J., et al. *Income and Welfare in the United States.* New York: McGraw Hill, 1962.

Murray, Janet. "Living Arrangements of People Aged 65 and Older: Findings from 1968 Survey of the Aged, *Social Security Bulletin.* XXXIV (September, 1971).

Sonquist, J. A., et al. *Searching for Structure.* Ann Arbor: Institute for Social Research, 1971.

Table 13-1

Money Income Measures within 1970 Money Income Deciles

(for all 1971 families)

Money Income Decile	Total Family Money Income (col. 1)	− Money Transfers Excluding Help from Relatives (col. 2)	− Help from Relatives (col. 3)	= Money Income Excluding Transfers (col. 4)	− Contributions to Outside Dependents (col. 5)	= Money Income Excluding Transfer System (col. 6)
First Decile (less than $2400)	$ 1,570	$ 996	$ 50	$ 524	$ 20	$ 504
Second Decile ($2400-4129)	3,260	1,339	76	1,845	20	1,825
Third Decile ($4130-5597)	4,850	1,299	93	3,458	46	3,412
Fourth Decile ($5598-7255)	6,446	1,154	61	5,231	41	5,190
Fifth Decile ($7256-8814)	8,025	1,059	37	6,929	57	6,872
Sixth Decile ($8815-10,551)	9,724	869	9	8,846	105	8,741
Seventh Decile ($10,552-12,689)	11,591	567	28	10,996	102	10,894
Eighth Decile ($12,690-15,049)	13,842	588	18	13,236	134	13,102
Ninth Decile ($15,050-19,199)	16,928	447	16	16,465	242	16,223
Tenth Decile ($19,200 or more)	26,692	529	3	26,160	504	25,656
TOTAL	$10,298	$ 883	$ 41	$ 9,374	$ 128	$ 9,246

Table 13-2

Money Income Measures within Age of Head
(for all 1971 families)

Age of Head	Total Family Money Income (col. 1)	−	Money Transfers Excluding Help from Relatives (col. 2)	−	Help from Relatives (col. 3)	=	Money Income Excluding Transfers (col. 4)	−	Contributions to Outside Dependents (col. 5)	=	Total Family Money Income Excluding Transfer System (col. 6)
Under 25	$ 6,924		$ 279		$ 131		$ 6,514		$ 25		$ 6,489
25-34	10,759		369		53		10,337		74		10,263
35-44	13,534		592		16		12,926		199		12,727
45-54	13,274		685		7		12,582		234		12,348
55-64	10,725		925		17		9,783		179		9,604
65-74	6,177		2,555		8		3,614		61		3,553
75 or older	4,265		2,215		87		1,963		14		1,949
TOTAL	$ 10,298		$ 883		$ 41		$ 9,374		$ 128		$ 9,246

Table 13-3

Trends in Transfer Payments Included in Official Statistics,
and Estimates of Two Excluded Transfers

	Billions of Dollars				
Year	Business Transfers	Government Transfers	Inter-family Transfers	Intra-family Transfers	Private Philanthropy[c]
1950	2.7	14.3			
1955	3.1	16.1			
1960	3.3	26.6			8.0[a]
1965	3.5	37.2			} 11.1[b]
1970	3.6	73.9	8.4	313.2	

SOURCE: First two columns: National Income Statistics (Statistical Abstract, 1971, p. 309)

Next two columns: Aggregate estimates from OEO Panel Study of Family Income Dynamics

Last column: [a]Estimated (excluding small amounts under $50) from data in Morgan, David, Cohen and Brazer, Income and Welfare in the United States, McGraw-Hill, 1962, p. 259.

[b]Estimated from "Statistics of Income", 1968, Individual Income Tax Returns, Internal Revenue Service, p. 75.

[c]For additional estimates of philanthropy, see Frank G. Dickinson, The Changing Position of Philanthropy in the American Economy (New York: National Bureau of Economic Research, 1970), pp. 208-209.

Transfers are one-way transactions, not exchanges, since nothing is given in return, at least at the time. (Contributory transfers like pensions have legal requirements, insurance a probabilistic one, and personal charity or family aid a cultural one.)

Table 13-4

Method of Calculating Net Contributions
of Individuals to Their Families

Family Member	Weekly Cost of Food Needs[1]	Fraction of Total Family Food Needs	Income Earned (col. 3)	Estimated Share of Family Income − (col. 4)[2] =	Net Contribution (col. 5)[3]
40 year old man	$ 6.90	.404	$ 7,000	$ 4,040	$ 2,960
38 year old wife	6.30	.368	3,000	3,680	− 680
2 year old child	3.90	.228	0	2,280	−2,280
	$ 17.10	1.000	$ 10,000	$ 10,000	0

---

[1]Estimated, at "Low Cost" Level by U. S. Department of Agriculture (Family Economics Review, March, 1967).

[2]Total Family Income allocated to members in proportion to food needs.

[3]Column 3 minus Column 4.

Table 13-5

Proportion of Families Who House Relatives by Age of Head
Unadjusted and Adjusted by Multiple Regression
for 12 Other Characteristics

Age	1960[1]				1970			
	Number of Family Heads	Percent of Family Heads	Unad-justed	Adjusted	Number of Family Heads	Percent of Family Heads	Unad-justed	Adjusted
Under 25	167	5.9	0.04	0.12	696	13.1	0.04	0.06
25-34	541	19.3	0.08	0.13	1,021	20.1	0.05	0.04
35-44	652	23.4	0.16	0.17	974	18.6	0.26	0.23
45-54	581	20.2	0.25	0.22	896	17.0	0.41	0.41
55-64	475	16.0	0.24	0.20	691	14.1	0.29	0.30
65-74	261	10.3	0.16	0.13	363	11.0	0.17	0.19
75 and older	123	4.9	0.17	0.13	198	6.0	0.16	0.16
Variance "Explained" $(Eta^2$ or $Beta^2)^2$		N.A.	0.01				0.11	0.10

---

[1] J.N. Morgan, et. al., Income and Welfare in the United States, (New York: McGraw-Hill, 1962), p. 171.

[2] Eta^2 is the proportion of the variance of the dependent variable explained by the unadjusted deviations. $Beta^2$ is analogous, but is the variance explained after adjustment for other predictors where inter-correlations among predictors is not serious. Beta approximates partial correlation coefficient.

Table 13-6

Proportion Who House Relatives by Race of Family Head
Unadjusted and Adjusted by Multiple Regression
for 12 Other Characteristics

Race	1960[1]				1970			
	Number of Family Heads	Percent of Family Heads	Unad-justed	Adjusted	Number of Family Heads	Percent of Family Heads	Unad-justed	Adjusted
White	2,402	89.4	0.16	0.17	3,018	86.4	0.18	0.19
Negro					1,669	10.8	0.34	0.30
Puerto Rican and Mexican	398	10.6	0.23	0.20	116	2.2	0.32	0.26
Others					36	0.5	0.37	0.36
Variance "Explained" $(Eta^2 \text{ or } Beta^2)$			N.A.	0.01			0.02	0.01

---
[1]

J.N. Morgan, et. al., Income and Welfare in the United States, (New York: McGraw-
Hill, 1962), p. 174.

Table 13-7

Proportion Who House Relatives by Taxable Income of Head and Wife
Unadjusted and Adjusted for 12 Other Characteristics

Taxable Income of Head and Wife	1960[1]				1970			
	Number of Family Heads	Percent of Family Heads	Unad-justed	Adjusted	Number of Family Heads	Percent of Family Heads	Unad-justed	Adjusted
None	103	3.2	0.09	0.05	523	7.4	0.29	0.20
$1 - 499	190	5.7	0.17	0.08	235	4.8	0.21	0.19
500 - 999	183	5.4	0.19	0.12	175	3.2	0.21	0.18
1,000-1,999	300	8.3	0.22	0.18	303	5.5	0.14	0.14
2,000-2,999	249	7.6	0.19	0.17	279	4.1	0.26	0.23
3,000-4,999	449	17.2	0.19	0.18	650	11.1	0.21	0.20
5,000-7,499	585	23.8	0.14	0.17	717	12.9	0.16	0.23
7,500-9,999	350	13.9	0.20	0.23	577	13.0	0.19	0.21
10,000-14,999	271	10.4	0.14	0.18	832	21.3	0.21	0.22
15,000 or over	120	4.5	0.15	0.15	549	16.8	0.20	0.20
Variance "Explained" $(Eta^2$ or $Beta^2)$			N.A.	0.01			0.01	0.003

---

[1] J.N. Morgan, *et. al.*, Income and Welfare in the United States, (New York: McGraw-Hill, 1962), p. 170.

Table 13-8

Individual Income* Before and After Contribution to Family** by Relation to Head
(1970)

Income Group	Head Before Contribution	Head After Contribution	Wife Before Contribution	Wife After Contribution	Children Before Contribution	Children After Contribution	Others Before Contribution	Others After Contribution	All Before Contribution	All After Contribution
Less than $250	0.1	0.0	1.2	0.0	87.2	0.1	66.3	0.3	39.1	0.0
$250-499	0.0	0.2	0.3	0.2	2.2	0.8	2.0	3.0	1.1	0.6
$500-749	0.1	0.4	0.6	0.3	2.1	2.3	3.4	6.1	1.2	1.4
$750-999	0.2	1.0	0.5	0.7	1.1	3.3	4.0	4.3	0.8	2.1
$1,000-1,499	0.9	2.7	3.1	2.3	1.8	10.7	7.4	12.6	2.0	6.4
$1,500-1,999	1.7	4.6	4.3	4.5	0.9	12.4	3.3	12.8	2.0	8.2
$2,000-2,499	2.2	6.0	6.3	7.0	0.8	14.4	4.3	11.0	2.6	9.9
$2,500-2,999	2.9	7.1	6.5	8.3	0.6	12.0	1.0	11.9	2.7	9.6
$3,000-3,499	3.5	7.8	8.4	10.2	0.6	10.0	1.1	9.4	3.3	9.3
$3,500-3,999	3.2	7.9	9.5	9.0	0.3	8.4	1.1	7.0	3.3	8.3
$4,000-4,499	4.0	8.1	8.5	8.6	0.5	6.0	0.0	6.1	3.4	7.3
$4,500-4,999	4.5	7.4	7.4	8.6	0.2	4.6	1.2	2.8	3.2	6.3
$5,000-6,249	11.0	15.1	16.8	16.2	0.9	6.4	1.7	7.5	7.7	11.4
$6,250-7,499	9.5	10.8	9.7	9.5	0.2	3.9	0.5	2.1	5.3	7.3
$7,500-8,249	6.6	4.5	4.4	3.5	0.2	1.3	0.4	0.5	3.2	2.8
$8,250-9,999	12.2	7.2	6.8	6.1	0.2	1.8	1.0	1.0	5.6	4.5
$10,000-12,499	14.5	4.7	4.5	2.8	0.1	0.7	0.9	1.3	5.7	2.5
$12,500-14,999	9.4	2.4	0.8	1.1	0.0	0.3	0.1	0.3	3.2	1.2
$15,000-19,999	7.2	1.2	0.3	0.7	0.0	0.2	0.3	0.0	2.6	0.6
$20,000 and over	5.6	0.7	0.0	0.4	0.0	0.1	0.0	0.0	1.8	0.3
Total	100.0	100.0	100.0	100.0	100.0	100.0	100.0	100.0	100.0	100.0
Number of cases	4,840		3,013		8,036		1,038		16,927	

*Income = Money + $ Imputed Rent + $ Housework

**Distribution of Income among family members assumed proportionate to food needs.

Table 13-9

Mean Income, "Consumption," and Net Contribution
to Family, by Age, Sex, and Relation to Head*

Age, Sex, Relation to Head	Money Income ($)	+ Imputed Rent ($)	+ House- work ($)	= Individual Income ($)	− Allocated Share of Income ("Consumption") ($)	= Net Contribution to Family ($)
Male Head						
Less than 35	8,163	242	307	8,712	5,666	3,046
35-54	11,991	767	222	12,980	5,488	7,492
55-64	10,110	890	352	11,352	7,331	4,021
65 and over	5,777	767	606	7,150	5,527	1,623
Female Head						
Less than 45	5,010	161	1,803	6,974	4,421	2,553
45 and over	3,998	538	1,829	6,365	5,263	1,102
Wife						
Less than 45	1,940	−	3,412	5,352	4,672	680
45 and over	1,470	−	3,000	4,470	5,765	−1,295
Others						
Less than 16	11	−		11	2,915	−2,904
16 and over	1,275	−		1,275	4,269	−2,994

*Income includes imputed rent and value of housework. Allocation of consumption is
calculated in proportion to food needs.

Table 13-10

Net Contribution to Family for Different Definitions of Income by Age, Sex and Relation to Head*

(1970)

Age, Sex, Relation to Head	Money Income Contribution		Money Income + $ Imputed Rent Contribution		Money Income + $ Housework Contribution		Money Income + $ Imputed Rent + $ Housework Contribution	
	Mean ($)	Aggregate** (Billion $)	Mean ($)	Aggregate** (Billion $)	Mean ($)	Aggregate** (Billion $)	Mean ($)	Aggregate** (Billion $)
Male Heads								
Less than 35	4315	60.02	4470	62.17	3656	50.86	3811	53.00
35-54	7864	163.10	8421	174.64	7181	148.93	7738	160.48
55-64	4624	37.60	5128	41.69	3734	30.36	4238	34.45
65 and over	2319	16.74	2686	19.39	1535	11.08	1902	13.73
Female Heads								
Less than 45	1591	6.52	1671	6.85	2598	10.65	2679	10.98
45 and	477	4.64	583	5.66	874	8.49	979	9.52
Wives								
Less than 45	-1608	-39.89	-1724	-42.78	835	20.71	718	17.82
45 and over	-3071	-58.44	-3431	-65.29	-1370	-26.07	-1730	-32.91
Others								
Less than 16	-2385	-132.13	-2491	-138.00	-3180	-176.17	-3287	-182.10
16 and over	-1734	-59.34	-1902	-65.09	-2431	-83.19	-2599	-88.94

* Consumption of income allocated equally per person

** Using population data from the current Population Reports Series P. 20, No. 198.

Table 13-11

Net Contribution to Family for Different Definitions of Income by Age, Sex and Relation to Head*
(1970)

Age, Sex Relation to Head	Money Income Contribution**		Money Income + $ Imputed Rent Contribution		Money Income + $ Housework Contribution		Money Income + $ Imputed Rent + $ Housework Contribution		Money Income + $ Imputed Rent + $ Housework Contribution - Adjustments***	
	Mean ($)	Aggregate** (Billion $)	Mean ($)	Aggregate** (Billion $)	Mean ($)	Aggregate** (Billion $)	Mean ($)	Aggregate** (Billion $)	Mean ($)	Aggregate** (Billion $)
Male Heads										
Less than 35	3,761	52.37	3,901	54.27	2,905	40.41	3,046	42.36	3,549	49.37
35-54	7,683	159.34	8,229	170.68	6,945	144.05	7,492	155.37	7,238	150.12
55-64	4,462	36.28	4,952	40.26	3,531	28.71	4,021	32.69	4,398	35.76
65 and over	2,144	15.48	2,488	17.96	1,279	9.24	1,623	11.72	2,611	18.85
Female Heads										
Less than 45	1,506	6.18	1,585	6.50	2,474	10.14	2,253	10.46	2,426	9.95
45 and over	565	5.49	678	6.59	989	9.61	1,102	10.71	1,053	10.24
Wives										
Less than 45	-1,616	-40.09	-1,733	-42.99	770	19.76	680	16.86	33	0.82
45 and over	-2,752	-52.37	-3,087	-58.74	-960	-18.26	-1,295	-24.64	-1,898	-36.12
Others										
Less than 16	-2,114	-117.12	-2,211	-122.49	-2,807	-155.51	-2,904	-160.88	-2,593	-143.65
16 and over	-2,034	-69.60	-2,217	-75.87	-2,811	-96.19	-2,994	-102.45	-2,641	-90.38

*Consumption of Income allocated in proportion to food needs.

**Using population data from the current Population Reports Series P.20, No. 198.

***Adjustments are deductions from income including commuting costs of head and wife, union dues of head, cost of child care when wife or single head works, and estimated federal income taxes paid by family.

Table 13-12

Aggregate Amounts of Income Given and Received by Age, Sex
and Relation to Head*

Age, Sex, Relation to Head	Amounts Given by Net Givers** (Billion $)	Amounts Received by Net Receivers** (Billion $)	Percent of Group Who Are Givers
Male Heads			
Less than 35	45.372	3.009	84.8
35-54	156.539	1.164	96.5
55-64	33.937	1.244	85.8
65 and over	12.981	1.260	81.0
Female Heads			
Less than 45	11.162	0.696	92.8
45 and over	12.000	1.293	90.9
Wives			
Less than 45	34.813	17.947	62.1
45 and over	13.380	38.019	36.5
Others			
Less than 16	0.002	160.866	.1
16 and over	7.672	110.132	9.5
Total	320.866	328.568	

*Consumption of income allocated in proportion to food needs

**Using population data from the current Population Reports,
Series P. 20, No. 198.

TABLE 13-13

Aggregate Amounts of Income Given and Received by Age,
Sex, and Relation to Head*

Age, Sex, and Relation to Head	Amount Given by Net Givers** Market Wage Rate	Amount Given by Net Givers** Opportunity Wage Rate
Male Heads		
Under 35	45.37	57.85
35-54	156.54	174.07
55-64	33.94	42.05
65 or older	12.98	19.91
Female Heads		
Under 45	11.16	11.99
45 or older	12.00	13.31
Wives		
Under 45	34.81	50.13
45 or older	13.38	19.10
Others		
Under 16	.00	.00
16 or older	7.67	10.10
	320.87	398.51

*Consumption of income allocated in proportion to food needs.

**Using population data from Current Population Reports, Series P. 20, No. 198.

Table 13-14

Opportunity Wage Rates

Female Heads:	Size of largest city in the area: (mostly county)					
	500,000 or more	100,000- 499,999	50,000- 99,999	25,000- 49,999	10,000- 24,999	Under 10,000
Education						
0-11 grades	2.09	1.67				
12 grades through college no degree	2.97			2.20		
College degree	4.09					
Wives:						
Education						
0-12 grades and non-academic training	2.39			2.01		
Some college through college, bachelor's degree	2.90					
College, advanced degree	4.32					

14

"LABOR FORCE PARTICIPATION OF WIVES: THE EFFECTS OF COMPONENTS OF HUSBANDS' INCOME."*

Katherine P. Dickinson, Jonathan G. Dickinson

Studies of the labor force participation of married women have occupied an important position in labor force literature since the 1930's. One of the major areas of interest has been the response of the wife's labor force status to her husband's income and, more importantly, to changes in her husband's income. The main emphasis has been on what is referred to as the added worker effect.[1] This hypothesis states that when the husband's income declines, the family may be reluctant to decrease its standard of living, and the wife may enter the labor force in order to compensate for the loss in the head's income.

---

*The research reported here was performed by the Survey Research Center at the University of Michigan under contract (OEO-4180) from The Office of Economic Opportunity.

[1]The term, "added worker effect" implies a model of wives' labor force behavior in which the head's working behavior is treated as exogenous. A more realistic model would allow for simultaneity in the labor force decisions of heads and wives. While a wife may go to work to offset the effect of her husband's unemployment, a husband might forego extensive overtime if his wife finds a good job. The authors plan further investigation of such a model, but in the current paper we relate our analysis to the simpler, single equation model. In following this model, we join the great majority of previous researchers.

One approach to studying the added worker effect has been to investigate the response of the labor force status of married women to the cyclical fluctuations in the economy. In these studies, attention has focused on the relative importance of the added worker effect, which tends to increase the labor force participation of wives in an economic downturn, and of the discouraged worker effect, which depresses married women's participation because jobs are harder to find in a recession. The results of these studies are often ambiguous because these two factors operate together during a cycle, so that it is very difficult to distinguish their independent effects.

A second approach has been to use cross-section data to study the added worker effect more directly. Instead of investigating the response of the wife's labor force status to the general employment rate, these studies looked specifically at her response to her husband's income. In his article, "Labor Force Participation of Married Women," Jacob Mincer states that, in general, one observes a negative relationship between the income of the head and the labor force participation of the wife. However, he hypothesizes that this observed relationship is not primarily a result of a wife's long-run response to her husband's "permanent" income, but rather the result of a short-run added worker effect.

To test this theory, Mincer regressed the labor force participation of wives on the weeks the head worked during the year and on the income he earned. He interpreted the results as follows:

> Now a decline in weeks, keeping total earnings constant, means a corresponding amount of increase in earning power, which is offset by a transitory loss of income of the same amount. The change in the permanent component of income is expected to bring about a *decrease* in labor force participation. The same change of the transitory component in the opposite direction is expected to stimulate an *increase* in market activities. The direction of the net outcome depends, therefore, on which income effect is stronger. Indeed, the negative sign of $b_{me.x}$ [the slope of regression of labor force rate on weeks worked, keeping earnings of head constant] provides evidence that the effect of the transitory income outweighs the permanent income effect! (Mincer, p. 82)

Subsequent investigators have also dealt with the question of temporary versus permanent added worker effect. Cain found temporary added worker effects which were significant but smaller than the permanent effects. Cohen, Rea and Lerman found a significant effect of the head's unemployment on wives' labor force participation, but the effect became insignificant when they controlled for the level of family income less the wife's earnings. These results tend to weaken Mincer's conclusions, but all of the studies share the difficulties which are inherent in indirect estimation.

It is clearly desirable to obtain more direct estimates of the permanent and transitory components of head's income in order to measure the added worker effect. The separation of these two components of head's income requires repeated observations on the same family units over a period of time. In this investigation of the labor force participation of wives, we make use of recently available data from the first three years of the "Panel Study of Income Dynamics," being conducted by the Survey Research Center at the University of Michigan. The currently available data from the survey include information on income, labor force, and demographic characteristics of families in each of the years, 1967, 1968, and 1969. The sample size is approximately 5,000, with over-sampling among low income families, which is compensated for by weighting the data. Our attention is restricted to families who had a married head under 65 and who had the same head and wife over the three year interviewing period. The sample for this analysis contains 2154 families.

The Model of Labor Force Participation

In order to obtain an unbiased measure of the response of the wife's labor force participation to her husband's income, we must specify an estimation model which accounts for the effects of all the important variables. When a married woman decides whether or not to enter the labor force, she is essentially making a choice among three things: market work, non-market home production, and leisure. If we consider the wife as the marginal worker, her labor force status can then be considered to be a function of four variables: the income of the family from sources other than the wife's market work, her market wage rate, her non-money home production wage rate, and her tastes.

The added worker hypothesis indicates that the family income variable should be divided into a transitory and a permanent component. For most families, the largest source of income other than the wife's market earnings is the earnings of the head. Therefore, although we control for the simple level of income from other sources, we restrict our attention to the earned income of the head in testing for differential effects of permanent and transitory components.

The derivation of permanent and transitory components of the head's earnings from three years' data requires some care. The simplest method would be to consider the head's three year average income as his permanent income and yearly deviations from that average as his transitory income. The problem with this method is that most incomes are rising over time and at different rates for different groups in the population. Thus "normal" income would appear to be transitorily low in the first year and transitorily high in the third, and this bias would be larger for those with greater rates of increase in income.

In order to get around this problem, we could calculate a time trend for each individual and then observe the yearly deviations from his average income plus his time trend. The individual trend, however, would be seriously biased by a large transitory component in the first or third year. This bais would largely obliterate the very transitory component which we wish to measure. The method which we use in this paper to circumvent the above difficulties involves the assignment of an "expected time trend" for each individual. The expected time trend is derived from a multivariate regression[2] of the time rate of change[3] of income for all married heads on occupation, age, race and other demographic characteristics. If we denote the expected time trend of the ith individual by $\hat{b}_i$, our estimate of the permanent component of his income at time t becomes:

1) $Y_{ti}^P = \overline{Y}_i + \hat{b}_i t$; where t = -1, 0, 1.

The transitory component of income is then the deviation of income in a given year from this trend adjusted average:

2) $Y_{ti}^T = Y_{ti} - (\overline{Y}_i + \hat{b}_i t) = Y_{ti} - Y_{ti}^P$.

At this point we should acknowledge the assumptions about an individual's perception of his permanent income and about the relevant "horizons" which are embodied in our method. First, we assume that income experience over three years adequately represents the "long run" for most individuals. If three years is too short a period, our measure of permanent income will be somewhat contaminated by a transitory component. The given measure of transitory income will pick up the major part of a true transitory component of income, however, and the observable relationship to wives' labor force participation should be substantially better than an order of magnitude estimate. The current results will, of course, be subjected to tests as further data become available.

Second, a different model of the way perceptions of permanent income are formed is implied for each of the three years. In the first year, the given measure of permanent income corresponds to that of an individual who bases his perception on the (correct) anticipation of the subsequent two years. The measure in the final year corresponds to the perception based on the past two years. In the middle year, the two are combined. To the extent that anticipations are based on extrapolations of the past and to the extent that they are correct, the models are esentially equivalent. In any case, we analyze each year separately so that any differences can be noted.

It may be that yet a third component of the head's earnings is important in explaining the wife's labor force participation. The Duesenberry relative

---

[2]The algorithm used was Multiple Classification Analysis which yields results equivalent to a dummy variable regression, but is computationally more efficient when the number of categories is large (see Andrews, Morgan, Sonquist).

[3]We estimated a simple linear time trend rather than a rate of growth. The differences for a three year period are minor and the reduction of complexity is substantial.

income hypothesis holds that families with incomes below that of families in their reference group are likely to save less in order to sustain consumption at a level commensurate with that of the other families. Similar reasoning applied to wives' labor force behavior suggests that if a husband's permanent income is low relative to that of his peers, the wife will be likely to enter the labor force, foregoing leisure and home production, in order to raise the family's total money income to the level of the peer group. In order to test this analogue of the "relative income" hypothesis, we separate the permanent income of the head into two components: the level to be expected on the basis of his personal characteristics and local market conditions, and the permanent deviations of his income from that expected level.[4]

We consider the head's expected permanent income to have the same form as his actual permanent income; that is, we use a trend adjusted average. Since the trend we are using for permanent income is an "expected" time trend, we need only develop a new measure for the head's expected average earnings. For this expected average, we take the predicted level from a regression of the head's three year average income based on age, education, occupation, other demographic characteristics, and variables representing local market conditions. The head's expected permanent income than has the form:

$$3) \quad \widehat{Y}_{ti}^{P} = \widehat{\overline{Y}}_{i} + \widehat{b}_{i}t.$$

The residual from the above equation for each individual is identified as his relative deviation from the expected level. Y_i^R then has the form:

$$4) \quad Y_i^R = (\overline{Y}_i + \widehat{b}_i t) - (\widehat{\overline{Y}}_i + \widehat{b}_i t) = \overline{Y}_i - \widehat{\overline{Y}}_i.$$

Clearly then, the individual's expected permanent income and his relative deviation sum to his permanent income in a given year:

$$5) \quad Y_{ti}^{P} = (\overline{Y}_i + \widehat{b}_i t) + (\overline{Y}_i - \overline{Y}_i) = \overline{Y}_i + \widehat{b}_i t.$$

Equations 2 and 5 taken together show that the observed income of the head in each year is the sum of the three components discussed above:

$$6) \quad Y_{ti} = \widehat{Y}_{ti}^{P} + Y_i^R + Y_{ti}^T.$$

---

[4]This procedure bears some similarity to one used by Cain. He separated the head's income in one year into expected level and a residual. The residual was considered to be a measure of transitory income. Our procedure goes a step further and distinguishes enduring personal differences in income from transitory variations about individual norms.

The three components are included in the estimating equation for the determinants of wives' labor force participation, and the acceptance or rejection of the various hypotheses depends on the comparative sizes and confidence intervals of the estimated coefficients. We should note at this point that our testing of the relative income hypothesis does not influence the simultaneous testing of the added worker hypothesis. The combined effect of $\hat{Y}_t^P$ and Y^R equals that of Y_t^P alone; and, since separation of these components is based on variables which are constant over the three years, transitory income is uncorrelated with the components just as it is uncorrelated with the whole of permanent income.

The measurement of the remaining variables in our model is much more straight-forward. We include the income from rent, interest, dividends, and income from the earnings of family members other than the head or wife as measures of the level of family income from other sources. In order to represent the market wage of the wife, we include several variables concerning her personal characteristics (her age, education, and race) as well as variables concerning the market conditions of the area in which she lives (the unemployment rate of the county, the size of the largest city in the county, and the region of the country).[5] As a measure of the wife's wage in home production, we consider the age of the youngest child, the number of children in the family, whether or not the head is disabled,[6] and the number of adults in the family. Tastes are unmeasured, except insofar as education represents a taste for market work. However, if it is safe to assume that tastes are not correlated with the other variables included, this omission should not bias the estimated coefficients. The dependent variable which we use is whether or not the wife was employed during the year in question.[7]

Estimation of the Model

In estimating the model of labor force participation of wives which was described above, we have used the Multiple Classification Analysis (MCA) algorithm as our primary analysis tool. In addition to computational efficiency, this method of estimation has the advantage of allowing for non-linearity in the effects of predictors.

---

[5]The unemployment rate of the county is collected each year by a questionnaire sent to the state unemployment commissions as part of the Panel Study of Income Dynamics.

[6]This is any disability which limits the amount or kind of work he can do.

[7]This is not an exact measure of wives' labor force participation, but it is a close approximation. To the extent that there are wives in the labor force who did not find work at any time during the year, our estimates of the employment rate of wives slightly understate the labor force participation rate. However, our estimates are comparable to those of Mincer and others who used the same dependent variable.

The estimation results for the second year[8] are presented in Table 14-1. The coefficients presented there for each category of a given variable are essentially equivalent to standard regression dummy variable coefficients for those categories.[9] The $\beta2$ statistic is a measure of the importance, or predictive power of a given variable.[10] Table 14-2 presents this statistic for all predictors in each of the three years.

The comparison of β^2 statistics indicates that transitory income is not an important variable in determining whether or not the wife is in the labor force during any of the three years. Out of 15 predictors, transitory income ranks 9th in importance in the first year, 12th in the second year, and 13th in the third year.

The relatively stronger showing of transitory income in the first year may be attributable to an error in our assumptions about the horizon for that year. Our measure of permanent income in that year assumes that the family correctly anticipates the head's income stream over the subsequent three years. To the extent that such foresight is imperfect, our measure of transitory income in that year is likely to be contaminated with what the family perceives to be permanent income.

An F test on the significance of transitory income in year 2, using a simplified model,[11] yields an F statistic of 2.05 which would be significant at a 5% level in a random sample, but which is quite marginal, considering our complex sample and dichotomous dependent variable. The credibility of transitory income as a predictor of wives' labor force participation is further weakened when we note that the coefficients for negative values are predominantly negative. Since most discussions of the added worker effect

---

[8]We have chosen to focus our attention on the middle year because the equation for this year does not contain the term for the estimated time trend. The comparative results for the other years, which are quite similar, are also discussed.

[9]The MCA coefficients represent deviations from the mean of the whole sample, rather than deviations from the mean of those in an excluded category. The adjusted mean can be interpreted as the predicted level of wives' labor force participation with other predictors held constant.

[10]The β^2 is computed as the weighted sum of squares of the coefficients of all the categories of a predictor, divided by the sum of squared deviations of the dependent variable. If the effect is linear, the β^2 is equivalent to the square of the normalized regression coefficient. It overstates the partial R^2 to the extent that predictors are intercorrelated. But in the absence of high negative intercorrelations of predictors, a condition satisfied in the current data, the β^2 provides a very useful measure of the relative importance of predictors.

[11]The weak predictors, number of adults, region, city size, county unemployment rate, taxable income of other than head and wife, and rent interest and dividends were omitted to facilitate repeated runs. The coefficients of the remaining predictors changed only negligibly upon simplification. In the regressions shown in 7a and 7b the variable rent interest and dividends was included as a linear predictor.

have emphasized the wife's response to downturns in the husband's income, we initially expected positive coefficients for this range of values. The anomalous effects in the negative range also account for a substantial portion of the variance explained by transitory income. When a single slope is fitted to transitory income using a conventional regression algorithm with dummies for the remaining predictors of the simplified model,[11] the coefficient is *positive* with a t value of 3.4. When a dummy variable is included for values of transitory income below -$2500, to avoid domination by the cases at the low extreme, the slope becomes negative, but has a t value of only 0.27. The coefficients are show below in equations 7a and 7b.

In contrast with transitory income, the head's expected permanent income, Y^P, and his deviation from it, Y^R, are very important predictors. And, the relationships, though irregular at lower values, have the expected negative slope over a large part of their range. We note, however, that the curves for both permanent income components are very similar in shape, which suggests that the distinction is not necessary. This point is supported by a second MCA run with observed permanent income, Y^P, substituted for its two components. A comparison of the explained variances of the two models yields an F statistic of less than 1.0. Therefore, the decomposition of permanent income into an expected and a residual component does not significantly increase the explanatory power of the model.

The results from the parallel regression mentioned above present the comparative effects in a form more familiar to many readers. Equation 7a shows the effects of transitory income and the two components of permanent income in year 2. The curvilinear effects at the low end of each component have been accounted for with dummy variables to avoid domination of the slope over the rest of the range.[12] The coefficients of demographic dummy variables are consistent with those in Table 14-1 and are not shown.

7a.

$$\text{WLFP2} = -0.0022 Y^T \quad -.15 \text{ (if } Y^T \quad -2500)$$
$$\phantom{\text{WLFP2} = }(.0083) \quad\quad (.07)$$

$$-0.219 \, \hat{Y}^P \quad -.15 \text{ (if } \hat{Y}^P \quad 4500)$$
$$(.0040) \quad\quad (.04)$$

$$-0.163 \, Y^R \quad -.17 \text{ (if } Y^R \quad -6000) \, -.019 \text{ rent interests, etc.}$$
$$(.003) \quad\quad).07) \quad\quad\quad\quad (.009)$$

$$+ \text{ coefficients for demographic variables.}$$

$$\left[\begin{array}{l} \text{Income measures in thousands of dollars} \\ \text{Standard errors in parentheses} \end{array} \right]$$

---

[12] When the dummies are omitted, the permanent income slopes decrease by about 25% in absolute value and the transitory slope becomes significantly positive as mentioned above.

The coefficient of transitory income is not significatnly different from zero. The coefficients of $\hat{Y}^P$ and Y^R are both highly significant, but they are not significantly different from each other.[13] When Y^P is substituted for $\hat{Y}^P$ and Y^R in equation 7b, the coefficient of transitory income is affected only slightly and the coefficient of Y^P is essentially the average of the two component slopes with a slightly tighter confidence interval.

7b.

$$\text{WLFP2} = -.002 \ Y^T \quad -.15 \ (\text{if } Y^T \ -2500)$$
$$\phantom{\text{WLFP2} = } (.0082) \qquad (.07)$$

$$-.0181 \ Y^P \quad -.16 \ (\text{if } Y^P \ 3500) \ -.020 \ \text{rent interest, etc.}$$

$$(.0023) \qquad (.08) \qquad\qquad (.009)$$
$$+ \ \text{coefficients of demographic variables}$$

The estimated slope for permanent income implies an elasticity of -.32 at the mean. The estimated elasticity with respect to transitory income (using the mean of Y^P) is less than one tenth the size and is not significantly different from zero.

Turning to sources of family income other than the earnings of the head and the wife, we note that the MCA results for dividends, interest and rent show an effect which is somewhat irregular, but which is predominantly in the expected direction. The slope coefficient estimated in the standard regression is -.019, which is quite close to that for permanent income. The lower confidence level ($t=2.3$) reflects the instability observed in the MCA results. No consistent effect is apparent in the MCA coefficients for the income of other earners in the family. This income may not be integrated into the family budget, so that the absence of an effect on the wife's labor force behavior is not surprising.

The estimation results pertaining to the wife's market wage are indicative of a strong positive substitution effect. Those variables representing her personal characteristics, age and education, equal or exceed the income variables in predictive strength in all three years. The race variable has a significant effect, but is somewhat lower in predictive power because of the relatively small percentage of nonwhites in the population. The variables representing local market conditions do not appear to have an important effect on whether or not the wife works.

---

[13]The observed small difference in the coefficients might be explained in terms of errors in variables. If transitory income has little or no effect on wives' labor force participation, any transitory contamination of our measure of permanent income will cause the usual errors in variables bias toward lower absolute value of the slope. When Y^P is separated into components, any contamination and associated bias will be concentrated in the residual component Y^R.

The true value of the wife's home production must be known as well as her market wage to explain fully her labor force participation. The demand for a wife's service at home increases with the number of children and declines as the youngest child reaches school age. As expected, wives' labor force participation shows a strong inverse relationship to this implicit home wage. The number of adults was included in our calculations to account for substitutes for the wife's services at home. There is a small effect in the expected direction when one extra adult is present, but for complex families with four or more adults, no simple relationship is apparent. A disabled family head is likely to require more care from a wife, and after controlling on income, we observed a small effect in this direction. The combination of a small effect and small numbers, however, yields a nearly negligible effect in the full sample.

Comparison with Mincer's Results

The results of our study on the relative importance of permanent and transitory components of family heads' income as determinants of wives' labor force participation are clearly contrary to Mincer's findings. If one accepts our results, one must question whether the discrepancies reflect true differences in wives' labor force behavior between 1950 and 1968, or whether Mincer's results for 1950 were, at least in part, an artifact of this method. To investigate this question, we endeavored to replicate Mincer's method with the current data.

The critical variables for Mincer's estimates are the head's labor income and the number of weeks for which the head was paid during the year. The former variable is available directly in the current data, but the latter variable is represented by the head's weeks of unemployment. This differs from the complement of the desired variable by the extent of unpaid sick time for which no measure is available. Barring extreme intercorrelations of variables, however, the estimated coefficient of weeks of unemployment will be of the same sign and of reasonably comparable magnitude to the desired coefficient of total weeks involuntarily lost from work. We also included a variable for total sick time, both paid and unpaid, to see if this would improve the estimate.

For comparable regressions we chose the modal population stratum on which Mincer focuses his discussion. This stratum includes married heads between the ages of 35 and 55 with a high school education, who live in regions other than the South. The estimated equation for 1968 is as follows:

8) $WLFP_2 = .77 - .027 \ Y_2 \quad .0036 \ U_2 \qquad R_2 = .04, \ n - 266$
$\qquad\qquad\quad (.009) \quad (.00088)$

U_2 = weeks of unemployment

Y_2 = head's labor income in 1968.

The positive coefficient on unemployment is consistent with Mincer's negative coefficient on weeks paid for. The coefficient is not significantly different from zero, however, and the inclusion of total sick time in the regression reduces the coefficient of unemployment still further, though it remains positive.

We do not find the strong added worker effect in the current data which Mincer observed in the 1950 data. But, by Mincer's reasoning, even an essentially zero coefficient on time involuntarily out of work, with observed income held constant, implies approximately equal effects of permanent and transitory income.

We did not observe this to be the case in our regressions on the full sample, and it is also not evident for the modal stratum, as indicated by the following simple regression of wife's employment on Y^P and Y^T for that group:

$$9)\ WLFP_2 = .81 - \underset{(.009)}{.031\ Y^P} - \underset{(.025)}{.005\ Y^T} \qquad R_2 - .04.$$

There is obviously a discrepancy between the observed inequality of coefficients of Y^P and Y^T in equation 9 and the equality of effects implied by the near-zero coefficient on weeks unemployed in equation 8. The key to the explanation lies in the fact that unemployment is more strongly correlated with permanent income than with transitory income in the given year. These correlations for the modal stratum in 1968 are as follows:

$$\rho\,U.YP = -.21, \quad \rho\,U.YT = -.17.$$

Apparently, unemployment is a recurring phenomenon for many who experience it, and it is frequently incorporated into long run income expectations.

Our approximation of Mincer's method then, yields a highly biased estimate of the relative strength of the transitory income effect on the level of wives' labor force participation in 1968. Inferences about Mincer's 1950 results must be qualified because the parameters of the model appear to have changed makedly since that time. In duplicating his method, we obtain not only a smaller estimate of the transitory effect, but also of the permanent effect: the elasticity with respect to permanent income is .44 in the current data, as opposed to .61 in 1950 for the modal group.[14] The overall impact of the head's income on the wife's labor force participation was greater in 1950, and it is possible that the transitory effect was stronger then also. A substantial likelihood remains, however, that Mincer's estimates exaggerate the magnitude of this effect.

---

[14]Comparable estimations based on the bivariate regression.

Conclusion

Most of the literature on wives' labor force participation has treated the wife as the marginal or "added" worker and regarded her income as a supplement to family income. Following this line, we have tested a number of hypotheses about the nature of this supplementation.

The temporary added worker hypothesis, developed for the most part by Mincer, views the wife's labor force participation as providing a temporary supplement to family income in response to transitory losses in the head's earnings. Mincer's estimate, using 1950 data, indicates that the effect of a husband's transitory income on a wife's labor force participation is significantly larger than the effect of his permanent income. Our estimates, using a more direct measure of the head's transitory income derived from three years of panel data collected in the late sixties, do not sustain Mincer's results. We find a consistently strong negative relationship between a wife's employment and the level of a husband's permanent income over the three years, but the relationship of a wife's employment to a husband's transitory income is weak in the first year and negligible in the other two.

By investigating the divergence in this results, we have approximated Mincer's indirect estimation of comparative permanent and transitory income effects. The latter method produces an estimate of the transitory income effect which is much closer to Mincer's original estimate. Further investigation reveals, however, that the proxy for transitory income used in the indirect estimation is also highly correlated with permanent income, so that the resultant estimates are biased in favor of a strong transitory effect. We remain confident then, in our finding that the transitory income of husbands is not an important determinant of the level of labor force participation by wives in the current U.S. population.

Our second hypothesis is that the wife is more likely to participate in the labor force to supplement family income if the husband's permanent income is below the level which would be expected on the basis of his demographic characteristics and local market conditions. This hypothesis is not supported by the empirical results. We do not find significant differences between the head's expected permanent income, and deviations from that expected level, in their effects on wives' employment in any of the three years. Further, the separation of permanent income into two components contributes only slightly to the explanatory power of the model of wives' labor force participation.

References

Andrews, Frank, Morgan, James N., and Sonquist, John. *Multiple Classification Analysis.* Ann Arbor: Institute for Social Research, 1967.

Cain, Glen G. *Married Women in the Labor Force.* Chicago: The University of Chicago Press, 1966.

Cohen, Malcolm S., Rea Jr., Samuel A., and Lerman, Robert I. *A Micro Model of the Labor Force.* Bureau of Labor Statistics, Paper No. 4. Washington, D.C.: U.S. Department of Labor, 1970.

_____. "The Effects of Family Conditions on Labor Force Participation: A Micro Study." Paper presented at the winter meetings of the Econometric Society, New York, December, 1969.

Mincer, Jacob. "Labor Force Participation of Married Women," in *Aspects of Labor Economics.* N.B.E.R. Princeton: Princeton University Press, 1962.

Morgan, James, et al. *A Panel Study of Income Dynamics: Study Design, Procedures, Available data 1968-1970 Interviewing Years.* Ann Arbor: Institute for Social Research, 1970.

TABLE 14-1

WHETHER OR NOT THE WIFE WAS EMPLOYED DURING 1968

Overall Percent Employed: 50%

Transitory Income $Y^T = Y_t - (\overline{Y} + \hat{b}t)$

$\beta^2 = .006$

	Coefficient	Adjusted Mean	Number of Cases
< -2000	-.14	.36	48
-2500 - -1500	.05	.55	91
-1499 - -1000	-.05	.45	143
-999 - -500	.02	.52	284
-499 - 0	.02	.52	687
1 - 500	.00	.50	532
501 - 1000	.03	.53	227
1001 - 1500	-.07	.43	125
1501 - 2500	-.06	.44	89
> 2500	.01	.51	68

Permanent Income $\hat{Y}^P = \hat{\overline{Y}} + \hat{b}t$ $\beta^2 = .015$

	Coefficient	Adjusted Mean	Number of Cases
< 3500	-.01	.49	174
3500 - 4500	-.03	.47	169
4501 - 5500	.05	.56	258
5501 - 6500	.04	.54	287
6501 - 7250	.07	.57	247
7251 - 8000	.01	.51	211
8001 - 9000	.05	.55	250
9001 - 10,000	.02	.52	191
10,001 - 12,000	-.02	.48	231
> 12,000	-.12	.38	276

TABLE 14-1 (Sheet 2 of 6)

	Coefficient	Adjusted Mean	Number of Cases
Deviation From Expected Income $\quad$ $Y^R = \hat{\bar{Y}} - \bar{Y}$ $\quad$ $\beta^2 = .020$			
< 6000	-.02	.48	60
-6000 − -3500	.07	.57	216
-3499 − -2000	.07	.57	380
-1999 − -1000	.07	.57	351
-999 − -500	.05	.55	214
-499 − 500	-.01	.49	346
501 − 1500	-.02	.48	256
1501 − 3500	-.09	.41	299
3501 − 6000	-.10	.40	100
> 6000	-.14	.36	72
Taxable Income of Other Than Head or Wife $\quad$ $\beta^2 = .007$			
0	-.01	.48	1776
1 − 249	.08	.58	92
250 − 499	-.09	.41	59
500 − 999	.10	.61	98
1000 − 1999	.08	.58	103
2000 − 3999	-.05	.45	80
4000 − 5999	-.01	.49	48
6000 − 8999	.03	.53	23
9000 − 12,999	.21	.72	11
$\geq$ 13,000	.03	.53	4

TABLE 14-1 (Sheet 3 of 6)

	Coefficient	Adjusted Mean	Number of Cases
Rent; Interest and Dividends of Head $\beta^2 = .007$			
0	.00	.50	1596
1 - 499	.02	.52	432
500 - 999	-.03	.47	105
1000 - 1999	.08	.58	62
2000 - 2999	-.10	.40	32
3000 - 4999	-.15	.35	20
5000 or more	-.18	.37	20
Not ascertained	-	-	26
Wife's Education $\beta^2 = .044$			
0-5 grades	-.16	.34	101
6-8 grades	-.14	.36	345
9 - 11 grades	-.10	.41	501
12, grades, H.S.	.01	.51	677
12 grades plus non-academic training	.11	.61	262
College, no degree	.05	.55	218
B.A.	.26	.76	107
B.A. plus graduate work	.06	.56	54
Wife's Age $\beta^2 = .069$			
< 25	.13	.63	294
25 - 34	.09	.59	600
35 - 44	.05	.55	665
45 - 54	-.08	.42	464
55 - 64	-.24	.26	244
Over 64	-.64	-.13	9
Not ascertained	-	-	18

TABLE 14-1 (Sheet 4 of 6)

	Coefficient	Adjusted Mean	Number of Cases
Race $\beta^2 = .011$			
White	-.02	.48	1617
Black	.18	.68	606
Mexican, Puerto Rican	.02	.52	52
Other	-.03	.47	19
County Unemployment $\beta^2 = .004$			
< 2%	-.02	.48	91
2% - 3.9%	.02	.52	1241
4% - 5.9%	-.02	.48	594
6% - 10%	-.03	.47	150
Over 10%	-.38	.11	4
Not ascertained	-	-	214
Size of Largest City in the County $\beta^2 = .007$			
Largest city $\geq$ 500,000	-.04	.46	812
100,000 - 499,999	.04	.54	469
50,000 - 99,999	-.06	.44	250
25,000 - 49,999	.04	.54	119
10,000 - 24,999	.06	.56	227
Under 10,000	.02	.52	417
Region $\beta^2 = .007$			
Northeast	-.03	.47	417
North Central	-.03	.47	565
South	.01	.51	967
West	.08	.58	345

TABLE 14-1 (Sheet 5 of 6)

	Coefficient	Adjusted Mean	Number of Cases
Age of Youngest Child in Family $\beta^2 = .032$			
No children	.05	.55	622
Under 2	-.12	.38	311
Two	-.16	.34	172
Three	-.11	.39	174
Four	-.08	.42	138
Five	-.04	.46	113
6 through 8	-.01	.50	279
9 through 13	.11	.61	297
14 through 17	.10	.60	187
Number of Children $\beta^2 = .026$			
None	.10	.60	578
One	.01	.51	418
Two	-.04	.46	449
Three	-.06	.44	337
Four	-.08	.42	194
Five	-.11	.39	136
Six	-.13	.37	92
7 - 9	-.12	.38	90
Number of Adults $\beta^2 = .004$			
Two	.00	.50	1779
Three	.04	.54	334
Four	-.05	.45	119
Five	.16	.66	33
Six	-.30	.19	11
Seven	-.38	.12	3
Not ascertained	-	-	15

TABLE 14-1 (Sheet 6 of 6)

	Coefficient	Adjusted Mean	Number of Cases
Disability of the Head $\beta^2 = .001$			
Head disabled	.03	.53	1878
Head not disabled	-.01	.49	416

Unadjusted $R^2 = .19$
Adjusted $R^2 = .15$

TABLE 14-2

WHETHER OR NOT WIFE WAS EMPLOYED IN 1967, 1968 and 1969

	B^2 for 1967	B^2 for 1968	B^2 for 1969
1) Transitory Income $Y_t - (\overline{Y} + \hat{b}t)$	.007	.006	.002
2) Permanent Income $\hat{\overline{Y}} + \hat{b}t$	.021	.015	.011
3) Deviation from Expected Income $\overline{Y} - \hat{\overline{Y}}$	.030	.020	.029
4) Taxable Income of Other Than Head or Wife	.006	.007	.007
5) Rent, Interest, Dividends of Head	.012	.007	.004
6) Wife's Education	.054	.044	.026
7) Wife's Age	.036	.069	.068
8) Race	.020	.011	.011
9) County Unemployment Rate	.005	.004	.008
10) Size of Largest City in the County	.005	.007	.003
11) Region	.006	.007	.009
12) Age of Youngest Child	.043	.032	.025
13) Number of Children	.027	.026	.033
14) Number of Adults	.003	.004	.002
15) Disability of the Head	.003	.001	.001

	1967	1968	1969
Unadjusted R^2	.21	.19	.17
Adjusted R^2	.17	.15	.13

15

"INDEX CONSTRUCTION: AN APPRAISAL OF THE INDEX OF CONSUMER SENTIMENT."

Richard T. Curtin

A focal point of the series of household surveys conducted by the Survey Research Center has been the analysis of discretionary consumer expenditures. To systematize and summarize the presentation of the collected data relevant to an understanding and prediction of changes in discretionary expenditures, the Index of Consumer Sentiment (ICS) was formulated. The construction of the ICS was guided by two major criteria: the constructed index should reflect in a systematic fashion the underlying behavior model, and it should provide an adequate summary measure for the analysis of aggregate fluctuations in consumer durable spending. As is the case with any constructed index, the ICS possesses both analytical advantages and limitations when it is incorporated into analysis models. The limitations result mainly from the fact that the quarterly surveys on changes in consumer attitudes yield much more information than what is summarized in the ICS; this additional information is sometimes crucial to an understanding of the behavioral implications of the quarterly movements in the ICS. Careful attention must also be paid to the behavioral model underlying the construction of the ICS to ensure that it is consistent with any analysis framework into which the ICS is incorporated for the explanation and/or prediction of consumer durable spending.

The analytical advantages of using the ICS stem mainly from its efficiency in providing a summary measure of consumer sentiment with respect to discretionary expenditures. The efficiency of an index to a large extent depends upon the weighting criterion and the functional form which is used to consolidate the available information from component questions. The major concern of this paper is to assess the ICS in terms of its efficiency in summarizing the available information from its five component questions. Factor analysis, a psychometric technique for index construction, is employed for this purpose. By using this technique, the variables contributing to a factor (i.e., the composite variable or index) emerge as the result of the underlying pattern of relationships among the observed variables (i.e., the component questions). In addition, the weights to be assigned are determined on the basis of the factor structure of the variables.

The ICS is based on the responses to five questions which relate to how people feel about their personal financial situation, business conditions, and the market conditions for major durables (see Table 15-1 for a listing of these questions and the notation employed to identify the individual questions). The index is constructed as follows:

$$ICS = \sum_{i=1}^{5} X_i(100) + 100,$$

where X_i equals the proportion of respondents giving favorable responses minus those giving unfavorable responses to each of the five questions. As indicated in the above formulation, each question is given equal weight in the construction of the ICS.

A constructed index of consumer sentiment should be unidimensional. That is, the observed inter-correlations among the component parts of the index should in principle be adequately represented in one dimensional space. Multi-dimensional indices (especially when the dimensions approach orthogonality) only add confusing "noise" to an analysis framework. This criterion reflects in part the nature of the data analyzed. Since the desired measurement is a syndrome of attitudes, consumer sentiment, no single question may adequately tap such an attitudinal complex. In such circumstances, the investigator usually chooses a set of questions which relate to the various aspects of the desired syndrome. If the chosen set of survey items forms a multi-dimensional index, movements in the individual components will not necessarily imply a direct and systematic relationship to changes in the desired measure of consumer sentiment.

For example, suppose a constructed index is two dimensional and may be represented by the general form

$$I = f(D_1, D_2),$$

where I equals the realized value of the consumer sentiment measure; D_1

TABLE 15-1

QUESTIONS COMPOSING THE INDEX OF CONSUMER SENTIMENT

B/W AGO: We are interested in how people are getting along financially these days. Would you say that you and your family are <u>better off</u> or <u>worse off</u> financially than you were a year ago?

B/W YR: Now looking ahead, do you think that <u>a year from now</u> you people will be <u>better off</u> financially, or <u>worse off</u>, or just about the same as now?

G/B 12 MO: Now turning to business conditions in the country as a whole, do you think that during the next 12 months we'll have <u>good</u> times financially, or <u>bad</u> times, or what?

G/B 5 YR: Looking ahead, which would you say is more likely: that in the country as a whole we'll have continuous good times <u>during the next five years</u> or so, or that we will have periods of widespread unemployment or depression, or what?

G/B HH: Now about the big things people buy for their homes, such as furniture, refrigerator, stove, television, and things like that. Generally speaking, do you think now is a good or a bad time for people to buy major household items?

FIGURE 15-1

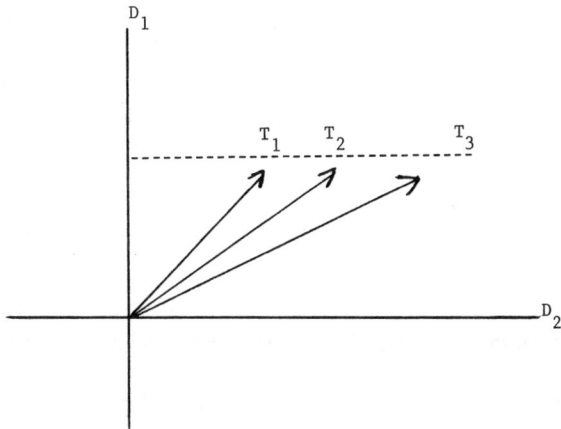

represents the desired (true) dimension of consumer sentiment; D_2 represents another dimension which the set of questions employed inadvertently measure and is not of direct interest nor related to the behavior under study. Additionally, let us assume for the sake of simplicity, that these dimensions are orthogonal and that the calculated measure of sentiment corresponds to the length of the vector from the origin to the observed data point. This situation is illustrated in Figure 15-1 in which the points T_1 - T_3 respresent data observations from three consecutive quarters. An inspection of this diagram reveals that the calculated measure of consumer sentiment increases over time while the desired measure of consumer sentiment, as represented by D_1, has shown no movement during these three quarters. In the context of the ICS, this may imply that if one item or some subset of the items either partially or effectively measures an extraneous dimension (i.e., D_2), the computed measure of sentiment will reflect variations which may not be systematically related to changes in the desired dimension of consumer sentiment.

The factor analytic procedure was employed to analyze the dimensionality of the ICS, and to examine the structuring of the variables in terms of the number of significant dimensions represented by the observed data points.[1] The factor model may be written, for the *common-factor portion alone,* as:

$$Z = AF.$$

The notation used is defined in Table 15-2.

In essence, the use of this technique is based on the assumption that the observed correlations among the five index questions mainly result from some underlying regularity in the data. The observed correlations are assumed to result from the variables sharing the same common determinant: consumer sentiment. The extent of these interrelationships can be seen by an examination of the correlation matrix for the five index questions:

B/W AGO	1.000				
B/W YR	0.656	1.000			
G/B 12 MO	0.638	0.753	1.000		
G/B 5 YR	0.569	0.665	0.903	1.000	
G/B HH	0.674	0.741	0.711	0.563	1.000

Note: Quarters covered are from 1954 through 1971:4.

---

[1] On this and other points concerning factor analysis, see Harman. In the following analysis, each sentiment variable's value for each quarter is defined as the proportion giving favorable responses minus those giving unfavorable responses (i.e., the x's). The quarters covered are from 1954 through 1971:4. Within this time span there are 15 missing observations on the ICS and its components out of a total of 72. Linear interpolation was used to estimate these missing data points.

TABLE 15-2

NOTATION USED IN FACTOR MODELS

R = Matrix of observed correlations among the five sentiment variables.

Z = Matrix of measurements on each of the sentiment variables in standardized form.

z = Column vector of the sentiment variables.

F = Matrix of measurements on each of the factors.

A = Matrix of the common factor coefficients ("factor loadings").

TABLE 15-3
COMMON FACTOR SOLUTION OF FIVE SENTIMENT QUESTIONS

Variables	Common Factor	Communality
B/W AGO	.736	.542
B/W YR	.843	.711
G/B 12 MO	.935	.874
G/B 5 YR	.853	.728
G/B HH	.801	.642
Contribution of Factor	3.50	
Percent of Total Common Variance	96.3%	

The total observed variance in the set of sentiment questions is seen as being decomposable into that variance which is "common" and into that which is "unique" for each variable in the set. Essentially these assumptions involve replacing the units in the diagonal of the observed correlation matrix with communalities for each variable. The communalities represent the proportion of common factor variance for each of the five questions. Thus, this procedure omits the unique and error contributions of their variance from the analysis model.

As an initial approximation for the communalities, the squared multiple correlation of each variable with the remaining four sentiment variables was used. The Kaiser criterion (the number of factors whose eigenvalue is greater than one) was used to determine the number of dimensions. The results of the analysis are shown in Table 15-3. Clearly, the five component questions of the ICS may be seen to form a one dimensional index: one dimension accounts for 96% of the common variance.

Up to this point, the analytic procedures employed have been mainly concerned with obtaining the linear resolution of the set of index questions in terms of a hypothetical factor: consumer sentiment. A description of the factor in terms of the observed variables is a relatively straightforward procedure. Conventional regression methods were employed to obtain estimates of the factor measurements. The estimate of the factor can be expressed as follows:

$$\overline{F} = S^1 \; R^{-1} \; Z$$

$$= A^1 \; R^{-1} \; Z$$

since the factor structure (S) and pattern (A) coincide. A measure of the accuracy of estimating a factor by means of the above equation is given by its coefficient of multiple correlation. The estimated consumer sentiment factor achieved a value of .97 for this coefficient.

A measure of the efficiency of the weighting criterion used to construct the ICS may be gained from a comparison of the ICS and the index based on the consumer sentiment factor. The major difference between these two procedures for constructing an index involves the weights attached to the individual component questions; each method assumes a linear additive model. The ICS gives equal weight to all component questions while the index based on the factor solution employs differential weighting based on the common factor structure. An examination of the time profile of these indexes showed them to be virtually identical. The serial correlation between these two indexes was .989 over a period covering the quarters 1954:1 - 1971:4. In view of this high correlation, Ockham's principle clearly suggests a preference for the relatively straightforward approach used currently in the construction of the Index of Consumer Sentiment over the more theoretically and statistically encumbered approach of factor analysis. (With the addition of each new data observation, the correlation matrix would need to be re-factored and a new index series developed.)

A significant aspect of the factorial solution is that it provides an estimate of the importance of each question for the determination of the common factor and its variance. Each of the five observed sentiment variables were described linearly in terms of a common factor (which accounts for the correlations among the variables) and a unique factor (accounting for the remaining variance, including error, of each variable). The variance of each variable may be expressed as:

$$S_j^2 = 1 = a_j^2 + u_j^2,$$

where a_j^2 is the communality and u_j^2 represents the unique variance of each variable. The data presented in Table 15-3 shows the communalities of the sentiment variables ranged from a high of .874 (G/B 12 MO) to a low of .542 (B/W AGO). These results indicate that expectations concerning business conditions during the next 12 months are most central to the sentiment factor, while only slightly over half of the variance of the measure associated with one's evaluations of past financial changes contributes to this factor.

The communalities may also be taken as a measure of the efficiency of the index in summarizing the available information from each question. A communality of unity is taken as being fully efficient (i.e., the inclusion of 100 percent of the variance of a variable in the common factor). Conversely, the more variance included in each unique factor, which is orthogonal to the common factor, and therefore provides additional independent information, the less efficient is the index in summarizing that measure. Based on this criteria, the index must be considered highly efficient: fully 70 percent of the total observed variance in the set of sentiment questions is accounted for by the common factor. Unique factors account for more than 30 percent of the variance of only two measures: B/W AGO, 45.8 percent; G/B HH, 35.8 percent.

In the Index of Consumer Sentiment the value of each sentiment variable is defined as the proportion giving favorable responses minus those giving unfavorable responses. This definition implicity assumes that equal proportions in each of these categories exactly offset each other in their impact on consumer sentiment, and, consequently, on aggregate measures of purchasing dispositions. A determination of whether or not the structuring of positive and negative effect fundamentally differs within the set of index questions would provide, to a large extent, a test for the truth of this assumption. The question is, would a consideration of positive responses alone, or of negative responses alone, to each of the five index questions, yield essentially similar structural results? In Table 15-4, the variables were defined as the proportion of respondents giving favorable responses; in Table 15-5, the variables represent the proportion giving unfavorable responses. The sample period used for this analysis was from 1954 - 1971:4. A comparison of these structures with that presented in Table 15-3 shows essentially similar structures, regardless of whether one considers the favorable or unfavorable responses separately or whether the analysis is case in terms of the difference between these responses. This conclusion is further substantiated by a comparison of the time profiles of the various indices which may be constructed from these factor structures, i.e., indices based on: the favorable responses only; unfavorable responses only; the difference between favorable and unfavorable responses. Presented below are the correlations among these indices and the ICS for the time period 1954 - 1971:4.

ICS	1.000			
Favorable Responses Only	0.957	1.000		
Unfavorable Responses Only	-0.945	-0.844	1.000	
Difference Between Responses	0.990	0.956	-0.960	1.000

It should be carefully noted that the analysis in this paper is simply descriptive of the observed measures and their correlations. An examination of the predictive value of the sentiment syndrome is not within the scope of this paper. It suffices to say that predictive ability is dependent upon the correspondence between the common factor extracted and the behavioral response under investigation. Unique variance is explicitly discounted. Predictive ability would reach a maximum if the factors accounting for unique variance were uncorrelated with the dependent variable. Positive correlation would indicate that some of the additional independent information incorporated in these measures would provide for increased explanatory power over that of the common factor alone.

References

Harman, H.H. *Modern Factor Analysis*, 2nd Edition. Chicago: The University of Chicago Press, 1967.

TABLE 15-4

COMMON FACTOR SOLUTION FOR FAVORABLE RESPONSES
TO FIVE SENTIMENT QUESTIONS

Variables	Common Factor
B:AGO	.646
B:YR	.762
G:12 MO	.863
G:5 YR	.824
G:HH	.794
Contribution of Factor	3.05
Percent of Total Common Variance	97.5%

TABLE 15-5

COMMON FACTOR SOLUTION FOR UNFAVORABLE RESPONSES
TO FIVE SENTIMENT QUESTIONS

Variables	Common Factor
W:AGO	.713
W:YR	.796
B:12 MO	.974
B:5YR	.861
B:HH	.729
Contribution of Factor	3.36
Percent of Total Common Variance	90.9%

16

"THE FUNCTION OF CONSUMER ATTITUDE DATA BEYOND ECONOMETRIC FORECASTS."

Burkhard Strumpel, Jay Schmiedeskamp, M. Susan Schwartz

Surveys of consumer attitudes have been firmly established as indispensable tools for forecasting changes in aggregate consumer spending and saving. These attitude surveys, which were first developed and implemented on a regular basis in the United States, have spread far beyond their country of origin. They have proselytized forecasters in many countries of the world. Remaining doubts about the usefulness of attitude surveys certainly cannot be attributed to any failure of the approach to produce a wealth of knowledge which is highly relevant to the understanding and prediction of important changes in mass consumer behavior. It is the dissemination of this knowledge which lags behind.

Therefore, it is not the objective of this paper to try to prove once again the statistical significance of attitudinal measures within econometric models of aggregate consumer spending. Instead, the focus is entirely upon the central objective of consumer attitude surveys: to achieve a greater understanding of *why* consumer attitudes change and *how* those changes influence consumer spending and saving behavior under various circumstances.

Section I of this paper discusses the theoretical model according to which unfolding events effect changes in consumer attitudes and expectations, and

*Paper presented to the Conference of CIRET (International Contact on Business Tendency Surveys) Brussels, September 1971. The authors gratefully acknowledge valuable advice from George Katona and Lutz Erbring.

consequent changes in consumer behavior. Section II focuses on the *source* of changes in consumer attitudes by analyzing the impact of various types of favorable and unfavorable news on different subgroups of consumers.

Section III deals with the usefulness of attitudinal data in making "conditional" forecasts of the probable change in consumer behavior if policy interventions or other "exogenous" events take place. Finally, Section IV considers the potential of consumer sentiment measures for analyzing changes in the savings rate (both long and short term), international differences in consumer behavior, and the impact of political attitudes on consumers.

I.

It is a basic principle of psychological economics that consumers' discretionary spending behavior is a function of both their "ability to buy" and "willingness to buy." (Katona, 1951) The precise meaning of these terms is frequently misunderstood.

The "ability" to buy does *not* mean the "capability" to buy. The fact is that at any time, the great majority of consumers in an affluent society have the capability to make a substantial purchase, either out of liquid assets or by incurring installment debt. This remains true for most families in times of recession as well as prosperity. In the context of psychological economics, a change in the "ability to buy" refers to a change in an economic variable which might ordinarily be expected to cause a change in spending behavior unless something else happens which causes consumers to react in a different manner. For example, if a change occurs so that many people have higher disposable incomes, they are likely, on the average, to spend some of the extra money, *all other things being equal.*

But all other things are *not* equal. There are times when consumers are much more willing than they are at other times to spend for discretionary items or to incur installment debt. This "willingness to buy" is a function of consumers' attitudes and expectations concerning (among other things) their personal financial situation, the trend of business conditions, and buying conditions for major consumer goods. The important points are that (a) these attitudes are subject to change under the impact of a continual flow of a variety of events, information, and personal experiences which affect the mass of consumers and (b) these attitudes can be measured by means of consumer surveys.

The process by which a news event (either economic or non-economic may cause a change in aggregate spending or saving behavior is represented through the following stimulus—➤intervening variable—➤response paradigm:

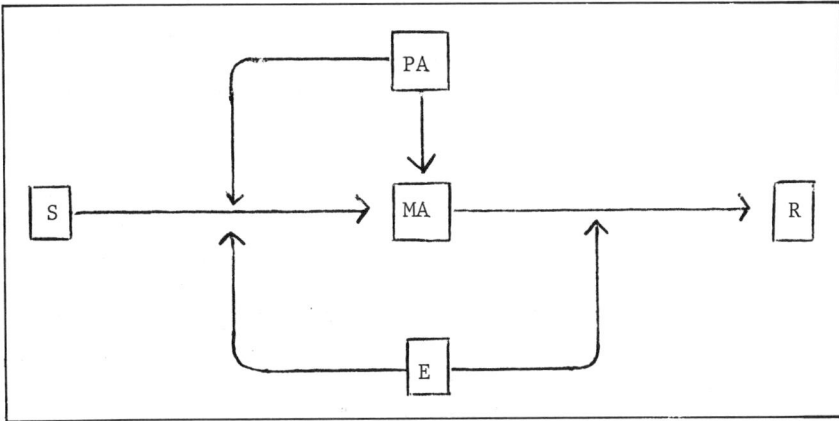

S   = Stimulus (new event, information, personal experience)
PA = Prior Attitudes (the previously existing set of attitudes, expectations, habits, motives, and beliefs held by consumers)
E   = Environment (the circumstantial situation in which consumers operate at the moment, e.g., the state of the business cycle, market supply conditions, credit availability, employment possibilities, etc.)
MA = Modified Attitudes (the set of attitudes, expectations, etc., as they are *changed* under the impact of the perceived stimulus)
R   = Response (change in spending or saving behavior, incurrence of debt)

How a given stimulus is perceived by consumers depends upon the environment within which it occurs and also upon how the stimulus may relate to the set of attitudes, expectations, habits, motives and beliefs which the consumers already hold. The stimulus (as perceived) will interact with the previously existing set of attitudes to form a modified set of attitudes. Consumers' response to the stimulus will then be determined by the modified set of attitudes and by the environment in which the stimulus occurs.

This way of looking at the world is useful because it suggests a number of questions which are important to ask when assessing the likely impact of an event on consumer sentiment, and therefore on spending and saving behavior:

1. To what extent are consumers aware of the event? Certainly, if consumers are not generally aware of a change, it can have little impact on their attitudes and expectations. This seems to have been the case, for example, with the elimination of the federal income tax surcharge in the U.S. in 1970.
2. Do consumers understand what has happened and does it make sense to them? If consumers do not have the ability or knowledge to comprehend the implications of an event, or if it makes little sense in the con-

text of what they know, the event is likely to have little effect. This may have been the case, for example, when Kennedy first proposed a tax cut in 1962 at a time when the federal budget was in deficit and when Kennedy was saying that the government needed to increase spending in order to solve numerous problems.

3. How does the event relate to already existing consumer attitudes: does it reinforce them or does it cause dissonance? For example, favorable news about an improvement in a single industry will have little impact if it is widely believed that conditions in other industries remain unfavorable.

4. Is the event a matter of important concern to many people? For example, not many people are greatly concerned when they read of a change in the prime interest rate; in contrast, news of a tighter home mortgage market arouses great concern.

5. What sort of expectations for the future are engendered by the event? For example, if incomes rise, do people believe that the increase will be followed by further increases?

Survey of consumer attitudes are in a unique position to answer these kinds of questions, not only for individual consumers, but also for the mass of the population. For the purposes of economic forecasting and macroeconomic analysis, it is attitude change and behavior change among the *mass* of consumers which is relevant. In a representative sample of consumers, the distribution of individual changes is equivalent to the change among the total population of consumers. In this sense, the S→O→R paradigm outlined above is as valid for the mass of consumers as it is for individuals.

The most important consideration is that surveys make it possible to assess the *net* impact of a stream of different kinds of events which occur during a given period of time; some of these events have a favorable effect, and some have an unfavorable effect on consumer attitudes and expectations. Furthermore, because the surveys include many open-ended questions in order to discover *why* consumers hold the attitudes and expectations they do, information is provided concerning the likely effect of future events, such as changes in government economic policy, the imposition of wage-price controls, or the end of a war. It is possible, therefore, to use data on consumer attitudes to formuluate "conditional forecasts" of changes in both attitudes and behavior.

In summary, the way in which consumers may respond to changes in economic variables (e.g., income or taxes) is heavily dependent upon the circumstances under which the changes occur and upon how consumers perceive the changes. Much of the rest of this paper is devoted to a discussion of these important considerations.

II.

For many years, the Survey Research Center has devoted a great deal of attention in its reports to the reasons *why* consumer attitudes and expectations have changed. The sources of attitude formation have been studied in two ways: first, by asking many open-ended questions which respondents answer in their own words, in order to discover which factors may have the most salient influence on attitudes at various times; and second, by cross-tabulating data on consumer attitudes with expectations about unemployment, inflation, interest rates, and other issues.

And yet, in contrast to the many econometric analyses which are concerned with the relationship between changes in consumer sentiment and changes in aggregate consumer spending behavior (Hymans, 1970; Katona, 1971; Maynes; Mueller; Shapiro and Angevine; Strumpel, Novy and Schwartz) (MA and R in the previous paradigm), there have been only a few attempts to explore quantitatively the sources of attitude change (S and MA), and all of these have focused on an attempt to find a few economic variables (for example, the unemployment rate and stock prices) which can serve as a proxy for measures of consumer sentiment (Adams and Green; Shapiro; Hymans, 1970; Katona, 1960, Chapter 5). Because of the great diversity of factors which cause changes in attitudes under various circumstances, there efforts have met with only very qualified success, especially at times when attitudes have undergone significant change.

An understanding of the sources of attitude formation involves more than a substantial theoretical interest. An increased knowledge of how various kinds of political and social events or changes in economic variables may affect consumer sentiment could result in forecasts with a longer time horizon, or in "conditional" forecasts of consumer sentiment and behavior. The following analysis studies the statistical relationships between the perception of political or economic news and attitude change in the United States during the period 1967-1971. This period includes an initial phase of favorable sentiment and another of substantially deteriorating sentiment with a slight recovery at the end.

For fifteen years, the Survey Research Center in most of its regular quarterly surveys has asked the following question: "During the last few months, have you heard of any favorable or unfavorable changes in business conditions?" This question is of a sufficiently general and exploratory nature to elicit a broad range of information on the kinds of news which link events with changes in some important consumer attitudes. Chart 16-1 exhibits the long-term trend in this question after the answers are grouped into two categories: favorable and unfavorable news. The proportion of answers is cyclically highly volatile. Major turning points in sentiment coincide with changes in the frequency of mention of unfavorable news heard.

The perception of the economic situation, like that of politics generally, seems to conform to Murry Edelman's thesis that in modern societies the ordinary citizen's relationship to public events is governed essentially by the interplay of subjective perceptions of threat and reassurance. Threat, we might add, is more likely to be perceived than reassurance. The worse the situation, the more central the economic environment becomes in people's life space. When unemployment or inflation is rising, larger portions of the public are recruited to attention; for example, reports of unfavorable news were given by many respondents in 1970.

Since early 1966, there has been a distinct increase in underlying, not just cyclically anchored, feelings of insecurity and pessimism. As Chart 16-1 shows, pessimistic expectations for business conditions over the long term (five years) deteriorated to an extent unprecedented during the last twenty-five years.

A change in economic sentiment is the product of news developments in various spheres: the economy, the society, the world. People tend to entertain a holistic view of their environment and future. Good news in one area spills over to perception in other areas, in a "generalization of affect" (Katona, 1964, Chapter 17). The end of World War II, rather than triggering a fear of unemployment caused by returning soldiers and cutbacks in the defense budget, stimulated consumer optimism, and not just patriotic satisfaction. It is not surprising, then, to find that news about "business conditions" includes frequent references to war, international tensions, civil disorder, presidential elections, the drug scene, crimes, pollution, etc. Naturally, classical business problems such as unemployment are mentioned most frequently.[1]

Five categories were formed:[2] references to prices and inflation; to employment and business conditions; to domestic political news (including references to civil disorder, crime, polution, etc.); to international news (including war); and finally to events related to the respondent's personal experience and not transmitted through the mass media, such as a relative losing a job, the availability of overtime in respondent's place of work, etc. ("prime sources"). Chart 16-2 exhibits the level and changes in the frequency of perception of particular types of favorable or unfavorable news, as well as a plot

---

[1] Even though the question about "business conditions" elicits a wide variety of different types of news, it should be kept in mind that the answers to this question do not fully reflect the impact of those types of news (e.g., inflation) which are more closely related to other important aspects of sentiment, for example, the personal financial situation or market conditions.

[2] News items which were mentioned in response to the previously quoted question or to the question, "Now turning to business conditions in the country as a whole - do you think that during the next twelve months we'll have good times financially, or bad times, or what? Why do you think that?" were combined to form the categories.

of the Index of Consumer Sentiment.

The frequency of perceptions of unfavorable news surged violently starting early in 1969. Concern with inflation started to move first, responding to the rapid rise in the Consumer Price Index. During 1969, favorable news of employment or business conditions became less frequent, while unfavorable reports of personal experiences became more frequent. Full-fledged recession psychology literally "broke out" between the fourth quarter 1969 and the first quarter 1970, when the proportion of people who had heard bad news about employment conditions jumped from 10 to 40 percent. The perception of favorable or unfavorable domestic and international news changed much less, both absolutely and relatively.

If, as we hypothesized in the first section of this paper, attitide formation is dependent not only upon the news itself, but also upon the situation in which it unfolds and upon how individuals may perceive it, a disaggregation of the population is required for understanding sources of consumer attitude formation. Different people react differently to the same news. We might expect people with lower educational backgrounds to be less intensively confronted by the printed mass media, to experience less news perception generally, and to be less articulate in voicing their perceptions. We might expect people in the blue-collar strata, those who are potentially most affected by unemployment, reduction in overtime, and an opportunity for second jobs, to be more sensitive to employment threats, particularly those which are transmitted through non-media experience.

Table 16-1 shows that news is in fact, reported with greater frequency by college educated, white-collar, and high income persons. Predictably, the difference in frequency of perception is most pronounced along educational lines (college/non-college). The difference tends to increase in times of high overall saliency. As measured by the frequency of reported news, higher status groups are more responsive to the changing news climate. Favorable news appears to penetrate least to low-status groups, a phenomenon which may provide for a lag in their psychological and behavioral response to signs of an impending upturn in the economy. If we look at the differences in the kinds of news which are referred to by different status groups, the relatively more intensive concern with employment (including prime sources) of lower status subgroups is conspicuous.

Compared with the differences which are attributable to economic and social status, the differences associated with age are small. It is hardly surprising that younger people are more likely to be susceptible to favorable news; they are also more responsive to international news (Vietnam).

We come now to the main topic of this section: the relationship of the type of news which is heard, to sentiment. Which economic trends or news perceptions have had a strong influence on consumers' psychological stance, and how do theoretical specifications describing these relationships differ among subgroups of the population?

Chart 16-2 and Table 16-1 show the importance of the employment issue during the 4-year period, not only in terms of frequency of mention, but also in terms of correlating with the index. The statistical results which are represented in Table 16-2, as well as the regressions which are contained in the Appendix, add further substance to our conclusion. The Index of Consumer Sentiment is highly correlated with unfavorable news about employment (Table 16-2). References to other types of news do not correlate as well with the sentiment index, but the mulitple regression formulations presented in the Appendix indicate that they do constitute an important factor in sentiment formation.[3]

Are more easily accessible statistical data, for example, on actual unemployment or inflation, a meaningful substitute for reported news in explaining changes in consumer sentiment? The survey question on news heard measures for the analyst not only the saliency of a particular event, but also the respondent's evaluation of its effect: was it favorable or unfavorable? The data in Table 16-2 and in the Appendix suggest that the recall or perception of events, rather than the events themselves, better reflect the influence of environmental changes on consumer sentiment. In addition, of course, statistical data comparable to "primary sources," the international situation, or domestic political policy are not available. These data demonstrate the need for an analysis of the relation between events and consumers' perception of news.

The Appendix contains separate sets of equations for various status subgroups.[4] The following conclusion emerges: the significant correlation between employment news and sentiment is repeated for each of the subclasses studies. However, for low-status subgroups, reported unfavorable news from prime sources is also highly correlated with the sentiment index.

----

[3]A stepwise regression search procedure was employed. The program operates as follows. The variable explaining the greatest proportion of the variance is selected for the first step. At each succeeding step, the program searches among the remaining variables for the one which adds the most to the explanatory power of the model, that is, results in the greatest reduction in error variance. It continues the process until the unexplained variance cannot be reduced within some prespecified confidence limit. The independent variables are ordered in the multiple regressions which are presented in the Appendix according to the step in which they entered the explanatory function. All five categories of news items were included as potential explanatory variables: one variable measured the proportion of respondents mentioning favorable news in the category; another measured the proportion reporting unfavorable news. However, unfavorable news of employment or business conditions was excluded on two grounds. First, the multicollinearity problem is substantially increased by its inclusion, and second, the strong bivariate relationship tends to preclude the identification of the importance of other effects.

[4]Data for the occupational and educational subgroups were not available for the first four quarters of the analysis period, so that the analysis for these groups was carried out on a reduced number of observations.

For these persons, the unfortunate experiences of one's contemporaries or one's self, which represent a threat to the status quo, are a critical determinant of sentiment changes. However, reassurance from favorable prime source news is less significant.

These data suggest that certain strata can be reached to only a marginal degree by economic news transmitted through the media. "Moral suasion" and "talking up the economy" may not be too promising a strategy for a substantial proportion of people who are accustomed to believe what they see and hear from others.[5]

Non-economic news, although it plays a secondary role to news of economic conditions, bears an important relationship to attitudes among high-status persons. The inclusion of perceived news of domestic political events and the international situation adds as much as twenty-four percent to the correlation with sentiment.

The previous analysis was concerned essentially with the relation between reported news and consumers' short-run attitudes toward business conditions. It is useful also to investigate how reported news relates to long-run expectations. Responses to the question "Looking ahead, which would you say is more likely—that in the country as a whole we'll have continuous good times during the next five years or so, or that we will have periods of widespread unemployment or depression or what?" during the last five years have exhibited a consistent and enduring deterioration of great potential significance (see Section IV of this paper). Respondents' answers to the question are coded as "good times" (optimistic expectations), an intermediate point ("some good, some bad"), "bad times" (pessimistic expectations), or uncertainty. These responses should not be taken as *bona fide* forecasts by respondents of what may actually happen to business conditions over a five-year period. Few people look that far ahead. Rather, this question provides a general measure of underlying optimism or pessimism, of faith that everything will work out all right in the long run. Therefore, it is reasonable to argue that some items of news which are thought to have only short-term effects might have little influence on people's long-run outlook. Instead, it might be presumed that the five-year question would be related to the general tenor of news in the recent past.

A number of different formulations were tested, among them the relationship of long-run expectations to news reported measured in the same quarter, lagged one quarter, and averaged over two quarters. The best relationship was found between the dependent variable and news perceptions which were averaged over the current and preceding quarter. Table 16-3 is a comparison of six-month average news and current news; the average variable shows at

---

[5]A very similar conclusion emerges from the research report by INFAS, p. 45.

least as strong a relationship as the concurrent measure for all news categories.

An interesting finding is the strong correlation between the long-run expectations and unfavorable primary sources of news. This relationship is significantly more pronounced than was evident in the case of the short-term sentiment index.

The test period of the preceding analysis covered a time of increasingly unfavorable news and a deterioration in consumer confidence. Yet, a cogent case may be made for expecting differences in the values of the system's parameters between upturns and downturns of the business cycle. Katona speaks of the habituation effect: "Only what is new is news" (Katona, 1964). Good news is big news during bad times, but loses its impact when favorable news and good times have persisted over long periods. Therefore, the marginal effect of good news on attitudes might be greater during times of pervasive bad news than it is when good news prevails.

The diffusion patterns of news and experience need extensive further study. The analysis of this paper has been suggestive of the ways in which perceptions of news contribute to attitude formation and how the patterns differ between subgroups of the population. Future research should endeavor an examination of how the relationship of sentiment of reported news differs between economic upturns and downturns, and, indeed whether or not the system parameters are stable even between like stages of the business cycle. Another potentially promising strategy is the standardized measurement of the impact of the events according to a content analysis of news sources. [6] Much work remains to be done in the analysis of the complex linkage between events, policy measures and consumer sentiment. An increased understanding of these interactions promises to increase greatly our ability to use current data on consumer attitudes and expectations in order to forecast future changes in consumer sentiment.

III.

Surveys of consumer sentiment provide information which is useful to government in formulating public policy. With respect to changes in consumer behavior, policy makers are in need of two types of information: (a) what will consumers do in the future, assuming no (change in) government intervention or other exogenous shock; and (b) how would consumers react to a specified *change* in government policy, or to specified important exogenous

---

[6]The only currently available method of machine content analysis which has been sufficiently tested and applied to be of general use is the system developed a number of years ago under the name "General Inquirer." It is based on a systematic assignment of individual words to particular categories of meaning, determined by the specific purpose of the investigation. For details see Erbring.

events, should they occur. The regular monitoring of consumer attitudes and expectations represents an "early warning system" of type a, so that the policy maker, by applying his criteria of judgement and evaluation, can decide whether or not there is a need for intervention. Information of type b, makes possible "conditional forecasts," helping the policy maker to select appropriate instruments for intervention and to apply them in the appropriate manner, at the appropriate time, and to the appropriate extent. The quarterly surveys of the Survey Research Center provide information of both types.

Open-ended questions particularly, including the one inquiring about business-related news heard (analyzed in detail in Section II of this paper contribute to information of type b). For example, by voicing concern over the Vietnam war or over the inertia of the government, respondents provide information about how and to what extent news of a relaxation of the war effort, a decisive step toward peace, or a vigorous stance of the government on the domestic economic front might be perceived.

The failure of the 1968 tax hike to dampen consumer demand provided a particularly obvious example of the need for information of type b. When Congress adopted the 10 percent income tax surcharge in mid-1968, many forecasts were promptly adjusted to show a slower economic growth rate in the second half of 1968 and early in 1969. In contrast, SRC data in May 1968 showed that many consumers anticipated that the surcharge would be passed by Congress and believed that it would have favorable rather than unfavorable effects on business. At the same time, many families enjoyed income gains which were larger than the amount of the surcharge, and entertained optimistic expectations because of political developments, as home as well as abroad. Under these circumstances, SRC predicted in early June, 1968 *before the surcharge was passed* that it would receive little notice from consumers and would not have much restraining effect on consumer spending and the use of credit after it was passed. Surveys which were conducted late in 1968 and early 1969 verified this forecast.

Repeatedly over the years, data from SRC surveys of consumer attitudes and expectations have shown that changes in incomes, taxes, or interest rates do not necessarily or mechanically result in corresponding changes in consumer behavior. The difficulties in forecasting the impact of income increases a prime target of discretionary fiscal policy, using conventional theoretical approaches, were summarized by the late William H. Chartener who tested Keynes' assumption that the marginal propensity to consume lies between 0 and +1. For the eighty-six quarters between 1948 and 1969, he said:

... this has been true only a little more than half the time. In thirty quarters, consumer spending actually increased *more* than income. In five quarters, income increased but spending went down. In six quarters income went down but spending increased anyway.

Quarterly behavior might be expected to be somewhat erratic and affected strongly by leads and lags. But even the annual comparisons are disconcerting. In six of the sixteen years since 1953 . . . consumer spending has risen more than disposable income.

It is of some significance in understanding the recent short-falls of economic forecasts that consumers behaved as they were supposed to in the years 1964 through 1967, when several of the best known models were being developed and tested. The ratio of the increase in consumption to the increase in disposable income for those four years ranged between .75 and .90. Then came 1968 with 1.02. In the first three quarters of 1969 the ratio is 1.05.

So it becomes understandable why the econometric forecasters were caught off guard by consumers' perverse reaction to the tax increase. Instead of pulling in their belts, they increased their spending in the quarter following passage of the tax bill by $14.6 billion (annual rate), or almost two-and-a-half times their increase in after tax income . . . . The savings rate dropped abruptly by more than enough to affect the rise in taxes. (Chartener, p. 94)[7]

What role did the surtax play in the unusual year of 1968? Two possible conditions can be singled out:

a) Consumer sentiment was not affected by the implementation of the tax increase. Although the prevailing widespread gains in disposable income were somewhat reduced by the surtax, in the short run, the tax increase was reflected in decreased saving. In summary, there was no "sentiment effect,"[8] and the income effect depressed consumption only with a time lag.[9]

b) The imposition of the surtax was counterproductive in the short run

---

[7]The national income and product data have been revised somewhat since Chartener spoke in November 1969, without, however, fundamentally affecting his conclusions. The revised data show that for the twelve months between mid-1968 and mid-1969, the ratio of the increase in consumption to the increase in disposable income was 1.24.

[8]The term "sentiment effect" is broader than Pigou's "announcement effect." The latter refers to changes in behavior in response to news which causes changes in specific expectations. The former refers to changes in behavior in response to news which interacts with and causes changes in a broad range of consumer attitudes and expectations; see the paradigm outlined in Section I.

[9]It is quite plausible on theoretical grounds, that in the absence of a change in sentiment, personal consumption expenditures should adjust to changes in income rather slowly. Much consumption is based on habit, and the decision making process for the purchase of discretionary items is too much rooted in past considerations to be quickly revised because of minor income changes which are not accompanied by changes in sentiment. This applies with particular force to a situation in which the tax hike did not reverse but only diminished widespread gains in real income.

because many consumers believed it would have a favorable effect on business and therefore became more confident, mainly with regard to inflation. The "sentiment effect" outweighed the income effect, at least at the time of implementation.

It is not possible to determine which of these two conditions provides a more realistic description of what went on in 1968. Probably, both played a role for different people. Yet is was possible to forecast in June, 1968 that the measure would not fulfill the hopes which it had raised within government and among the economic profession.

Important sentiment effects which stemmed from the 1968 tax increase occurred long before the implementation of the measure. Similarly, the tax cut of 1964 had an impact on consumer sentiment and behavior long before withholdings from pay were actually reduced.[10]   Expenditures on durable goods and the incurrence of installment debt increased in the winter of 1963-1964 in anticipation of the tax cut, which was seen as a contributor to improvement in business conditions. However, during the first few months following the enactment of the measure, at a time when income gains were widespread, a sizable proportion of the additional gains in disposable income went into liquid assets rather than into expenditures. Later in 1964 and in 1965, the frequent and substantial increases in wages and salaries, in combination with the slowly accumulating gains from the tax cut, again greatly stimulated consumer demand.

An aftermath of the satisfaction American taxpayers felt with the tax cut of 1964 was noticeable in 1966. Surveys conducted in that year disclosed that a majority of consumers believed that an increase in income tax rates would occur. Many informed people thought that a tax increase would depress economic activity, not simply because they did not cherish the prospect of paying higher taxes, but also and primarily, because they viewed the tax increase as an act which was opposite in nature to the tax cut of 1964, which they still remembered clearly as having been favorable to the economy (Katona, Strumpel, Zahn, p. 86).

In summary, with respect to both the 1964 tax cut and the 1968 tax increase, the sentiment effect occurred long before implementation, while the income effect on consumption (not on saving) occurred only after a time lag. In 1968, the year when the tax hike was enacted and when a restrictive effect on consumer spending was most needed, the implementation paradoxically fell within a period which was not governed by either of the two effects.

During the sixties, the sentiment effects of measures of discretionary fiscal policy in the short run, which is relevant here, were more important than the income effect. To quote Ray Fair of Princeton University, a member of the econometric model fraternity:

---

[10]For a microanalysis of the reactions to the tax cut in 1963-65 see Katona and Mueller.

Tax law changes affect the forecasts of GNP and related variables indirectly through the effects they have on consumer sentiment and plant and equipment investment expectations. Since tax laws are generally debated and discussed considerably ahead of their actual enactment, these debates and discussions may affect the consumer sentiment and investment expectations variables far enough ahead so that these effects are reflected in the forecasts of the model. Personal tax law changes in the quarter in which they are enacted do not appear to have any systematic effect on personal consumption expenditures, and the argument given here for why this is so is that consumers to some extent have already discounted these changes. In other words, it is argued here that in explaining or forecasting short-run changes in consumption, it is more important to explain or forecast consumer sentiment than it is to account for the direct effects of tax rate changes on disposable personal income (Fair, p. 245).

If this is true, the question must be raised: can economic confidence be "fine-tuned"? Consumer reactions to government measures can now, to a considerable extent, be predicted from surveys of attitudes and expectations, given the present state of knowledge. However, before consumer sentiment can be purposefully activated and directed, there is much need for further research on the sources and operating mechanisms of attitude change. The recognition of this need led to the analysis in Section II of this paper.

IV.

Other sections of this paper have been concerned with short-run changes in consumer attitudes, and with forecasting consumer behavior. In this concluding section, we explore the potential of consumer sentiment in contexts other than demand analysis: longer-term shifts in saving; relatively stable international differences in consumer behavior; and voter preferences and political stability.

It has been argued that good years, years of upturn and prosperity, are years of spending, and bad years, those of downturn or recession, are years of saving. This is unquestionably true regarding one item that enters into personal saving, namely the negative item of incurrence of new debt. In good years, the purchase of durable goods and borrowing for that purpose is more extensive than in bad years; therefore in bad years, a smaller debt incurrence item is deducted from total personal saving than the one in good years. But with respect to financial saving in banks, bonds and stocks, the relationship is much more complex. There are powerful forces which promote financial saving in good years, and others that promote it in bad years.

During prosperous years, saving is reduced because of the competition of purchases of durable goods; part of these purchases are financed by drawing on liquid assets. At the same time, however, saving is promoted because income increases are frequent and substantial in good years and part of the income increments are saved. In years of recession or of threatening recession the relatively infrequent and small income increases impair people's latitude to save. At the same time, however, saving is promoted by the decision of many people not to spend (to postpone the purchase of cars, appliances, etc.). Moreover, motives to save are particularly strong when a recession is feared; people save as much as they can when they hear that unemployment is growing in the country (Katona, 1971).[11]

The preceding discussion provides some clues as to the role of consumer sentiment in the conspicuous and quite persistent shift in the rate of saving out of disposable income, amounting to more than 2 percentage points (from under 6 to over 8 percent) since early 1969. The last two years brought a substantial drop in consumer sentiment, which, however, was *not* accompanied by a corresponding decrease in income, or even by a substantial slowdown in income advances for the majority of the population. Both of the above identified variables, insecurity *and* continuing income increases, jointly provided for a stepped-up saving activity.

There may have been more factors which contributed to this condition than depressed short-term consumer confidence. Chart 16-2 shows the substantial deterioration in long-term expectations for business during the last two years, coupled with unusual "attentism," i.e., with an increased reporting of news influencing business conditions. There can be little doubt that the joint impact of the war in Southeast Asia, the protracted coexistence of high rates of inflation and unemployment, civil disorder, crime and pollution have profoundly, and not just cyclically, changed the Amercian people's outlook toward the future, and created a climate of insecurity and frustration which plausibly breeds an increased desire for savings. This is a phenomenon of at least medium-range duration which will not disappear earlier than its causes. To be sure, changes in sentiment which are connected with short-term cyclical economic phenomena naturally may cause temporary downward adjustments in the rate of saving.

Evidence that consumer sentiment may make for long-term differences in economic behavior is also found through international comparisons (Katona, Strumpel, Zahn, Chapter 4) The proportion of people approaching their economic future with optimism has some bearing on the degree to which a population is willing to participate in economic processes, i.e., to render productive service in order to satisfy their aspirations. There are indeed drastic intercontinental differences in consumer psychology, in spite of rapid and steady rises in mass incomes on both sides of the Atlantic. While in 1968, close to half (43 percent) of American heads of households anticipated that

---

[11]For earlier formulations, see Katona, 1960, Chapter 7.

they would be better off four years later, the same answer was given by only a third of the Britons, and a quarter of the French, the Germans, and the Dutch who were interviewed. Every third (31 percent) American both felt better off than he did four years ago and anticipated being better off four years hence, but only every fourth (24 percent) Briton, every fifth (19 percent) Frenchman, every sixth (16 percent) Dutchman, and every eighth (12 percent) German believed in the same continuum of personal progress. Correspondingly, in Germany the saving rate has been more than one-and-a-half times as high as the rate in the United States, while installment debt is of only marginal importance, and the proportion of households feeling "saturated" is large, and increasing with prosperity.

The consequences of changes in consumer attitudes extend far beyond economics to the political system. Economic dissatisfaction demonstrably makes for societal and political discontent (Strumpel, 1972) and places an effective constraint upon policy makers. If it is ignored, it threatens, at least in a democracy, the grip of power of the current rulers, if not the system itself. A clear indication of this condition for the United States was the outcome of the mid-term national elections in 1970 in favor of the Democrats, which was overwhelmingly attributed to dissatisfaction with the economic policies of the government. The seemingly harsh way in which the present administration publicized its "game plan," explicitly advocating the necessity for fighting inflation at the expense of employment, added a poignant note to the perception of actual government policies.

In the public mind, the responsibility for economic prosperity and recession largely rests with the government, which is readily blamed for the evils of inflation and unemployment. Responding to the question: "As to the economic policy of the government—I mean steps taken in regard to inflation or unemployment—would you say the government is doing a good job, only a fair, or a poor job?" only 14 percent of American heads of households in Spring 1971, responded with "a good job"; 28 percent spoke of "a poor job," and the rest (52 percent) said the government was doing "only a fair job." (See Table 16-4) Yet the disenchantment or even disillusionment with government economic policies seems to extend beyond the present administration. Pessimism about business conditions during the next five years is particularly high among those who feel that the government is doing a poor job. This suggests that adverse economic experience can be translated not only into votes against the incumbent administration, but also into apprehensions over the governmental system.

This effect can also be demonstrated by the political experience of Germany during the sixties. While the Christian Democrats were the ruling party, dissatisfaction with economic performance correlated highly with preference for the Socialist party, which picked up most of the protest vote. After the downfall of the Erhard government which was prompted mainly by the mismanagement of economic policies, the Socialists in 1966, entered into a coalition government with the Christian Democrats. In subsequent years, which coincided with a period of pessimistic consumer sentiment, an intimate association between economic dissatisfaction and preference for the Neo-Nazi party (NPD) emerged (Liepelt, pp. 257-71).

The present German Socialist Government, albeit belatedly, seems to have recognized the dynamite resting in people's perception of the performance of the economy. The recent drastic revamping of domestic policies, focusing on economic stabilization at the expense of the extensive and ambitious reform program, can be viewed as a reaction to a drop in the popularity of the left-wing coalition because of a loss of confidence in current economic policies. A drastic decline in consumer sentiment was signaled in early spring of this year. The parallels with the American scene in 1971, culminating in President Nixon's radical change of economic policies in August 1971, are striking. A thorough analysis of these measures' impact on sentiment, and their likely repercussions on behavior, is currently being conducted at the Survey Research Center.

CHART 16-1

ATTITUDES AND NEWS HEARD

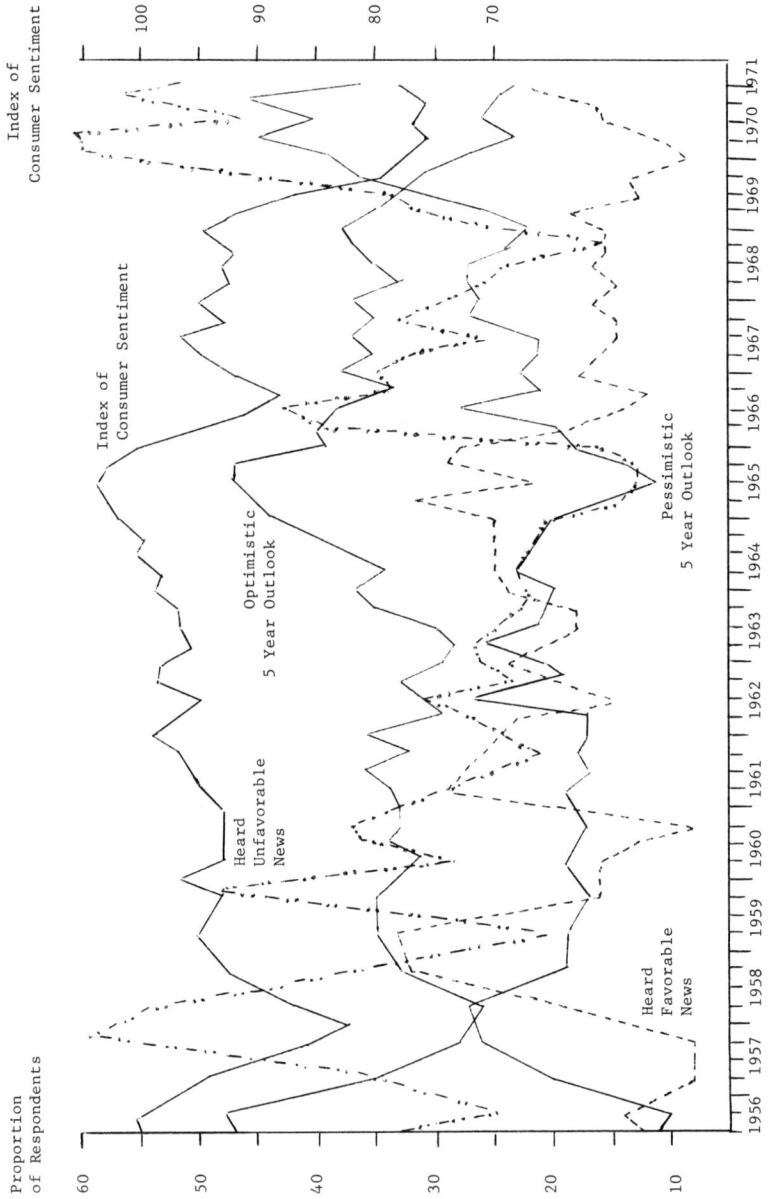

CHART 16-2

REPORTED NEWS AND CONSUMER SENTIMENT

Percent Reporting News:
Unfavorable Favorable

Index of Consumer Sentiment

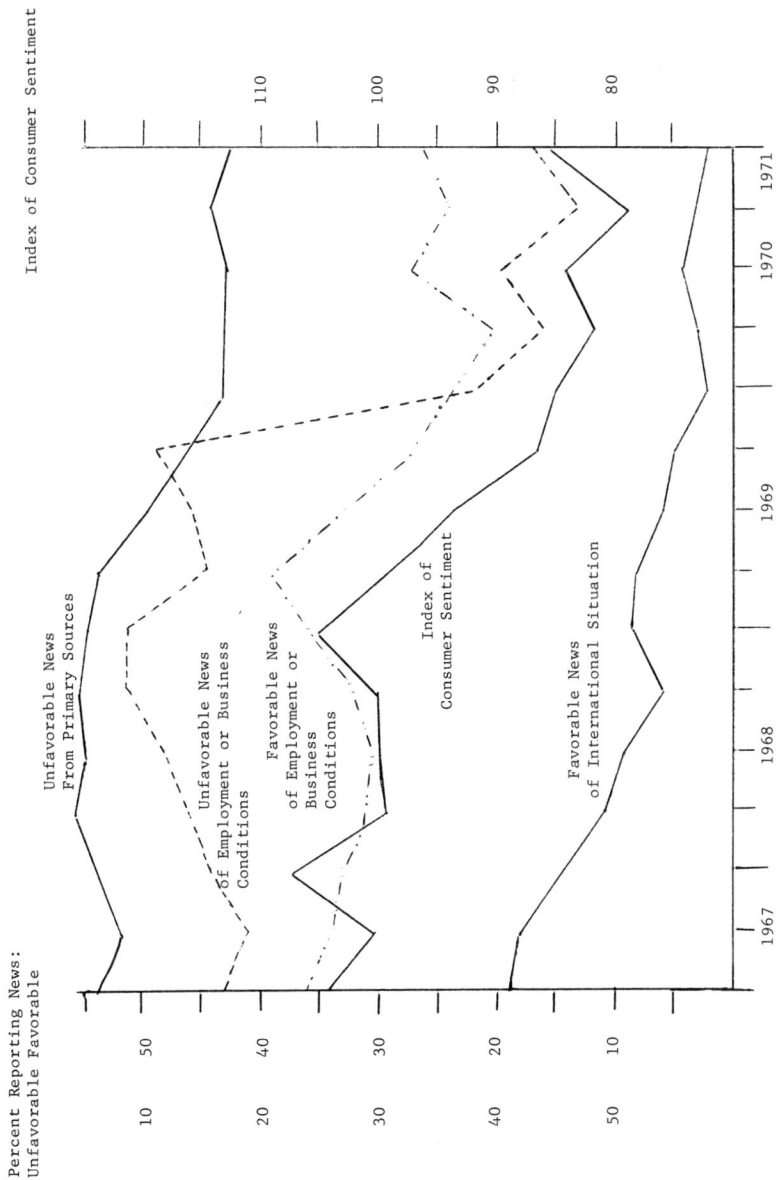

Unfavorable News
From Primary Sources

Unfavorable News
of Employment or Business
Conditions

Favorable News
of Employment or
Business
Conditions

Index of
Consumer Sentiment

Favorable News
of International Situation

TABLE 16-1 (Page 1 of 2)

REPORTED NEWS: DIFFERENCES BETWEEN POPULATION SUBGROUPS

Average and maximum proportion of respondents reporting
news during the period third quarter 1967 to first quarter 1971

	All persons	High income[1]	Low income[1]	Younger[1]	Older[1]	White collar workers[2]	Blue collar workers[2]	College educated[2]	Non-college educated[2]
Proportion reporting news heard:[3]									
Favorable									
Average	16	18	12	16	13	18	13	22	13
Maximum	28	30	17	29	21	34	14	43	19
Unfavorable									
Average	35	38	26	32	32	42	31	48	32
Maximum	57	59	39	46	50	52	44	66	46
News of employment or business conditions:[4]									
Favorable									
Average	31	35	29	33	30	33	29	33	29
Maximum	40	46	38	43	40	44	41	48	40
Unfavorable									
Average	24	26	24	24	27	31	29	33	29
Maximum	47	52	47	46	48	52	48	58	46
News from prime sources:									
Favorable									
Average	6	8	5	6	6	6	7	5	6
Maximum	8	12	8	8	8	9	9	8	8
Unfavorable									
Average	8	10	8	8	9	11	10	11	9
Maximum	12	15	12	12	12	14	13	15	12
News of prices and inflation:									
Favorable									
Average	5	7	4	7	5	8	5	11	5
Maximum	8	10	6	12	7	12	7	14	6
Unfavorable									
Average	14	15	14	16	15	18	14	21	15
Maximum	22	23	21	24	21	24	20	30	21

TABLE 16-1 (Page 2 of 2)

REPORTED NEWS: DIFFERENCES BETWEEN POPULATION SUBGROUPS

Average and maximum proportion of respondents reporting
news during the period third quarter 1967 to first quarter 1971

	All persons	High income[1]	Low income[1]	Younger[1]	Older[1]	White collar workers[2]	Blue collar workers[2]	College educated[2]	Non-college educated[2]
News of international situation:[4]									
Favorable									
Average	7	9	7	9	7	6	5	6	5
Maximum	19	22	18	26	18	10	10	15	8
Unfavorable									
Average	4	4	4	5	4	4	4	5	4
Maximum	7	7	7	9	7	7	7	10	7
News of domestic political policy and events:[4]									
Favorable									
Average	9	11	8	9	9	10	8	13	8
Maximum	16	18	15	16	16	18	14	21	16
Unfavorable									
Average	10	11	9	11	10	10	10	12	9
Maximum	12	15	12	16	12	12	13	17	12

[1]The subgroups are defined as: High Income: $10,000 or more
Low Income: Less than $10,000
Younger: Under 35
Older: 35 and older

[2]Proportions cover the period third quarter 1968 to first quarter 1971.

[3]The question: "During the last few months, have you heard of any favorable or unfavorable changes in business conditions? What did you hear?"

[4]News items mentioned in response to the above quoted question and the question "Now turning to business conditions in
the country as a whole – do you think we'll have good times financially, or bad times, or what? Why do you think that?"

TABLE 16-2

MEASURES OF ASSOCIATION BETWEEN REPORTED NEWS,
EVENTS AND INDEX OF CONSUMER SENTIMENT

	Correlations with the Index of Consumer Sentiment
	r^2
Reported News:	
Favorable news of employment and business conditions	.67
Unfavorable news of employment and business conditions	.71
Favorable news from primary sources	.24
Unfavorable news from primary sources	.59
Favorable news of prices and inflation	.49
Unfavorable news of prices and inflation	.34
Favorable news of international situation	.56
Unfavorable news of international situation	.28
Favorable news of domestic political policy or events	.30
Unfavorable news of domestic political policy or events	.10
Events	
Unemployment rate	.64
Inflation rate	.30

TABLE 16-3

LONG-RUN EXPECTATIONS AND REPORTED NEWS

	Correlation (r^2) with:	
Concurrent news of:	Optimistic long-run expectations[1]	Pessimistic long-run expectations[1]
Favorable employment or business conditions	.63	.67
Unfavorable employment or business conditions	.87	.77
Favorable primary source news	.04	.16
Unfavorable primary source news	.67	.64
Favorable international situation	.46	.44
Favorable domestic political policy or events	.34	.54
Six-month average news of:		
Favorable employment or business conditions	.65	.60
Unfavorable employment or business conditions	.87	.73
Favorable primary source news	.15	.64
Unfavorable primary source news	.83	.80
Favorable international situation	.47	.45
Favorable domestic political policy or events	.54	.71

[1]The frequency of optimistic/pessimistic answers in response to the question "Looking ahead, which would you say is more likely - that in the country as a whole we'll have continuous good times during the next five years or so, or that we will have periods of widespread unemployment or depression or what?"

TABLE 16-4

FIVE YEAR BUSINESS EXPECTATIONS
AND WHETHER GOVERNMENT IS DOING A GOOD JOB
(May 1971)

Business Conditions Expected During the Next 5 years	All	Government is doing a		
		Good Job	Only Fair Job	Poor Job
Good times	20%	33%	22%	12%
Pro-con	17	10	15	13
Bad times	37	28	35	45
Don't know, not ascertained	26	29	28	30
Total	100%	100%	100%	100%
Percent of families	100%	15%	52%	28%

The question was: "Looking ahead, which would you say is more likely - that in the country as a whole we'll have continuous good times during the next 5 years or so, or that we will have periods of widespread unemployment or depression or what?"

Appendix

APPENDIX (Page 1 of 2)

CONSUMER SENTIMENT AND REPORTED NEWS:
RELATIONSHIPS WITHIN DEMOGRAPHIC SUBGROUPS

A. All Persons

$I - .557 + 1.225$ FAVEMP $\qquad\qquad\qquad \bar{R}^2 = .64$
$\quad\quad (.248)$
$I = 1.053 - .499$ UNFEMP $\qquad\qquad\qquad \bar{R}^2 = .68$
$\quad\quad (.093)$
$I = .766 + 2.892$ FAVPRIM $\qquad\qquad\qquad \bar{R}^2 = .17$
$\quad\quad (1.502)$
$I = 1.107 - 2.172$ UNFPRIM $\qquad\qquad\qquad \bar{R}^2 = .56$
$\quad\quad (.519)$
$I = .683 + .601$ FAVEMP $- .620$ UNFPRIM $= .664$ FAVINTL $+ .706$ FAVDOM $\bar{R}^2 = .90$
$\quad\quad (.174) \qquad\quad (.358) \qquad\quad (.200) \qquad\qquad (.293) \quad$ D.W. $= 2.21$

B. Persons With High Income ($10,000 and over)

$I = .571 + 1.021$ FAVEMP $\qquad\qquad\qquad \bar{R}^2 = .67$
$\quad\quad (.194)$
$I = 1.057 - .506$ UNFEMP $\qquad\qquad\qquad \bar{R}^2 = .76$
$\quad\quad (.076)$
$I = .715 + 2.680$ FAVPRIM $\qquad\qquad\qquad \bar{R}^2 = .35$
$\quad\quad (.926)$
$I = 1.092 - 1.697$ UNFPRIM $\qquad\qquad\qquad \bar{R}^2 = .40$
$\quad\quad (.440)$
$I = .594 + .620$ FAVEMP $+ .660$ FAVINTL $+ .565$ FAVDOM $\qquad \bar{R}^2 = .83$
$\quad\quad (.187) \qquad\quad (.224) \qquad\quad (.288) \qquad\qquad$ D.W. $= 1.45$

C. Persons With Low Income (Less than $10,000)

$I = .499 + 1.451$ FAVEMP $\qquad\qquad\qquad \bar{R}^2 = .44$
$\quad\quad (.331)$
$I = 1.068 - .645$ UNFEMP $\qquad\qquad\qquad \bar{R}^2 = .76$
$\quad\quad (.078)$
$I = .818 + 2.140$ FAVPRIM $\qquad\qquad\qquad \bar{R}^2 = .04$
$\quad\quad (1.855)$
$I = 1.142 - 3.090$ UNFPRIM $\qquad\qquad\qquad \bar{R}^2 = .81$
$\quad\quad (.413)$
$I = .869 - 1.976$ UNFPRIM $+ .549$ FAVEMP $+ .420$ FAVINTL $\qquad \bar{R}^2 = .93$
$\quad\quad (.351) \qquad\qquad (.174) \qquad\quad (.188) \qquad\qquad$ D.W. $= 2.82$

D. White Collar Workers

$I = .497 + 1.202$ FAVEMP $\qquad\qquad\qquad \bar{R}^2 = .84$
$\quad\quad (.168)$
$I = 1.089 - .631$ UNFEMP $\qquad\qquad\qquad \bar{R}^2 = .89$
$\quad\quad (.069)$
$I = .630 + 4.133$ FAVPRIM $\qquad\qquad\qquad \bar{R}^2 = .56$
$\quad\quad (1.122)$
$I = 1.210 - 2.990$ UNFPROM $\qquad\qquad\qquad \bar{R}^2 = .65$
$\quad\quad (.677)$
$I = .540 + .983$ FAVEMP $- 1.007$ UNFPRIM $+ .725$ FAVDOM $+ 1.421$ FAVINTL $\bar{R}^2 = .98$
$\quad\quad (.087) \qquad\qquad\qquad\qquad (.119) \qquad\quad (.374) \qquad$ D.W. $= .55$

APPENDIX (Page 2 of 2)

E. Blue Collar Workers

$I = .573 + 1.088$ FAVEMP $\bar{R}^2 = .54$
       (.304)
$I = 1.048 - .572$ UNFEMP $\bar{R}^2 = .81$
       (.087)
$I = .662 + 3.395$ FAVPRIM $\bar{R}^2 = .59$
       (1.503)
$I = .863 - 2.999$ UNFPRIM $\bar{R}^2 = .82$
       (.464)
$I = .978 - 2.323$ UNFPRIM $+ .426$ FAVEMP $\bar{R}^2 = .87$
       (.512)   (.207)   D.W. = 1.55

F. College Educated

$I = .615 + .947$ FAVEMP $\bar{R}^2 = .60$
       (.247)
$I = 1.082 - .467$ UNFEMP $\bar{R}^2 = .85$
       (.064)
$I = .892 + .822$ FAVPRIM $\bar{R}^2 = .03$
       (1.454)
$I = 1.113 - 1.690$ UNFPRIM $\bar{R}^2 = .46$
       (.549)
$I = .667 + .630$ FAVEMP $+ .828$ FAVINTL $\bar{R}^2 = .84$
       (.261)   (.408)   D.W. = 1.55

G. Non-College Educated

$I = .574 + 1.132$ FAVEMP $R^2 = .55$
       (.309)
$I = 1.061 - .572$ UNFEMP $R^2 = .86$
       (.067)
$I = .653 + 4.262$ FAVPRIM $R^2 = .39$
       (1.557)
$I = 1.162 - 2.902$ UNFPRIM $R^2 = .86$
       (.388)
$I = 1.221 - 2.840$ UNFPRIM $- 1.493$ UNFINTL $R^2 = .91$
       (.614)   (.306)   D.W. = 1.97

    I = Index of consumer sentiment

  FAV = Favorable news perceived

  UNF = Unfavorable news perceived

  DOM = Domestic Political policy and events

INTL = International situation

  EMP = Employment or business conditions

PRIM = News from primary sources

[a]The independent variables are the proportion of the subgroup population mentioning the news items. See text for the wording of the survey questions.

References

Adams, F. Gerard, and Green, E.W. "Explaining and Predicting Aggregative Consumer Attitudes," *International Economic Review*, VI (September, 1965).

Chartener, William H. "The Trouble with Econometric Forecasts," *The Economic Outlook for 1970*, Seventeenth Annual Conference on the Economic Outlook. Ann Arbor: Department of Economics, The University of Michigan, 1970.

Ebring, Lutz. "Mass Publics and Political Events, On Modeling the Dynamics of Public Opinion: Theoretical Considerations, Research Design and Progress." Unpublished report, University of Michigan, 1971.

Fair, Ray C. *A Short-Run Forecasting Model of the United States Economy*. Lexington, Massachusetts: D.C. Heath and Company, 1971.

Hymans, Saul H. "Consumer Durable Spending: Explanation and Prediction," Brookings *Papers on Economic Activity*, No. 2. Washington, D.C.: The Brookings Institution, 1970.

Strumpel, Burkhard, Morgan, James N., and Zahn, Ernest (eds.). *Human Behavior in Economic Affairs: Essays in Honor of George Katona*. Amsterdam: Elsevier Publishing Company, 1972.

INFAS (Institut fuer Angewandte Sozialwissenschaft, Bad Godesberg) Research Report. Konjunktur: Meinungen et Erwartungen, 1968.

Institute for Social Research. *Survey of Consumer Finances*. Ann Arbor: The University of Michigan, published annually since 190.

Katona, George. *The Mass Consumption Society*. New York: McGraw-Hill, 1964.

――――. *The Powerful Consumer*. New York: McGraw-Hill, 1960.

――――. *Psychological Analysis of Economic Behavior*. New York: McGraw-Hill, 1951.

――――. Reply to Saul H. Hymans' Paper "Consumer Durable Spending." Brookings Papers on Economic Activity, No. 1. Washington, D.C.: The Brookings Institution, 1971.

Katona, George, and Mueller, Eva. *Consumer Response to Income Increases*. Washington, D.C.: The Brookings Institution, 1968.

Katona, George, Strumpel, Burkhard, and Zahn, Ernest. *Aspirations and Affluence*. New York: McGraw-Hill, 1971.

Liepelt, Klaus. "Anhaenger der Neven Rechtspartei," *Politische Vierteljahrschrift*, VIII (July, 1967).

Maynes, E. Scott. "An Appraisal of Consumer Anticipation," *1967 Proceedings of the Business and the Economic Statistics Section*. American Statistical Association, 114 ff.

Mueller, Eva. "Ten Years of Consumer Attitude Surveys: Their Forecasting Record," *Journal of the American Statistical Association*, LVIII (December, 1963), 899-917.

Shapiro, Harold T. "The Index of Consumer Sentiment and Economic Forecasting: A Reappraisal," in Strumpel, Burkhard, Morgan, James N., and Zahn, Ernest (eds.). *Human Behavior in Economic Affairs: Essays in Honor of George Katona*. Amsterdam: Elsevier Publishing Comapny, 1972.

Shapiro, Harold T., and Angevine, G.E. "Consumer Attitudes, Buying Intentions and Expenditures: An Analysis of the Canadian Data," *Canadian Journal of Economics* (May, 1969).

Strumpel, Burkhard. "Economic Stress as a Source of Societal Discontent." Paper Presented at the Annual Meeting of the American Sociological Association, New Orleans, August, 1972.

Strumpel, Burkhard, Novy, Klaus, and Schwartz, M. Susan. "Consumer Attitudes and Outlays in Germany and North America." Paper presented to the 9th Conference of CIRET (International Conference on Business Tendency Surveys), Madrid, 1969, and published in *Jahrbuch fuer Sozialwissenschaft*, I, 1970.

PART 4

METHODOLOGY

17

SURVEY METHODS

Sampling and Interviewing

The samples of the Survey Research Center represent cross-sections of the population living in private households in the United States, excluding Alaska and Hawaii. Transients, residents of institutions, and persons living on military bases are not included. The method known as multistage area probability sampling is used to select a sample of dwelling units representative of the nation. First, 74 primary sampling units (each composed of a county or group of counties) are selected: 12 of the largest metropolitan areas are selected with certainty, and 62 other sampling units are selected by probability methods from among all remaining counties in the coterminous United States.

In each primary sampling unit three to six secondary selections of cities, towns, census tracts, or rural areas are made. In the third stage of sampling, urban blocks, or small portions (blocks) of rural areas are chosen. Finally, for each new survey a sample of dwelling units in clusters of about four, is drawn from the block selections—always by a process of random choice.

The basic unit for sampling is the dwelling unit, and for interviewing, the family unit. A family unit is defined as all persons living in the same dwelling unit who are related to each other by blood, marriage, or adoption. A single person who is unrelated to the other occupants of the dwelling, or who lives along, is a family unit by himself. In some dwelling units there are two or even several family units. Early in 1971 about 1.6 percent of all family units were secondary units unrelated to the primary family occupying the dwelling unit. The total number of family units in the coterminous 48 states can be estimated from survey data and from census data relating to the number of occupied dwelling units. Over the last few years there has been a steady and substantial increase in the number of families. Tentative expansions indicate that there were about 65.6 million family units early in 1971.

The head of the family unit is designated as the respondent. Five calls, and in some cases more, are made at different times in the day at dwelling units at which no one has been found at home. If a designated respondent refuses to give relevant information, a letter is sent urging him to reconsider. The letter is followed by another visit.

The Survey Research Center maintains a nationwide staff of interviewers, selected and trained by a staff of traveling supervisors. The interviewers are instructed in the careful and uniform use of the fixed-question open-answer technique. They pay particular attention to the establishment of rapport with respondents. Many questions are answered in the respondent's own words, which the interviewers record verbatim (or as nearly verbatim as possible). Nondirective probes are used to clarify the answers received.

The Content of the Surveys

The Survey Research Center in its studies of consumer behavior concentrates on the major volatile money outlays by consumers and the factors influencing them. Studies of the distribution of everyday expenditures—on food, clothing, incidentals, etc.—are not included in the survey program because (a) they change gradually and need not be studied at frequent intervals, and (b) their determination would require different methods (for instance, diaries left with respondents). In our affluent society discretionary outlays, both expenditures and amounts saved, played an important role. They require special attention and fortunately most of them are usually well remembered.

In addition to questions on a variety of demographic characteristics questions are asked in the annual financial surveys on the following major topics:
1. Income in the calendar year prior to the interview.
2. Housing status and debt on homes owned at the time of the interview, and purchases, sales, or additions and repairs in the preceding year.
3. Automobile ownership as well as purchases, sales, and debt incurred or repaid in the preceding year.
4. Purchases, sales, and debt on other durable goods for the previous year.
5. Other major transactions and other debt.
6. Financial assets and life insurance at the time of the interview.

In order to assess changes in consumers' opinions and feelings of optimism and confidence, quarterly rather than annual surveys are conducted. Each of the quarterly surveys contains about 30 periodically repeated questions. All questions are concerned with attitudes toward and expectations about personal finances, the national business situation, price changes, and market conditions. Taken together, observed changes in these measures of consumer sentiment provide an indication of changes in consumer willingness to make major discretionary expenditures. Questions on buying intentions—for houses, automobiles, household goods—throw light on consumer inclinations to buy certain specific items as of the time of the survey.

Direct questions are supplemented with open-ended probes, or *"why"* questions, which respondents answer in their own words. These probes serve to uncover the reasons behind attitudes; it is just as important to know why consumers feel as they do as it is to know how they feel. Answers to *"why"* questions turn up cue words like recession, cold war, unemployment, stock market, inflation. The frequency of these cues, available from a content analysis of answers, provides a useful measure of the extent to which changes in attitudes are salient to consumers.

Surveys of this kind are not intended to establish an absolute measure of the state of consumer sentiment at a given time. They are intended to measure *change.* Comparison with previous measurement indicates the direction of change in consumer optimism and to some extent also the degree of change.

In order to measure change in attitudes it is necessary to use identical methods in repeated surveys—in sampling, question formulation, and the analysis of replies. Since, however, each new period brings forth new problems, many surveys also contain new questions in addition to the trend questions.

Index of Consumer Sentiment

Change in consumers' willingness to buy may best be determined by making use of the answers to all questions asked in the quarterly surveys. Nevertheless, in order to make available a summary measure of change in consumer sentiment, the Survey Research Center uses the answers to five questions to calculate an Index. The five questions are:

1. "We are interested in how people are getting along financially these days. Would you say that you and your family are better off or worse off financially than you were a year ago?"
2. "Now looking ahead—do you think that a year from now you people will be better off financially, or worse off, or just about the same as now?"
3. "Now turning to business conditions in the country as a whole—do you think that during the next twelve months we'll have good times financially, or bad times, or what?"
4. "Looking ahead, which would you say is more likely—that in the country as a whole we'll have continuous good times during the next five years or so, or that we will have periods of widespread unemployment or depression, or what?"
5. "About the big things people buy for their homes—such as furniture, house furnishings, refrigerator, stove, television, and things like that. For people in general, do you think now is a good or a bad time to buy

major household items?"

To construct the Index, a relative score is calculated for each question separately, by taking the percentage giving favorable or optimistic answers, subtracting the percentage giving unfavorable answers, and adding 100. (It will be noted that this procedure is equivalent in effect to assigning a value of 2 to favorable responses, of 1 to "same" or "don't know" responses, and of 0 to unfavorable answers.) An average is then taken over the five relative scores, and the result is adjusted to the base (February 1966 survey = 100).

As with all the questions on consumer attitudes and expectations studied in connection with the outlook for consumer demand, absolute values of the Index are of less importance than its changes.

Survey Errors

Properly conducted sample interview surveys yield useful estimates, but they do not yield exact values. Errors may arise from several sources: sampling nonresponse, reporting, and processing. Each source of error must be considered in evaluating the accuracy of survey information. Because of these different kinds of error, differences between current and past findings may not be significant.

Sampling errors arise in surveys because only a fraction of the population is interviewed. Since the data obtained in successive surveys are based on representative samples drawn by probability methods, the size of the sampling errors can be calculated. The magnitude of the sampling error depends on the size of the sample and its geographic spread, and on the magnitude of the reported percentage in question.

Sampling errors are presented in two ways; first, as they relate to survey findings (Table 17-1); second, as they relate to differences in survey findings, either differences between independent samples or differences between subgroups of the same sample (Table 17-2). Sampling errors are not a measure of the actual errors involved in specific survey measurements. They mean that, except for nonsampling errors, errors greater than those shown in Table 17-1 or differences larger than those found in Table 17-2 will occur by chance in only five cases out of one hundred.

In order to determine the sampling errors of specific findings it is necessary to know the size of the sample on which the finding is based. Table 17-3 presents the number of cases in the 1971 financial survey for several important subgroups of the sample.

The Sampling Section of the Survey Research Center has made elaborate calculations to determine the sampling errors of the major attitudinal and expectational measures used by the Center.[1]   Averaging a number of such

---

[1] See Leslie Kish, "Standard Errors for Indexes from Complex Samples," *Journal of the American Statistical Association*, June 1968.

calculations, the size of one standard error was found to be 1.65 whenever the reported percentage is near 50 percent (see Table 17-4). For some purposes a measure of two standard errors should be used, i.e., the figures in Table 17-4 should be multiplied by two. The chances are 19 out of 20 that answers obtained from the entire population would lie within two standard errors. The sampling error for families with over $10,000 income is half again as high as it is for the entire sample.

From the individual attitudinal measures, a relative score may be constructed by adding 100 to the percentage of optimistic replies and subtracting the percentage of pessimistic replies. For instance, if 50 percent say that they are better off than a year ago and 15 percent say they are worse off, the relative score would be 135. Table 17-5 shows the standard error of the relative scores for the five questions used in calculating the Index of Consumer Sentiment, and also the standard error of the Index itself.

The standard error for intentions to buy automobiles is also shown in Table 17-5. In this case the relative score consists of the percentage of families who report they will or probably will buy a car during the next twelve months, plus one-half of those saying they might buy.

Nonresponse errors arise because some persons selected for the sample refuse to be interviewed, are not at home after repeated callbacks, are ill, or do not speak English. The response rate in the four surveys conducted in 1971 was approximately 80 percent. Nearly two-thirds of the nonresponse resulted from refusal to be interviewed or to give important data. Much of the remainder resulted from inability of the interviewer to contact anyone at the dwelling unit.

Reporting errors—due to misunderstanding of questions or answers, lack of interest by the respondent, or intentional falsification—are kept at a minimum by careful training of interviewers, by attempting to gain the confidence and cooperation of the respondent so that he will answer to the best of his ability, and by watching for inconsistencies in the process of coding and analysis. Because answers are influenced by the wording of questions, conclusions based on answers to a single question are less reliable than those emerging from answers to several questions or from the interrelationship of answers to several questions. Reporting errors are minimized when comparisons are made between answers to identical questions obtained in successive surveys making use of the same methods; there is reason to assume that reporting errors have the same direction and similar magnitudes under these circumstances.

TABLE 17-1

APPROXIMATE SAMPLING ERRORS[a] OF SURVEY FINDINGS

(In percentages by size of sample or subgroup)

Reported percentages	Number of interviews							
	3,000	2,000	1,400	1,000	700	500	300	100
50	2.5	2.8	3.2	3.6	4.2	4.9	6.2	10.5
30 or 70	2.3	2.5	2.9	3.3	3.8	4.5	5.7	9.6
20 or 80	2.0	2.2	2.6	2.9	3.4	3.9	4.9	8.4
10 or 90	1.5	1.7	1.9	2.2	2.5	2.9	3.7	6.3
5 or 95	1.1	1.2	1.4	1.6	1.8	2.1	2.7	4.6

[a]The figures in this table represent two standard errors. Hence, for most items the chances are 95 in 100 that the value being estimated lies within a range equal to the reported percentages, plus or minus the sampling error.

TABLE 17-2

APPROXIMATE SAMPLING ERRORS[a] OF DIFFERENCES

(In percentages)

Size of group	Size of group						
	3,000	2,000	1,400	1,000	700	500	200
For percentages from 35 percent to 65 percent							
3,000	3.5	3.7	4.0	4.4	4.9	5.5	7.9
2,000		3.9	4.2	4.6	5.0	5.6	8.0
1,400			4.5	4.8	5.3	5.8	8.1
1,000				5.1	5.5	6.1	8.3
700					5.9	6.4	8.6
500						6.9	8.9
200							11.0
For percentages around 20 percent and 80 percent							
3,000	2.8	3.0	3.2	3.5	3.9	4.4	6.3
2,000		3.2	3.4	3.7	4.0	4.5	6.4
1,400			3.6	3.8	4.2	4.7	6.5
1,000				4.1	4.4	4.9	6.7
700					4.8	5.2	6.9
500						5.5	7.2
200							8.5
For percentages around 10 percent and 90 percent							
3,000	2.1	2.2	2.4	2.6	2.9	3.3	4.7
2,000		2.4	2.5	2.7	3.0	3.4	4.8
1,400			2.7	2.9	3.2	3.5	4.9
1,000				3.1	3.3	3.6	5.0
700					3.6	3.9	5.2
500						4.1	5.4
200							6.4
For percentages around 5 percent and 95 percent							
3,000	1.6	1.7	1.8	2.0	2.2	2.5	3.6
2,000		1.8	1.9	2.0	2.3	2.5	3.6
1,400			2.0	2.2	2.4	2.6	3.7
1,000				2.3	2.5	2.7	3.8
700					2.7	2.9	3.9
500						3.1	4.0
200							4.8

[a]The values shown are the differences required for significance (two standard errors) in comparisons of percentages derived from two different subgroups of a survey.

TABLE 17-3

NUMBER OF FAMILIES IN VARIOUS DEMOGRAPHIC GROUPS

(1971)

Group characteristic	Number of families	Group characteristic	Number of families
All families	1327	Occupation of family head	
1970 family income		Professional and	
		technical	169
Less than $1,000	16	Managers and officials	93
$1,000-1,999	68	Self-employed	74
$2,000-2,999	65	Clerical and sales	114
$3,000-3,999	94	Craftsmen and foremen	189
$4,000-4,999	98	Semiskilled	163
$5,000-5,999	77	Unskilled	153
$6,000-7,499	148	Farmers	44
$7,500-9,999	184	Miscellaneous	72
$10,000-14,999	309	Retired	256
$15,000 or more	268		
		Age of family head	
Life cycle stage of family head			
		Younger than age 25	116
Younger than age 45		25-34	254
		35-44	243
Unmarried, no children	75	45-54	261
Married, no children	109	55-64	203
Married, youngest child		65-74	167
under age 6	239	Age 75 or older	83
Married, youngest child			
age 6 or older	135	Education of family head	
Age 45 or older		0-5 grades	90
		6-8 grades	242
Married, has children	162	Some high school	222
Married, no children,		High school	226
head in labor force	217	Completed high school plus	
Married, no children,		other noncollege training	156
head retired	115	Some college	195
Unmarried, no children,		College, bachelor's degree	131
head in labor force	75	College, advanced or	
Unmarried, no children,		professional degree	59
head retired	122	Not ascertained	6
Any age		Race of respondent	
Unmarried, has children	78	White	1179
		Negro	121
		Other	27

Note: The term "no children" means no children younger than age 18 living at home.   Unemployed people and housewives age 55 or older are considered retired; unemployed people and housewives younger than age 55 are considered to be in the labor force.

TABLE 17-4

AVERAGE SAMPLING ERRORS OF THE MAJOR ATTITUDINAL VARIABLES,
BASED ON 1,350 CASES

If the percentage is near

50	20 (or 80)	10 (or 90)	5 (or 95)

then the standard error of that percentage is

1.65	1.3	1.0	0.7

and the standard error of a difference (change) in that percentage is

2.0	1.65	1.2	0.9

TABLE 17-5

STANDARD ERRORS OF THE INDEX OF CONSUMER SENTIMENT
AND ITS FIVE COMPONENTS

	Standard error of	
	Value	Change
Index of Consumer Sentiment	1.2	1.3
	Relative score	Change of relative score[a]
Components of the index:		
Evaluation of financial situation as compared with a year earlier	2.3	3.0
Expected change in financial situation	1.7	2.4
Business conditions expected over the next 12 months	2.3	2.9
Business conditions expected for the next 5 years	2.4	2.5
Good or bad time to buy large household goods	2.7	3.1
Intentions to buy automobile during the next 12 months	1.9	2.4

[a]See the text of Chapter 14 for the method used to calculate relative scores for the various questions.

18

QUESTIONNAIRE

The questionnaire used in the financial survey conducted early in 1971 is reproduced here. The surveys conducted late in 1971 contained a few additional questions which are reproduced under the tables reporting the findings.

1971 SURVEY OF CONSUMERS -- FIRST QUARTER

PROJECT 46606

January - February 1971

SURVEY RESEARCH CENTER
INSTITUTE FOR SOCIAL RESEARCH
THE UNIVERSITY OF MICHIGAN
ANN ARBOR, MICHIGAN 48106

(Do not write in above space)

---

1. Interviewer's Label

2. **P S U** _____

3. Your Interview No. _____

4. Date _____

5. Length of Interview _____
(Minutes)

INTERVIEWER: LIST <u>ALL</u> PERSONS, INCLUDING CHILDREN LIVING IN THE DWELLING UNIT,
BY THEIR RELATION TO THE HEAD.

6. All persons, by relation or connection to head	7. Sex	8. Age	9. Family Unit No.	10. Indicate Resp. by Check
1. HEAD OF DWELLING UNIT			1	
2.				
3.				
4.				
5.				
6.				
7.				
8.				
9.				
10.				
11.				
12.				

2

SECTION A: GENERAL ATTITUDES

A1. We are interested in how people are getting along financially these days. Would you say that you (and your family) are <u>better off</u> or <u>worse off</u> financially than you were a <u>year ago</u>?

| 1.   BETTER NOW | 3.   SAME | 5.   WORSE NOW | 8.   UNCERTAIN |

A2. Why do you say so?   _____

_____

A3. Now looking ahead - do you think that <u>a year from now</u> you (and your family) will be <u>better off</u> financially, or <u>worse off</u>, or just about the same as now?

| 1.   WILL BE BETTER OFF | 3.   SAME | 5.   WILL BE WORSE OFF | 8.   UNCERTAIN |

A4. Thinking about prices of things you buy in general, do you think they will go up in the next year or so, or go down, or stay where they are now?

| 1.   GO UP | 3.   SAME | 5.   GO DOWN | 8.   DON'T KNOW |

GO TO Q. A7

(IF WILL GO UP)

A5. How large a price increase do you expect? Of course nobody can know for sure, but would you say that a year from now prices will be about 1 or 2% higher, or 5%, or closer to 10% higher than now, or what?

_____

A6. Do you expect that the overall price increase during the next twelve months will be larger, the same, or smaller than during the past twelve months?

_____

_____

A7. Now turning to business conditions in the country as a whole - do you think that during the next 12 months we'll have <u>good</u> times financially, or <u>bad</u> times, or what?

| 1.   GOOD TIMES | 2.   GOOD WITH QUALIFICATIONS | 3.   PRO-CON |

| 4.   BAD WITH QUALIFICATIONS | 5.   BAD TIMES | 8.   UNCERTAIN |

A8. Why do you think that?   _____

_____

A9. Would you say that <u>at the present time</u> business conditions are better or worse than they were <u>a year ago</u>?

| 1. BETTER NOW | 3. ABOUT THE SAME | 5. WORSE NOW |

A10. During the last few months, have you heard of any favorable or unfavorable changes in business conditions?

_____

(IF YES)
A10a. What did you hear? _____

_____

_____

_____

> IF NOT CLEAR WHETHER A CHANGE R MENTIONS IS FAVORABLE OR UNFAVORABLE, PROBE:
> "Would (MENTION CHANGE) be favorable or unfavorable?"
> AND NOTE "favorable" OR "unfavorable".

A11. Speaking now about the international situation - Vietnam, Cambodia, and the Middle East - How do you think the way these things are going affect <u>business conditions</u> here at home? (Do you think the way things are going make for good times, or bad times or what?)

_____

_____

_____

A12. And how about <u>a year from now</u>, do you expect that in the country as a whole business conditions will be better or worse than they are <u>at present</u>, or just about the same?

| 1. BETTER A YEAR FROM NOW | 3. ABOUT THE SAME | 5. WORSE A YEAR FROM NOW |

A13. How about people <u>out of work</u> during the coming 12 months - do you think that there will be <u>more</u> unemployment than now, about the <u>same</u>, or <u>less</u>?

| 1. MORE | 3. ABOUT THE SAME | 5. LESS |

A14. Looking ahead, which would you say is more likely - that in the country as a whole we'll have continuous good times <u>during the next 5 years</u> or so, or that we will have periods of widespread unemployment or depression, or what?

_____

(IF DON'T KNOW   A14a. What does it depend on, in your opinion? _____
OR DEPENDS)

_____

4

A15. Here are some imaginary headlines you might see in the next few years (HAND
CARD A). We are interested in how the events they describe might influence
business.

Which of these would in your opinion have a great influence, which some
influence, and which only a little influence on business conditions?

A15a. First, which of these would have great influence? (INTERVIEWERS CHECK
ITEMS BELOW)

A15b. Next, which of the others would have some influence? (INTERVIEWERS
CHECK ITEMS BELOW)

A15c. Finally, which would have a little influence? (INTERVIEWERS CHECK
ITEMS BELOW)

	GREAT INFLUENCE ON BUSINESS CONDITIONS	SOME INFLUENCE ON BUSINESS CONDITIONS	A LITTLE INFLUENCE ON BUSINESS CONDITIONS
a. Fighting in Vietnam stops			
b. Somewhat more people out of work			
c. Cities report more racial problems			
d. Taxes to be lower next year			
e. Prices not rising as fast as before			
f. Rioting hits campuses across nation			
g. Government cuts spending for military equipment			
h. Large government spending to fight air and water pollution			

A16. How about a recession and unemployment like we had in 1958 and in the winter of
1960-61: do you think this will happen again?

A17. No one can say for sure, but what do you think will happen to interest rates
during the next 12 months?

| 1. GO UP | | 3. STAY THE SAME | | 5. GO DOWN | | 8. DON'T KNOW |

B. HOUSING

B1. Now I'd like to talk with you about things here at home. First about housing.
When did you move into this (house/apartment)?

_____(YEAR)

B2. Do you (FAMILY UNIT) own this (home/apartment), pay rent, or what?

☐ OWNS OR IS BUYING THIS (HOME/APARTMENT) - (GO TO Q. B4 OR Q. B5)

☐ PAYS RENT ON THIS (HOME/APARTMENT) - (GO TO Q. B3)

☐ NEITHER OWNS NOR RENTS THIS (HOME/APARTMENT) - (GO TO Q. B9)

(IF
RENTS)   B3. About how much rent do you pay a month? $_____
                                                          (GO TO Q.B9)

(IF OWNS
OR IS   IF R LIVES IN MULTIPLE DU STRUCTURE. TRY TO GET VALUE FOR
BUYING)   ONLY R'S DU. HOWEVER IF R CAN GIVE YOU ONLY VALUE OF ENTIRE
           STRUCTURE, BE SURE TO NOTE THAT FIGURE IS FOR WHOLE STRUCTURE.

| (IF MOVED IN DURING 1969 OR EARLIER) | B4. Could you tell me what the present value of this house (farm) is? I mean, about what would it bring if you sold it today? $_____ |
| (IF MOVED IN DURING 1970 OR 1971) | B5. How much did the house (farm) cost? $_____ |

(IF OWNS OR IS BUYING)

B6. Do you have any mortgages on this property?

[1. YES]   [5.   NO] - (GO TO Q. B9)
   ↓
B7. About how much is your total mortgage now? $_____

B8. How much are your monthly payments? $_____

6

(ASK EVERYONE)

B9.   Generally speaking, do you think now is a good time or a bad time to buy a house?

| 1.   GOOD | 3.   PRO-CON | 5.   BAD | 8.   DON'T KNOW |

B10. Why do you say so? _____

_____

B11. Do you expect to buy or build a house for your own year-round use during the next twelve months?

_____

(IF NO)

B12. How about during the year after that? _____

_____

(ASK EVERYONE)

B13. Did you have any expenses for work done on this (house and lot/apartment) in 1970 - things like upkeep, additions, improvements, or painting and decorating? (FARMERS -- EXCLUDE FARM BUILDINGS; LANDLORDS -- EXCLUDE INCOME PROPERTY)

| 1.   YES | | 5.   NO | - (GO TO Q. B16) |

B14. How much did it cost altogether? _____

B15. Did you borrow or finance any of it?

| 1.   YES | 5.   NO |

(ASK EVERYONE)

B16. Do you expect to make any large expenditures for work on this (house and lot/apartment) during the next 12 months -- things like upkeep, additions, or improvements, or painting and decorating? (FARMERS -- EXCLUDE FARM BUILDINGS: LANDLORDS EXCLUDE INCOME PROPERTY)

| 1. YES; PROBABLY | 3.   POSSIBLY, IT DEPENDS | 5.   NO |

(INTERVIEWER: ENCOURAGE WIFE TO HELP WITH THIS SECTION)

C. DURABLES

C1. How about large things for the home -- did you buy anything in 1970 such as furniture, a refrigerator, stove, washing machine, television set, air conditioner, household appliances, and so on?

| 1. YES | 5. NO - (GO TO Q. C5) |

C2. What did you buy? -- anything else? (ENTER EACH ITEM)			
C3. How much did it cost, not counting financing charges?	$_____	$_____	$_____
C4. Did you buy it on credit, or pay cash, or what?	CASH ONLY CREDIT	CASH ONLY CREDIT	CASH ONLY CREDIT

INTERVIEWER: REPEAT Q'S C3 AND C4 FOR EACH ITEM MENTIONED, THEN GO TO Q. C5

TC ☐☐☐☐

(ASK EVERYONE)
C5. Now about the big things people buy for their homes -- such as furniture, refrigerator, stove, television, and things like that. <u>Generally speaking</u>, do you think now is a good or a bad time for people to buy major household items?

| 1. GOOD | 3. PRO-CON | 5. BAD | 8. UNCERTAIN |

C6. Why do you say so? _____

_____

_____

8

C7. During the next 12 months do you, or anyone else in the family living here, expect to buy any large household items such as furniture, a TV set, or a major appliance?

_____

(IF YES OR MAYBE) C7a. What do you expect to buy? (CHECK ITEMS IN LEFT COLUMN BELOW)

(ASK EVERYONE - HAND CARD B)

C8. Looking at the items on this list (other than NAME ITEMS ALREADY MENTIONED), is there any possibility that you might buy any of these items during the next 12 months? (READ LIST-- (CHECK ITEMS IN SECOND COLUMN)

(ASK FOR EACH ITEM CHECKED IN EITHER Q. C7-7a OR Q. C8)

C9. (HAND CARD C) Looking now at this card, what would you say are the chances that you will buy (ITEM) during the next 12 months-- would you say you are almost certain to buy, or that it is very unlikely that you will buy, or would one of the answers in between best describe the chances that you will buy (ITEM)?

(ASK Q. C10 IF LIKELIHOOD OF BUYING THE ITEM IS 1 THROUGH 5)

C10. When do you think you might buy (ITEM)?

QC7-7a Expect to buy	Q C8 Some possi- bility		QC9 Likelihood of buying							
			1	2	3	4	5	6	7	
☐	☐	TV Set	☐	☐	☐	☐	☐	☐	☐	_____
☐	☐	Refrigerator	☐	☐	☐	☐	☐	☐	☐	_____
☐	☐	Automatic Washing Machine	☐	☐	☐	☐	☐	☐	☐	_____
☐	☐	Clothes Dryer	☐	☐	☐	☐	☐	☐	☐	_____
☐	☐	Kitchen Oven or Range	☐	☐	☐	☐	☐	☐	☐	_____
☐	☐	Room Air Conditioner	☐	☐	☐	☐	☐	☐	☐	_____
☐	☐	Dishwasher	☐	☐	☐	☐	☐	☐	☐	_____
☐	☐	Furniture (except kitchen or porch)	☐	☐	☐	☐	☐	☐	☐	_____
☐	☐	Phonograph, stereo or hi-fi equipment	☐	☐	☐	☐	☐	☐	☐	_____

(IF NO ITEMS CHECKED ABOVE, GO TO Q. C15)

CARD C

1. Almost certain
2. Probably will
3. Better than even chance
4. Even chance; may or may not
5. Less than even chance
6. Probably will not
7. Very unlikely

CHECK
ONE:

| 1. TV SET MENTIONED WITH LIKELIHOOD OF 1 THROUGH 5 | | 2. OTHER RESPONDENTS (GO TO Q. C15) |

C11. If you do buy a TV set, do you think it will be black and white, or will it be a color set?

| 1. BLACK & WHITE | | 2. COLOR | | 8. UNDECIDED |

C12. Why do you make that choice?

_____

_____

C13. On what does that choice depend?

_____

_____
(GO TO Q. C15)

(IF COLOR) C14. Will it be a console model that sits on the floor, a set that sits on a table or stand, or a smaller portable model with a carrying handle on top?

| 1. FLOOR | | 2. TABLE OR STAND | | 3. PORTABLE |

C15. How many TV sets in working order do you and your family living here own?

| 0. NONE (GO TO Q. D1) | | 1. ONE | | 2. TWO (GO TO Q. C17) | | 3. THREE (GO TO Q. C17) | | 4. FOUR OR MORE (GO TO Q. C17) |

C16. Do you think you may have two sets sometime within the next year or so?

_____

C17. Is the TV set (Are the TV sets) you now own black and white or color?

| 1. BLACK & WHITE | | 2. COLOR | | 3. BOTH |

10

D. CARS

D1. Do you or anyone else here in your family own a car?

YES   NO - (TURN TO Q.D26)

D2. Altogether, how many cars do you and your family living here own? _____
(CARS)

(INTERVIEWER: ASK Q.D3-D8 FOR EACH CAR OWNED BY FU)

	MAIN FAMILY CAR		
Now I'd like to ask a few questions about the car(s) you have now. (First, about the main family car...)			
D3. What year model is it?	19____	19____	19____
D4. What make of car is it? (2 WORD ANSWER)			
D5. Is it a 2-door sedan, a 4-door sedan, a station wagon, convertible, or what?			
D6. Is it a small car, a compact, a regular size car, something in-between, or what?			
D7. Did you buy this car new or used?	1. NEW 2. USED	1. NEW 2. USED	1. NEW 2. USED
D8. In what year did you buy it?	19____	19____	19____

ASK Q's D9-D11 FOR EACH CAR BOUGHT IN 1969 OR EARLIER.
ASK Q's D12-D21 FOR EACH CAR BOUGHT IN 1970 OR 1971.

LIST ALL CARS BOUGHT IN 1969 OR EARLIER (FROM Q.D8), AND ASK D9-D11 FOR EACH CAR

LIST MODEL YEAR AND MAKE ⟶			
D9. Do you (R AND FU) owe money on that car now?	NO (GO TO BOX A) YES ↓	NO (GO TO BOX A) YES ↓	NO (GO TO BOX A) YES ↓
D10. How much are your payments?	$_____ per _____	$_____ per_____	$_____ per _____
D11. How many payments do you have left to make?	_____	_____	_____

BOX A	(INTERVIEWER: ASK QUESTIONS D9-D11 FOR EACH CAR BOUGHT IN 1969 OR EARLIER AND THEN TURN TO NEXT PAGE)

RID ☐☐☐☐ ☐☐☐☐ ☐☐☐

LIST CARS BOUGHT IN 1970 OR 1971 (FROM Q.D8), AND ASK D12-D21 FOR EACH CAR.

Now about the cars you bought in 1970 or already this year--

LIST MODEL YEAR AND MAKE

D12. What was the total price of this car? TP	$_____	$_____	$_____
D13. When you bought this car did you trade-in or sell a car?	1. TI 2. S 5. NEITHER	1. TI 2. S 5. NEITHER	1. TI 2. S 5. NEITHER
(IF TRADE-IN OR SALE) D14. What did you get for the trade-in or sale? TI	$_____	$_____	$_____
D15. How much did you pay down in cash?	$_____	$_____	$_____
D16. Did you borrow or finance part of the total price?	5. NO –(GO TO BOX B) 1. YES	5. NO –(GO TO BOX B) 1. YES	5. NO –(GO TO BOX B) 1. YES
(IF BORROWED) D17. How much did you borrow, not including financing charges? AB	$_____	$_____	$_____
D18. How much are your payments and how often are they made?	$_____ PER_____	$_____ PER_____	$_____ PER_____
D19. How many payments did you agree to make altogether?	_____	_____	_____
D20. How many payments have you made?	_____	_____	_____
D21. How many payments do you have left to make?	_____	_____	_____

BOX B	ASK Q.D12-D21 FOR EACH CAR BOUGHT IN 1970-71. THEN TURN TO NEXT PAGE.

RID ☐☐☐☐ ☐☐☐☐ ☐☐☐☐

12

IF TRADE-IN OR SALE FROM D13 FOR ANY CAR, ASK D22-D25.
ALL OTHERS GO TO D26.

LIST ALL CARS BOUGHT IN 1970 OR 1971 <u>WITH A TRADE-IN OR SALE</u> (FROM D13). ASK D22-D25 ABOUT THE <u>TRADE-IN OR SALE.</u>		
Now about the car(s) you traded-in/sold when you bought your⎯⎯⎯⎯⎯⎯⎯⎯⎯⎯⎯⎯⎯⟶ (LIST MODEL YEAR AND MAKE OF CAR <u>BOUGHT</u>)		
D22. What year model was the car you traded-in/sold? D23. What make was it? (2 WORD ANSWER)	19____ (YEAR) _____	19____ (YEAR) _____
D24. What year did you buy the <u>car you</u> traded-in/sold? D25. Did you buy it new or used?	19____ (YEAR) 1.NEW 2.USED	19____ (YEAR) 1.NEW 2.USED

D26. We've been talking about cars. Now I'd like to ask you about other types of
vehicles. Do you or anyone else in the family here own any kind of a truck,
or a jeep-type vehicle?

            1. YES   5. NO
              ↓   (GO TO Q.D29)
             D27. How many do you own?_____

             (ASK ABOUT   D28. Is it a pick-up, or van, or jeep-type
             EACH ONE)   or what?

             _____ _____ _____

D29. Speaking now of the automobile market - do you think the next twelve months
or so will be a good time or a bad time to buy a car?

    1. GOOD   3. PRO-CON   5. BAD   8. DON'T KNOW
      ↓   ↓   ↓   ↓
   D30. Why do you say so?   _____

                                   _____

D31. Do you or anyone else in the family living here expect to buy a car during the next 12 months?

_____

D32. (HAND CARD C) Just to give us a better idea of what you think are the chances that you will buy a car during the next 12 months, would you please tell me which answer on this card best describes the likelihood that you will buy?

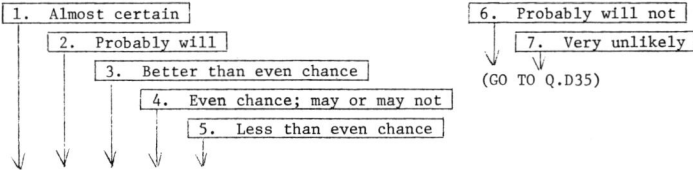

| 1. Almost certain |

| 2. Probably will |

| 3. Better than even chance |

| 4. Even chance; may or may not |

| 5. Less than even chance |

| 6. Probably will not |

| 7. Very unlikely |

(GO TO Q.D35)

D33. Will it be a brand new car or a used car? (IF TWO CAR PURCHASES PLANNED, USE MARGIN FOR SECOND)

| 1. NEW | | 2. USED | | 8. UNCERTAIN |

D34. When do you think you might buy this car?

_____

(GO TO Q. D36)

D35. How long do you think it will be before you people buy a car?

_____

D36. INTERVIEWER CHECK ONE: | 1. R OWNS A FOREIGN CAR (FROM Q.D4) | | 5. R DOES NOT OWN A FOREIGN CAR |

(GO TO Q.D39)

D37. When did you first buy a foreign-made car? (How many years ago?)

_____ (YEARS)

D38. Do you think you will buy another foreign car again sometime in the future?

| 1. YES | | 5. NO |

D38a. Why do you say so? _____

_____

14

D39. INTERVIEWER, | 1. R OWNS AT LEAST ONE CAR | 5. R NEITHER OWNS NOR
      CHECK ONE: | OR PLANS TO BUY WITHIN | PLANS TO BUY WITHIN
                       | THREE YEARS | THREE YEARS
                              ↓   (TURN TO Q. E1)

D40. Last year American manufacturers introduced a new type of car, smaller than
      those which had been made in this country. Have you seen any of these new
      American cars such as the Ford Pinto, the Chevrolet Vega, or the American
      Motors Gremlin?

            | 1. YES | | 5. NO |

D41. We are interested in finding out how people think the new small American
      cars compare with small foreign cars imported into this country. First,
      for a person like yourself, what do you think are some of the advantages
      of the small foreign cars over the new small American cars?

      _____

      _____

D42. For a person like yourself, what do you think are some of the disadvantages
      of the small foreign cars in comparison with the new small American cars?

      _____

      _____

D43. Would you be interested in having one of these small American cars, or would
      you be interested in having a small foreign car, or wouldn't you be interested
      in either one?

      | 1. SMALL AMERICAN CAR | | 2. SMALL FOREIGN CAR | | 5. NOT INTERESTED
                                                                     IN EITHER ONE |

D44. Some foreign cars, for example a Volvo, cost about as much to buy as many
      medium-size cars made in the United States, even though they are somewhat
      smaller in size. Do you think you might ever buy one of these medium priced
      foreign cars?

      _____

      _____

      (IF YES, PROBABLY OR MAYBE)
      D44a. For a person like yourself, what would be some of the advantages of
             buying one of these cars in comparison with a medium size American-
             made car for about the same price? (Anything else?)

             _____

      (IF NO)
      D44b. For a person like yourself, what would be some of the disadvantages of
             buying one of these cars in comparison with a medium size American-made
             car for about the same price? (Anything else?)

             _____

             _____

D45. Do you think the quality of medium priced foriegn cars generally is better,
      worse, or about the same as American-made cars?

      _____

E. INSTALLMENT DEBT

E1. There is a lot of talk about credit cards these days, and we're interested in what you think about them. Would you say that using credit cards is a good thing or a bad thing or what?

| 1. GOOD | | 2. GOOD, WITH QUALIFICATIONS | | 3. PRO-CON |

| 4. BAD, WITH QUALIFICATIONS | | 5. BAD | | 8. UNCERTAIN |

E2. Why do you say this? _____

_____

_____

E3. Does anyone in this family use a gasoline card? | 1. YES | | 5. NO |

E4. Does anyone in this family use a bank card? | 1. YES | | 5. NO | -(GO TO Q.E5)

(ASK ONLY IF R USES BANK CARD)

E4a. How many bank cards do you use? _____

E4b. During 1970 would you say that you used your bank card(s) nearly every month, or did you use it (them) about every other month or did you only use it (them) a few months during the year?

| 1. NEARLY EVERY MONTH | | 2. EVERY OTHER MONTH | | 3. A FEW MONTHS | | 5. DID NOT USE IN 1970 | (GO TO Q. E5)

E4c. On the average, how much did you buy on your bank card(s) in those months when you used it (them)? $_____

E4d. In terms of the types of things you used your bank card(s) for such as clothing, appliances, travel, restaurants, etc., on which three did you spend the most money?

_____ _____ _____

E4e. Do you always pay your bank card bill in full by the time it is due, or do you sometimes pay only part of what you owe in one month and pay the rest later?

| 1. ALWAYS IN FULL | | 5. DOES NOT ALWAYS PAY IN FULL |

E4f. Do you pay the balance off as soon as you can, or do you sometimes pay it a little at a time like an installment loan?

| 1. SOON AS CAN | | 5. LITTLE AT A TIME |

E4g. Do you ever use the cash advance feature of your card to get money at a bank?

| 1. YES | | 5. NO |

16

E5. Does anyone in this family use a credit card or charge card issued by a department store, chain store or other retail outlet?

| 1. YES | | 5. NO | – (GO TO Q. E6)

E5a. Is it for a local store or stores found only in your area, or is it for a big national chain such as Sears, Penneys or Montgomery Wards?

| 1. LOCAL | | 2. NATIONAL | | 3. BOTH | | 4. OTHER |

E5b. How many of these cards do you have? _____

E5c. During 1970, would you say that you used your store card(s) nearly every month, or did you use it (them) about every other month, or did you use it (them) only a few months during the year?

| 1. NEARLY EVERY MONTH | 2. EVERY OTHER MONTH | 3. A FEW MONTHS | 5. DID NOT USE IN 1970 | (GO TO Q. E6)

E5d. In terms of the types of things you used your store card(s) for, such as clothing, appliances, sporting goods, etc., on which three did you spend the most money?

_____   _____   _____

E5e. On the average, how much did you buy on your store card(s) in those months when you used it (them)? $_____

E5f. Do you always pay your store card bill in full by the time it is due, or do you sometimes pay only part of what you owe in one month and pay the rest later?

| 1. ALWAYS PAY IN FULL | | 5. DOES NOT ALWAYS PAY IN FULL |

(GO TO Q. E6)

E5g. Do you pay the balance off as soon as you can, or do you sometimes pay it a little at a time like an installment loan?

| 1. SOON AS CAN | | 5. LITTLE AT A TIME |

E6. Does anyone in this family use a travel and entertainment card such as American Express, Diners Club, Carte Blanche? (I mean a personal card rather than a business card)

| 1. YES | | 5. NO | – (GO TO Q. E7)

E6a. How many do you use? _____

E6b. In 1970, about how much did you charge on the card(s) altogether? $_____

E7. Aside from payments on autos and credit card payments, are you currently making any payments on the installment plan for appliances or any other goods you and your family have bought, or for any other reason?

| 1. YES | | 5. NO | - (GO TO Q. E11) |

(IF YES TO E7)

E8. What items are you buying? (ENTER IN TABLE)

E9. How much are your payments per month? (ENTER IN TABLE)

E10. How many months do you have left to pay? (ENTER IN TABLE)

E8. ITEMS	E9. HOW MUCH/MONTH	E10. HOW MANY MONTHS LEFT	TD	(SRC use only)

E11. Do you owe any money on revolving credit from stores?

| 1. YES | | 5. NO | - (GO TO Q. E14) |

E12. How much do you still owe on this revolving credit? $_____

E13. How much are your monthly payments? $_____

TMP ☐☐☐☐   TD ☐☐☐☐

E14. Suppose you needed a thousand dollars for a car which you would repay in ttwelve monthly payments. About how much do you think the interest or carrying charges would be? (IF DEPENDS ON WHERE BORROWED -- ASK FOR SOURCE)

E14a. (If respondent gives a dollar answer) About what percent interest rate would that be?
_____ PERCENT

18

F. INCOME, OCCUPATION AND EMPLOYMENT

(ASK Q. F1 - F7 ABOUT HEAD)

F1. Next we would like to talk with you about your work and the employment of others in the family. How about your present job? Are you (HEAD) working now, unemployed or laid off, retired and not working, or what?

| 1. RETIRED |

| 2. PERMANENTLY DISABLED |

| 3. HOUSEWIFE | (GO TO Q. F8)

| 4. STUDENT |

| 5. WORKING NOW |

OCC B

| 6. UNEMPLOYED, SICK, OR LAID OFF TEMPORARILY |

F2. What is your (HEAD'S) main occupation - that is, the kind of work you (HEAD) have been doing to earn a livelihood?

_____

_____

F3. What kind of business is that in?

_____

_____

F4. Do you (HEAD) work for someone else, or yourself, or what?

| 2. SOMEONE ELSE | | 3. BOTH SOMEONE ELSE AND SELF | | 1. SELF ONLY |

F5. In 1970, how many hours a week did you (HEAD) usually work when you were working on your main job?

_____ HRS./WK.

F6. Did you (HEAD) also have a second job in 1970?

| 1. YES | | 5. NO |

F7. What would you say was the total amount of your (HEAD) wages and salaries including second job, overtime and bonuses in 1970? $ _____

(IF R IS UNWILLING TO GIVE DOLLAR AMOUNT, HAND R SHOW CARD D AND ASK WHICH LETTER IS CLOSEST TO INCOME. ENTER LETTER IN SPACE FOR DOLLAR AMOUNT)

F8.   (INTERVIEWER: CHECK BOX)

☐ MALE FU HEAD HAS WIFE   ☐ MALE FU HEAD   ☐ FEMALE HEAD
                                 HAS NO WIFE   (GO TO Q. F11)
                                 (GO TO Q. F11)

F9.   Did your wife do any work for money during 1970?

☐ 1. YES   ☐ 5. NO   - (GO TO Q. F11)

F10. How much did she **earn** in 1970? $_____
      (IF R IS UNWILLING TO GIVE DOLLAR AMOUNT, HAND R SHOW CARD D AND ASK
      WHICH LETTER IS CLOSEST TO INCOME. ENTER IN SPACE FOR DOLLAR AMOUNT).

F11. Did you or anyone else in the family living here own a business at any
      time in 1970, or have a financial interest in any business enterprise?

☐ 1. YES   ☐ 5. NO   - (GO TO Q. F13)

F12. How much was your family's share of the total income from the business
      in 1970--that is, the amount you took out plus any profit left in?

                                              $_____
      (IF R IS UNWILLING TO GIVE DOLLAR AMOUNT, HAND R SHOW CARD D AND ASK
      WHICH LETTER IS CLOSEST TO INCOME. ENTER IN SPACE FOR DOLLAR AMOUNT)

F13. Did anyone else in your family beyond you and your wife, earn $1000 or
      more in 1970?

☐ 1. YES   ☐ 5. NO   - (GO TO F15)

F14. Who did this? (list below)

RELATION TO HEAD

20

F15. Did you (HEAD) receive any other income in 1970?

    a. professional practice or trade. . . . .   1. YES   5. NO

    b. farming or market gardening,
       roomers or boarders . . . .   1. YES   5. NO

    c. dividends . . . .   1. YES   5. NO

    d. interest, trust funds,
       royalties, or rent. . . . .   1. YES   5. NO

F16. Did you receive any income from social security, pensions or annuities, other retirement pay, alimony, child support, unemployment compensation, welfare, or help from relatives, or anything else?

          1. YES   5. NO   (GO TO Q. F17)

> F16a. Would you say the total amount you received was less than $1000, between $1000 and $3000, or was it more than $3000.
>
>   1. LESS THAN $1000   2. $1000-$3000
>
>   3. MORE THAN $3000

F17. Now taking into consideration all these things we've just discussed, as close as you can estimate, what was your total family income before taxes in 1970? $_____

    (IF R IS UNWILLING TO GIVE DOLLAR AMOUNT, HAND R SHOW CARD D AND ASK WHICH LETTER IS CLOSEST TO INCOME. ENTER IN SPACE FOR DOLLAR AMOUNT)

F18. Was your family's total income higher in 1970 than it was the year before that (1969), or lower, or what?

    1. HIGHER IN 1970   2. LOWER IN 1970   3. SAME -(GO TO Q.F20)

> F19. About how much did your family income go (up/down) from 1969 to 1970; did it (increase/decrease) by just 1 or 2 percent, or by 5 percent, by 10 percent or what?
>
>   _____

F20. How do you think your total family income for this year, 1971, will compare with the past year, 1970 - will it be higher, about the same, or lower?

    1. 1970 HIGHER   3. ABOUT THE SAME   5. 1971 LOWER
                  (GO TO Q.G1)   (GO TO Q.G1)

> F21. (IF HIGHER) About how much do you expect your 1971 income will be higher than last year, 1970; will it be 1 or 2 percent higher, or 5 percent, or 10 percent higher, or what?
>
>   _____

G. ASSETS

G1. Does anyone in your family have any certificates of deposit?

| 1. YES | | 5. NO |

G2. Do you or others in your family now have any savings accounts at banks, savings and loan associations, mutual savings banks, or credit unions, not including certificates of deposit? (CHECK WHICH APPLY)

| BANK | SAVINGS AND LOAN ASSN. | MUTUAL SAVINGS BANKS | CREDIT UNION | NO | (IF NO TO Q. G1, GO TO Q. G5, IF YES TO Q. G1, GO TO Q. G4) |

G3. How many accounts do you have? _____

(ASK IF R HAS SAVINGS ACCOUNT(S) OR CERTIF-ICATES OF DEPOSIT)

G4. About what is the total amount you have in all your savings accounts including any certificates of deposit that you may have? $_____

G5. Do you or others in your family have any checking accounts at banks?

| 1. YES | | 5. NO | — (GO TO Q.G7)

G6. About what is the total amount in the checking accounts? $_____

G7. Do you or others in your family own any United States Government Savings Bonds?

| 1. YES | | 5. NO |

G8. Do you (R AND FU) own any other types of bonds such as municipal or corporate bonds?

| 1. YES | | 5. NO |

G9. Do you (R AND FU) own any common or preferred stock in a corporation, including companies you have worked for, or own mutual fund shares, or own stock through an investment club?

(CHECK THE APPROPRIATE BOXES)

a) Common or preferred stock in a corporation, including companies you have worked for? | YES | | NO |

b) Mutual fund shares? | YES | | NO |

(IF 'YES' TO G8, G9a OR G9b)

G10. How much would you say you have invested altogether in stocks, municipal and corporate bonds, and mutual funds? _____

22

H. INFORMATION ABOUT FAMILY

(ASK EVERYONE)

H1. Now I have just a few more questions. Are you (HEAD) married, single,
widowed, divorced, or separated?

| 1. MARRIED | 2. SINGLE | 3. WIDOWED | 4. DIVORCED | 5. SEPARATED |

(GO TO Q. H3)

H2. How long have you been married? _____ (YEARS)

(ASK HEAD ONLY)   (HEAD)

H3. How many grades of school did you finish?	_____ (GRADES)
(IF MORE THAN 8) H4. Have you had any other schooling or training?	NO YES
(IF YES TO Q. H4) H5. What other schooling did you have?	_____ (COLLEGE, SECRE-TARIAL, BUSINESS, TRADE SCHOOL, NURSING, ETC.)
(IF ANY COLLEGE) H6. Do you have a college degree?	NO YES
(IF YES TO Q. H6) H7. What degrees do you have?	_____ _____

J1. Do you have a telephone here at home?

| 1. YES | | NO |

> J2. Is there any way you can be reached by
> telephone?
>
> | 2. YES | | 5. NO | (GO TO Q. J5)

J3. We are particularly interested in changes in people's financial situation
and opinions. Therefore, we might want to make a <u>very brief</u> phone call to
you in a few months to see how you are getting along and whether your ideas
have changed. Would you give me your phone number please? (IF NECESSARY,
ASSURE R THAT THE NUMBER WILL BE HELD IN STRICT CONFIDENCE AND NOT USED FOR
<u>ANY</u> OTHER PURPOSE)

| 1. GIVEN | | 5. REFUSED |

J4. Just so that we will be sure to get the right person if we do call again,
would you please give me your name? (IF NECESSARY ASSURE R THAT THE NAME
GOES ON A SEPARATE SHEET OF PAPER AND WILL BE KEPT APART FROM THE INTERVIEW)

| 1. GIVEN | | 5. REFUSED |

(IF TELEPHONE NUMBER OR NAME GIVEN, FILL OUT A TELEPHONE SHEET)

(IF R REFUSES, EXPLAIN): _____

_____

J5. These are all the questions I have. When we are finished with this survey we
can send you some of our findings as our way of thanking you, if you will send
this card. (HAND REPORT REQUEST CARD TO R)

(INTERVIEWER: CHECK TO MAKE SURE Q's 2, 3, 4, 5, on PAGE 1 ARE COMPLETE.
REMEMBER TO FINISH OBSERVATION SHEET AND THUMBNAIL SKETCH).

24

K. OBSERVATION DATA

(INTERVIEWER: BY OBSERVATION ONLY)

K1. Sex of <u>Head</u> of Family Unit:

        | 1. MALE | | 2. FEMALE |

K2. Sex of Respondent:

        | 1. MALE | | 2. FEMALE |

K3. Race:

    | 1. WHITE | | 2. NEGRO | | 3. OTHER | -(Specify) _____

K4. Number of calls: _____

K5. Who was present during the interview: _____

K6. TYPE OF STRUCTURE IN WHICH FAMILY LIVES:

    [_] TRAILER

    [_] DETACHED SINGLE FAMILY HOUSE

    [_] 2-FAMILY HOUSE, 2 UNITS SIDE BY SIDE

    [_] 2-FAMILY HOUSE, 2 UNITS ONE ABOVE
        THE OTHER

    [_] DETACHED 3-4 FAMILY HOUSE

    [_] ROW HOUSE (3 OR MORE UNITS IN AN
        ATTACHED ROW)

    [_] APARTMENT HOUSE (5 OR MORE UNITS,
        3 STORIES OR LESS)

    [_] APARTMENT HOUSE (5 OR MORE UNITS,
        4 STORIES OR MORE)

    [_] APARTMENT IN A PARTLY COMMERCIAL
        STRUCTURE

    [_] OTHER (Specify) _____

_____

THUMBNAIL SKETCH

BIBLIOGRAPHY

Each of the *Survey of Consumer Finances* monographs contains a bibliography, listing publications by the staff of the Economic Behavior Program of the Survey Research Center. Listed below are books and articles which were published or prepared in 1971.

Katona, George. "A Communication: Consumer Durable Spending." *Brookings Papers on Economic Activity.* Washington, D.C.: The Brookings Institution, 1971, p. 234-239.

———. "Consumer Expectations and Forecasting," in *The Economic Outlook for 1972.* Nineteenth Annual Conference on the Economic Outlook, November 1971, pp. 89-98.

———. "Consumption," *Encyclopedia of the Twentieth Century.* Encyclopedia Italiana, forthcoming.

———. "The Human Factor in Economic Affairs," in Campbell, Angus and Converse, Philip E. (eds.). *The Human Meaning of Social Change.* Russell Sage Foundation, 1972. pp. 229-267.

———. "Theory of Expectations." Forthcoming chapter in Morgan, James N., Strumpel, Burkhard, and Zahn, Ernest (eds.). *Human Behavior in Economic Affairs: Essays in Honor of George Katona.* Amsterdam: Elsevier Publishing Company, 1972.

Mandell, Lewis. *Credit Card Use in the United States.* Ann Arbor: Institute for Social Research, 1972.

———. "The Changing Role of the American Consumer," *Michigan Business Review.* (January 1972).

———. "Changing Consumer Needs: Problems and Opportunities for Small Business," *The Journal of Small Business Management.* (July 1972).

———. "Consumer Knowledge and Understanding of Consumer Credit," *Journal of Consumer Affairs.* (Scheduled for publication in summer, 1973).

Mandell, Lewis and Messenger, Robert. "A Modal Search Technique for Predictive Nominal Scale Multi-variate Analysis," *Journal of the American Statistical Association.* (Scheduled for publication in December, 1972).

Mandell, Lewis and Marans, Robert W. *Participation in Outdoor Recreation: A National Perspective.* Ann Arbor: Institute for Social Research, (Scheduled for publication in spring 1973).

Marans, Robert W., Scott, John C. and Driver, B. L. *Youth and the Environment.* Monograph. Ann Arbor: Institute for Socail Research, Summer 1972.

Marans, Robert W. "Outdoor Recreation Behavior in Residential Environments," in Carson, D., and Wohlwill, J.F. (eds.). *Environment and the Social Sciences: Prospectives and Ap-*

plications. Washington: American Psychological Association, 1972.

_____. "Research on New Community Development: Opportunities and Results," in *Housing Market Opportunities*. Bernhardt, K. (ed.). Ann Arbor: Institute for Science and Technology, The University of Michigan, 1972.

_____. "Influence of Physical Environment on Behavior: Planned vs. Unplanned Communities," in Weiss, S., Kaiser, E., and Burby, R. (eds.). *New Community Development: Planning Process, Implementation and Emerging Social Concerns*. Chapel Hill: Center for Urban and Regional Studies, 1972.

Marans, Robert W. and Mandell, Lewis. "The Relative Effectiveness of Density—Related Measures for Predicting Attitudes and Behavioral Variables," *Proceedings of the American Statistical Association*, 1972.

Marans, Robert W. and Rodgers, Willard. "Toward a Theory of Community Satisfactions," in Hawley, Amos, Morgan, Strumpel, Zahn (eds.). *Significance of the Community in the Metropolitan Environment*. Washington: National Academy of Sciences, 1973.

Morgan, James N. "A Quarter Century of Behavioral Research in Economics, Persistent Programs and Diversions." Forthcoming chapter in Hawley, Morgan, Strumpel and Zahn, *op cit*.

Morgan, James N. and Staff. *A Panel Study of Income Dynamics: Study Design, Procedures, Available Data, 1968-1971 Interviewing Years*. Monograph. Ann Arbor: Institute for Social Research, 1971.

Schmiedeskamp, Jay. "The Short-term Outlook for the Consumer Sector," in *The Economic Outlook for 1972*. Nineteenth Annual Conference on the Economic Outlook, 1971.

Strumpel, Burkhard. "Higher Education and Economic Behavior," in Withey, Stephen (ed.). *A Degree and What Else: Correlates and Consequences of a College Education*. New York: McGraw-Hill, 1971.

_____. "The Aged in an Affluent Economy," in Eisdorfer, Carl and Lawton, M. Powell (eds.). *Task Force on Aging Report*. American Psychological Association, 1972. (in publication).

_____. "Economic Behavior and Economic Welfare: Models and Inter-disciplinary Approaches." Forthcoming chapter in Morgan, Strumpel and Zahn, *op. cit.*

WORKING PAPERS

These papers were recently completed by members of the Economic Behavior Program. Reasonable numbers are available upon request to the Economic Behavior Program, Survey Research Center, Institute for Social Research, P.O. Box 1248, The University of Michigan 48106.

Baerwaldt, Nancy A. and Morgan, James N. "Trends in Inter-Family Transfers," March, 1972.

Baerwaldt, Nancy A. "Distribution of Individuals in 1968 and 1969."

Benus, Jacob. "Transportation of the Poor," July, 1970.

_____. "Local Data," February, 1971.

_____. "Static and Dynamic Responses of Food Consumption to Income," June, 1962.

Benus, Jacob and Morgan, James N. "Income Instability as a Dimension of Welfare," September, 1972.

Brazer, Marjorie. "Profile of the 1968 Family Sample," July, 1970.

Dickinson, Jonathan. "Estimates of Individual Labor Supply Based on a Cobb Douglas Utility Function," February, 1970.

_____. "Underemployment," August, 1970.

Dickinson, Katherine. "Investigation of the Attitudinal and Behavioral Indexes," July, 1972.

Dickinson, K.P. and Dickinson, J.G. "Labor Force Participation of Wives: The Effects of Components of Husband's Income," June, 1971.

Katona, George. "Inflation and the Consumer," 1972.

_____. "Persistence of Belief in Personal-Financial Progress," 1972.

Lansing, John B. and Dickinson, Katherine. "A Description of Eight Categories of the Poor," August, 1970.

_____. "Consumption Patterns of the Poor," August, 1970.

Mandell, Lewis. "Weighting for Non-Response: Objective Criteria for Survey Researchers," August, 1972.

Marans, Robert W. "Measuring Responses to Residential Environments with National Sample Data." Paper presented at The University of Maryland Symposium on Housing and Mental Health, March, 1972.

Morgan, James N., Harris, Beverly and Schrader, Tecla. "A Comparison of the Census and Survey Research Center Measures of Poverty Levels, on the Same Set of Data," January, 1971.

Morgan, James N. and Schrader, Tecla. "Two Notes on Earnings Differentials by Sex and Race," January, 1971.

Morgan, James N. "Static and Dynamic Responses of Food Consumption to Income," February, 1971.

_____. "Housing: The Relation of Quantity to Quality (cost to number of rooms) and the Relation of Housing Consumption (costs) to Income," February, 1971.

_____. "Income and Welfare of the Aged," January, 1972.

_____. "The Retirement Process in the United States," January, 1972.

_____. "The Distribution of the Poor," February, 1972.

_____. "An Initial Search for Any Attitudes or Behavior Patterns That Seem to Lead to Improvement in Economic Well-Being," March, 1972.

_____. "Change in Family Composition as a Behavior to be Explained," June, 1972.

Morgan, James, N. and Benus, Jacob. "Time Period, Unit of Analysis and Income Concept in the Analysis of Income Distribution," September, 1972.

Smith, James D. "Birth Control and Economic Well-Being," April, 1972.

Strumpel, Burkhard. "Economic Stress as a Source of Societal Discontent." New Orleans: Annual Meeting of the American Sociological Society, August, 1972.

SURVEY RESEARCH CENTER PUBLICATIONS

Survey Research Center Publications should be ordered by author and title from the Publications Division, Department B, Institute for Social Research, The University of Michigan, P.O. Box 1248, Ann Arbor, Michigan 48106.

1960 Survey of Consumer Finances. 1961. (paperbound), 310 pp.

1961 Survey of Consumer Finances. G. Katona, C. A. Lininger, J. N. Morgan, and E. Mueller. 1962. (paperbound), 150 pp.

1962 Survey of Consumer Finances. G. Katona, C. A. Lininger, and R. F. Kosobud. 1963. (paperbound), 310 pp.

1963 Survey of Consumer Finances. G. Katona, C. A. Lininger, and E. Mueller. 1964. 262 pp. (May be ordered only from University Microfilms, Zeeb Rd., Ann Arbor, Mich.)

1964 Survey of Consumer Finances. G. Katona, C. A. Lininger and E. Mueller. 1965. (paperbound), 245 pp.

1965 Survey of Consumer Finances. G. Katona, E. Mueller, J. Schmiedeskamp, and J. A. Sonquist. 1966. (paperbound), 263 pp.

1966 Survey of Consumer Finances. G. Katona, E. Mueller, J. Schmiedeskamp, and J. A. Sonquist. 1967. (paperbound), 303 pp.

1967 Survey of Consumer Finances. G. Katona, J. N. Morgan, J. Schmiedeskamp, and J. A. Sonquist. 1968. (paperbound), 343 pp.

1968 Survey of Consumer Finances. G. Katona, W. Dunkelberg, J. Schmiedeskamp, and F. Stafford. 1969. (paperbound), 287 pp.

1969 Survey of Consumer Finances. G. Katona, W. Dunkelberg, G. Hendricks, and J. Schmiedeskamp. 1970. (paperbound), 331 pp.

1970 Survey of Consumer Finances. G. Katona, L. Mandell, and J. Schmiedeskamp. 1971. (paperbound), (clothbound), 293 pp.

Credit Card Use in the United States. L. Mandell. 1972.   (paperbound), 115 pp.

Economic Survey Methods. John B. Lansing and James N. Morgan. 1971. (paperbound),   (clothbound), 448 pp.

Searching for Structure. John Sonquist, Elizabeth L. Baker and James N. Morgan. 1971.   (paperbound),   (clothbound), 287 pp.

Working Papers on Survey Research in Poverty Areas. John B. Lansing and Stephen Withey. 1971.   (paperbound), 629 pp.

Planned Residential Environments. John B. Lansing, Robert W. Marans and Robert B. Zehner. 1970.   (paperbound),   (clothbound), 283 pp.

The Automobile Worker and Retirement: A Second Look. Richard E. Barfield. 1970.   (paperbound), 56 pp.

Technological Advance in an Expanding Economy: Its Impact on a Cross-Section of the Labor Force. Eva Mueller. 1969.   (paperbound), (clothbound), 254 pp.

Non-Market Components of National Income. Ismail Sirageldin. 1969. (paperbound), 127 pp.

New Homes and Poor People. John B. Lansing, Charles W. Clifton, and James N. Morgan. 1969.   (paperbound), 136 pp.

Early Retirement: The Decision and the Experience. Richard Barfield and James N. Morgan. 1969.   (paperbound),   (clothbound), 289 pp.

Multiple Classification Analysis. James N. Morgan, John A. Sonquist and Frank M. Andrews. 1967.   (paperbound), 221 pp.

Automobile Ownership and Residential Density. John B. Lansing and Gary Hendricks. 1967.   (paperbound), 230 pp.

The Geographic Mobility of Labor. John B. Lansing and Eva L. Mueller. 1967.   (paperbound), 421 pp.

Productive Americans: A Study of How Individuals Contribute to Economic Progress. James N. Morgan, Ismail Sirageldin, and Nancy Baerwaldt. 1966.   (paperbound), 546 pp.

Residential Location and Urban Mobility: The Second Wave of Interviews. John B. Lansing, 1966.   (paperbound), 115 pp.

Private Pensions and Individual Saving. George Katona. 1965.   (paperbound),   (clothbound), 114 pp.

Consumer Behavior of Individual Families Over Two and Three Years. Richard F. Kosobud and James N. Morgan (Editors). 1964.   (paperbound),   (clothbound), 208 pp.

Residential Location and Urban Mobility. John B. Lansing and Eva Mueller. 1964.   (paperbound), 142 pp.

Residential Location and Urban Mobility: A Multivariate Analysis. John B. Lansing and Nancy Barth. 1964.   (paperbound), 98 pp.

The Travel Market, 1964-1965. John B. Lansing. 1965.   (clothbound), 112 pp.

The Changing Travel Market. John B. Lansing and Dwight M. Blood. 1964. (paperbound), 374 pp.

The Detection of Interaction Effects. John A. Sonquist and James N. Morgan. 1964. (paperbound), 292 pp.

The Travel Market, 1958, 1959-1960, 1961-1962. John B. Lansing, Eva Mueller, and others. Reprinted 1963 (originally issued as three separate reports). (paperbound), 388 pp.

The Travel Market 1955, 1956, 1957. John B. Lansing and Ernest Lillienstein. Reprinted 1963 (originally issued as three separate reports). (clothbound), 524 pp.

Location Decisions and Industrial Mobility in Michigan, 1961. Eva Mueller, Arnold Wilken, and Margaret Wood. 1962. (paperbound), (clothbound), 115 pp.

Survey of Consumer Finances data are available on computer tapes, together with a detailed code decribing the content of the tapes. Thus, interested scholars or other parties may obtain or prepare further analysis beyond that presented in this volume.

OTHER BOOKS BY MEMBERS OF THE ECONOMIC BEHAVIOR PROGRAM

Aspirations and Affluence: Comparative Studies in the United States and Western Europe. George Katona, Burkhard Strumpel and Ernest Zahn. McGraw-Hill, 1971.

Consumer Response to Income Increases. George Katona and Eva Mueller. Washington, D.C.: Brookings Institution, 1968.

Living Patterns and Attitudes in the Detroit Region. John B. Lansing and Gary Hendricks. A report for TALUS (Detroit Regional Transportation and Land Use Study), 1967, 241 pp. (Available only from TALUS, 1248 Washington Blvd., Detroit, Mich. 48226.)

Economic Behavior of the Affluent. Robin Barlow, H. E. Brazer, and J. N. Morgan. Washington, D.C.: Brookings Institution, 1966.

Transportation and Economic Policy. John B. Lansing, Free Press, 1966.

The Mass Consumption Society. George Katona. McGraw-Hill, 1964.

Income and Welfare in the United States. J. N. Morgan, M. H. David, W. J. Cohen, and H. E. Brazer. McGraw-Hill, 1962.

An Investigation of Response Error. J. B. Lansing. G. P. Ginsburg, and K. Braaten. Bureau of Economic and Business Research, University of Illinois, 1961.

The Powerful Consumer. George Katona. McGraw-Hill, 1960.

Consumer Economics. James N. Morgan. Prentice-Hall, 1955.

Contributions of Survey Methods to Economics. G. Katona, L. R. Klein, J. B. Lansing, and J. N. Morgan. Columbia University Press, 1957.